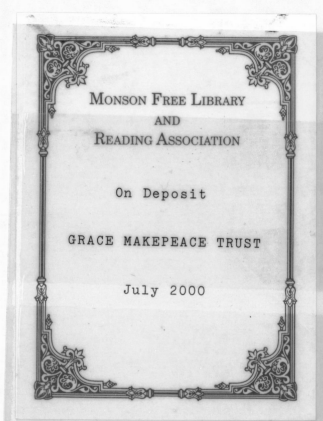

BEGINNINGS
OF
SISTERHOOD

KEITH E. MELDER

BEGINNINGS
OF SISTERHOOD

THE AMERICAN WOMAN'S
RIGHTS MOVEMENT, 1800-1850

STUDIES IN THE LIFE OF WOMEN
GENERAL EDITOR: Gerda Lerner

SCHOCKEN BOOKS

NEW YORK

First published by SCHOCKEN BOOKS 1977

Copyright © 1977 by Schocken Books Inc.

Library of Congress Cataloging in Publication Data

Melder, Keith.
  Beginnings of sisterhood.

  (Studies in the life of women)
  Bibliography: p.
  Includes index.
  1. Women's rights—United States—History.
  2. Feminism—United States—History. I. Title.
  HQ1426.M44   301.41'2'0973   76-53611

Manufactured in the United States of America

In Memory
of
KATHLEEN ADAMS

Acknowledgements

Portions of chapter 2 have appeared previously in different form as: "Woman's High Calling: The Teaching Profession in America, 1830-1860," *American Studies* (University of Kansas) 13, no. 2 (Fall 1972): 19-32; and "Mask of Oppression: The Female Seminary Movement in the United States," *New York History* 55, no. 3 (July 1974): 261-79.

A portion of chapter 3 was previously published as "Ladies Bountiful: Organized Women's Benevolence in Early 19th-Century America," *New York History* 48, no. 3 (July 1967):231-54.

Major portions of chapter 6 were previously published as "Forerunners of Freedom: The Grimké Sisters in Massachusetts, 1837-38," *Essex Institute Historical Collections* 103 (July 1967): 223-49.

Institutions permitted quotations from manuscripts in their custody as follows: the Abigail Kelly Foster Papers in the American Antiquarian Society; Catherine Beecher Papers in the Collection of American Literature, The Beinecke Rare Book and Manuscript Library, Yale University; antislavery collections in the Boston Public Library by courtesy of the Trustees of the Boston Public Library; Weld-Grimké Papers in the Clements Library, University of Michigan; Sidney Howard Gay Papers in the Columbia University Libraries; records of the Philadelphia Female Anti-Slavery Society in the Historical Society of Pennsylvania; Margaret Fuller Papers in the Houghton Library of Harvard College Library; collections in the Manuscript Division, Library of Congress; College History Collection, Mount Holyoke College Library; Robert S. Fletcher Papers in the Oberlin College Archives; collections in the Archives-Manuscript Division, Ohio Historical Society; collections in the Presbyterian Historical Society; Hooker Collection, Schlesinger Library, Radcliffe College; journal of Lydia Ann Stow, Whittemore Library, Framingham State College (Mass.); Kelly-Foster Collection, Worcester Historical Society. All these institutions gave generously of their resources as research for this study went forward.

Permission to quote from manuscripts also came from Willard P. Fuller, Jr., custodian of the Fuller Family Papers. Mrs. Robert Ticknor, owner of the Betsey Cowles Papers, loaned many of these manuscripts to the Smithsonian Institution and gave permission for their quotation. Her collection is now deposited in the American History Research Center, Kent State University (Ohio).

Over a period of years the National Museum of History and Technology in the Smithsonian Institution provided time, facilities, and a favorable environment for research. The Smithsonian Libraries, and especially librarians Jack S. Goodwin and Charles G. Berger, helped in obtaining much information.

The grant of a Lena Lake Forrest Fellowship by the Business and Professional Women's Foundation supported research during an earlier phase of the work.

Many individuals contributed ideas and encouragement over the years. The late David M. Potter helped design the project and asked the right questions at the outset. Along the way, the late Norman Holmes Pearson, the late Adrienne Koch, and Patricia Watlington offered criticism, support, and suggestions. Publication of this work owes much to Gerda Lerner, who had faith in the project and served constantly as a constructive critic and supporter when the manuscript took final form. Others, too numerous to mention, helped to discover facts and give them meaning. Omissions and errors of fact and interpretation are solely the responsibility of the author.

Contents

BEGINNINGS
OF SISTERHOOD

1

HER APPROPRIATE SPHERE

NINETEENTH-century Americans faced changes in virtually all phases of their lives, changes that seemed unprecedented in number and impact. Politically, they had dissolved one set of loyalties in the Revolution and were seeking to establish a new national allegiance to coexist with strong regional identities. Their government remained experimental and uncertain through much of the century. Physically, the young nation grew from an area of settlement confined chiefly to the Atlantic coast into a continental power stretching to the Pacific Ocean. The nation's population multiplied many times, augmented by diverse cultural and racial minorities from abroad. Americans increasingly accepted the values of progress, welcoming change, anticipating improvements in their lives and their children's lives. A restless, unsettled society, nineteenth-century America promised almost un-limited opportunities, yet left its people with profound anxieties.

Women were deeply involved in all of these changes. In theory they lived sheltered lives, protected by stronger men from the most disruptive effects of political, economic, and social change. In fact, however, they suffered the effects of change and found their lives profoundly disturbed, their emotions alienated. How were they to respond to change? By what standards would wlmen govern themselves in the face of social turmoil? Many Americans of both sexes sought to answer these fundamental questions.

Nineteenth-century women learned an ideology, calling it "The Appropriate Sphere of Woman," whichwould resolve their doubts and order their lives. Defining womean's sphere as subordinate to the domain of man, most Americans assumed the existence of a natural order in society, a hierarchy in which stations were assigned immutably and beneficently. Wrote one commentator: "Each creature in the universe finds itself in that position for which its peculiar organization has fitted it, and discovers in its offices the exact correlatives of its powers."[1] The inequality of the sexes was ordained when God said to woman, "He shall rule over thee." Men and women occupied totally different social situations:

> Females fill a peculiar station in society. They move in a sphere of their own which they, and they alone, were designed to occupy. It would be singular, if we did not find in woman, powers as different from those of man as the station which she is required to fill is different from his. [2]

Woman's virtues, according to the most acceptable definition of her sphere, were those of submission: "Meekness, humility, gentleness, love, purity, self-renunciation, subjection of will....The fairest flowers which our fallen world can produce." [3]

Between 1750 and 1850 the circumstances of women's lives changed in a number of ways, especially in the economy, under the law, and in the attitudes influencing woman's social status. Wherever it flourished—on the frontier or in long-settled areas—the agrarian economy depended on woman's contributions. Agricultural families functioned as economic units, with each member sharing in the work. A division of labor existed and distinctions were made between men's and women's work, but much overlapping of function could occur. Thus, to some extent, agricultural society brought a form of occupational equality to the sexes. The tasks of both husband and wife were essential to the successful operation of each family farm: both worked at home, and, although one labored generally in the fields or the barns while the other was confined within the house or nearby, their jobs were similar in being menial, unskilled or semi-skilled, and laborious.

Industrialization brought changes for women, both within and outside the domestic circle, expanding occupational opportunities in some fields and diminishing them in others. The development of factory production between 1800 and 1860 reduced the variety of labor performed in traditional women's household tasks of spinning, weaving, sewing, and food processing. Such production did not suddenly leave the home, but gradually, as machinery and new techniques of production were applied in factories, housewives found their workloads eased. To a great extent, as Edith Abbott has indicated, textiles remained women's work:

> It may . . . be said . . . the work which women had been doing in the home could be done more efficiently outside of the home, but women were carrying on the same processes in the making of yarn and cloth. The place and conditions of labor had been changed, but women's work continued to be an important factor in the industry. [4]

Some single women gained a measure of independence from their work in the factories—"They were no longer obliged to finish out their faded lives mere burdens to male relatives." Although textile labor offered an alternative to domesticity to young women in some areas of the country, most mill girls viewed their factory employment as temporary, to help out their parents on marginal farms, "to secure the means of education for some male members of the family," to earn a dowery, or for some other purpose. [5]

Textile-mill jobs did not mean personal independence or a break with restrictive home environments. At Lowell, the most famous of the mill towns, the girls were treated as wards both on and off the job—their employers supervised their conduct, their home lives in company boarding houses, their religious behavior, and their friendships. For a time, Lowell was a model town, impressing numerous visitors from the United States and abroad with its respectable young ladies, who edited and wrote their own literary magazine, the famous *Lowell Offering*. But all too quickly, under the pressure of industrial competition, conditions in the mills deteriorated, the work was speeded up, wages fell, and the sturdy New England farm girls disappeared from Lowell to be replaced by poverty-striken Irish immigrants.

Few industrial communities were as attractive and "elevating" to ambitious women as Lowell had been. Elsewhere, mill owners employed entire families—men, women, and children—rather than single individuals, and female inequality was emphasized by the lower wages and less-desirable jobs given to women. Early statistics indicate little about women's economic independence; the first statistics on female industrial labor, from the census of 1850, do not distinguish factory employment from domestic industry, although they report 225,922 women employed in industry, constituting 24% of all industrial workers. [6] The notion that industry "emancipated" women from household slavery appears to be largely mythological. Nevertheless, factory employment offered alternatives to domestic service for selected groups of American women. Over a period of many years some traditional domestic tasks were removed from the home, altering women's housekeeping responsibilities, especially among urban families. With its concentration of production in cities and towns, mechanized industry brought profound changes in the lives of men and women, and in the family as a social and economic institution. Industrialization upset the deep-seated economic partnership of the family, separating men's and women's work, giving to masculine labor a higher obvious value, symbolized by the pay envelope.

Significant changes also occurred in women's nonindustrial occupations. Among traditional female vocations, medicine was largely affected, as it became professionalized through the institution of formal medical training. Excluded from most of this training, women could not obtain certification as professional physicians. Perhaps the growing emphasis on female "modesty" and "delicacy" were equal barriers to the practice of medicine by women. Male physicians even took over one of the traditional women's specialties, obstetrics. Innkeeping and shopkeeping lost respectability as occupations for women. Other changes in women's nonindustrial working patterns actually enlarged the scope of their influence. Their employment as teachers, their involvement in voluntary religious and reformist organizations, and their literary endeavors will be considered later in this narrative. Taken as a whole, the changes in women's occupations of the late eighteenth and early nineteenth centuries seem to have clarified and separated women's laboring "sphere" from that of men. By apparently diminishing the economic significance of domestic tasks and establishing a nearly universal disparity of wages between the sexes, these changes gave the advocates of equality an obvious grievance.

Further evidence of the changing status of American women in the colonial and early national periods may be found in the law. Contrary to widespread assumptions, English common law, with its traditional submergence of women, was not the only legal pattern transmitted to the American colonies. Married women, against whom common law discriminated most heavily, could gain control over their separate property through the use of ante-nuptial contracts or by the establishment of trusts. In acquiring the privileges of *femme sole* traders, in gaining the right to testify in some courts concerning controversies which involved their husbands, and in receiving special court protection when widowed, many colonial wives obtained considerable freedom under the law. In part, these modifications of common law arose because of the scarcity of lawyers in the colonies. In many instances, local customs probably replaced the common law in governing women's legal rights, and custom often treated women more generously than did the law.

The rise of equity jurisprudence had an important influence on the changing legal situation of American women. Beginning in the Courts of Chancery in the late sixteenth century, British equity law superseded the common law regulation of married women's property. In contrast to the common law's assumption of the unity of husband and wife, equity often treated married women as if they were independent. Married women might sue their husbands, they could make contracts, a husband might give his wife funds or goods for her separate use, a wife could hold and maintain an independent estate, disposing of its returns as she saw fit. When wives granted control of their separate property to their husbands, equity courts examined the transactions "with an anxious watchfulness and caution, and dread of undue influence." [7] Although early American jurisprudence did not recognize equity as a distinct field of law, its principles became intermingled with the common law in many courts. Justice Joseph Story, equity's greatest American exponent, found it "difficult to resist the impression that [equity's] interposition is founded in wisdom, in sound morals, and in a delicate adaptation to the exigencies of a polished and advancing state of society." [8]

Legislation contributed to the transformation of women's legal status. As early as 1823 Maine gave legal protection to the property rights and personal independence of married women who had been deserted by their husbands, and Massachusetts followed with a similar law in 1835. Throughout the 1840s, preceding the attacks of organized feminists, agitation resulted in married women's property bills in several states. Two of the most notable early women's property laws were passed in New York and Pennsylvania in 1848 after years of controversy, *before* Elizabeth Cady Stanton's assertion at Seneca Falls that man had made woman "civilly dead," that "he has taken from her all right in property...." Motivations for new women's property legislation were not necessarily liberal, however, as suggested by the argument that such laws were needed to protect family fortunes against improvident husbands. [9]

Despite a trend toward greater equality in treating women under the law, the conservative influence of Blackstone's *Commentaries* remained powerful in American legal circles. Blackstone was particularly popular and useful among America's self-trained lawyers:

It reduced to a moderate compass, digested, organized, and expounded a vast mass of old laws, rulings, and precedents. Moreover, for a law work, it was written in free, flowing, and popular style, so that any literate person of a little more than ordinary intelligence could by a few months close study make himself master of its leading principles. [10]

Blackstone's interpretation of woman's legal condition offered her little freedom:

By marriage, the husband and wife are one person in law; that is, the very being or legal existence of the woman is suspended during the marriage, or at least is incorporated and consolidated into that of the husband; under whose wing, protection, and cover, she performs everything.... [11]

Thus legal definitions of women's rights and duties were ambiguous, guided both by the looser views derived from equity and legislation, and the tight restrictions dictated by Blackstone's assumptions of married women's civil annihilation. Given the tension between differing approaches to the law, it is little wonder that legal status became one of the early issues for advocates of women's rights.

Socially, woman's position also changed considerably during the late colonial and early national periods of American history. The first century of settlement was a period of hardship and toil, when men and women alike expended their energies in creating a viable society. During the eighteenth century, as commerce brought wealth to the middle Atlantic region and the New England colonies, and Southern planters consolidated their lands and came to rely on enslaved Africans for their labor force, new expectations of wealth and social standing took hold in America. The living standards of merchants and planters swelled to include elaborate town houses and country seats patterned after English examples, and the imitation of dress and fashionable leisure-time activities of the English gentry.

These developments in colonial society had important consequences for eighteenth-century American women of the middle and wealthy classes. The older Puritan and agrarian notion of marriage as a domestic partnership, which had given security and purpose to women's lives, was seriously questioned. In contrast to this concept of women's situation were upper-class ideas of femininity which valued women chiefly as creatures of the fashionable and social world. For the "best" people, women's functions moved from the family into society, from the performance of physical labor and managerial duties in the home to pursuits that were chiefly ornamental. Instead of contributing to the family economy, women sought leisure for the cultivation of their femininity, in order to prove that, as wealthy individuals, they could afford to be unproductive. These new social patterns, like the development of industry, contributed toward a more rigid separation of men's and women's spheres.

Providing additional support for a distinct woman's sphere was romanticism, with its emphasis on imagination, emotion, diversity, and exotic principles. Romantic ideals easily assimilated the growing cult of female weakness and the separation between men's and women's lives. Although it idealized the frail female, romanticism put strong emphasis upon woman's moral role, encouraging positive duties for women which were not menial or strictly domestic in the older sense of contributing to the household economy, but which were meaningful, respectable, and morally acceptable.

After 1800, middle class American women apparently developed a distinct sense of their appropriate sphere. With husbands engaged in commerce or one of the professions, they were eager for the benefits of wealth—fine clothing, large and well-furnished houses, servants, and good prospects for their children. To some degree they represented the pattern described by Thorstein Veblen in his analysis of leisure-class social life, in which woman's enforced idleness and conspicuous display represented the emulation of upper-class behavior by members of the middle class.[12] But the new fashionable and ornamental views of women, assuming physical and mental weakness, repelled many conscientious, pious Americans.

Nineteenth-century theories of femininity, developing gradually out of the separation of men's and women's lives during the eighteenth century, emphasized a great division in American culture in which men and women played contrasting roles. Men were aggressive, exploitive, materialistic. physical, unchaste, impious, and mobile; women were pious, pure, selfless, delicate, domestic, nurturant, passive, conservative. Thus, middle class women faced a new series of expectations, defined by their sex roles. Paradoxically, since men should be aggressive and women passive, the new attitudes deplored idleness, and demanded that women be up and doing, exercising their particular virtues;

The urgent, crying wants of the community, and of the age in which we live, are not an increase of physical power, of intellectual wealth. . . . They are an increased diffusion of the spirit of kindness and compassion, sympathy and love. [13]

And these wants were the special business of women. Thousands of essays, newspaper articles, domestic manuals, and other specimens of popular literature urged women to help civilize their age.

Responding to nineteenth-century notions of their appropriate sphere, middle-class women answered a series of demands. They were thought to be particularly responsible for the maintenance of evangelical Protestantism. Not that they should usurp the authority of the clergy; rather that with clerical guidance and patronage they should be assistants and bearers of the church's message throughout the land by indirect and subtle influences. Faced with a male population increasingly attracted by the allurements of the world, clergymen made no secret of enlisting women in the great revival of the early nineteenth century. They appealed successfully for female support of benevolent and religious enterprises of every variety. But women would remain subordinate to men in carrying out their responsibilities:

While the pious female, therefore, does not aspire after things too great for her, she discovers that there is a wide field opened for the exercise of all her active powers. . . . Knowing that her true dignity and usefulness consist in filling that station marked out for her by the God of nature and of grace, she is satisfied in being an assistant of man. [14]

Practical piety tended to become feminized and, while religious leadership remained man's prerogative, women formed the majority of many congregations.

Interpreters of woman's appropriate sphere emphasized her moral superiority and her role as guardian of the nation's virtue. Because they were more sheltered, more protected from the world's vices and passions, women owed a solemn duty to protect their families from evil. Where would a worldly man find honor and integrity? "At home—in the wife of his bosom. It is for her to keep man within the sphere of duty, of charity, of virtue, religion, and peace...."[15] Woman's moral superiority gave her a special role as culture bearer, capable of doing "more toward forming the manners and regulating the customs of society, than all our public functionaries."[16] Special obligations existed toward unfortunate classes of the population, such as slaves, for "nothing is more underrated than the power of female influence, when exerted in a righteous cause," or merchant seamen whose condition might be improved "spiritually and temporally" by the efforts of generous women.[17] With pardonable exaggeration one female writer gave almost cosmic proportions to the moral responsibilities of her sex: "Woman was destined to a holy and honourable office...as the most effective instrument in the moral regeneration of a fallen world...."[18]

Woman's crowning glory was motherhood: in the bearing, nursing and rearing of her offspring she could most fully carry out the responsibilities of her appropriate sphere. To the mother was ascribed a profound influence—greater than that of kings, armies, statesmen—for she held sway over the cradle, guiding, forming, instructing the shapeless infant. Lydia Maria Child dedicated her *Mother's Book,* a manual filled with helpful practical hints and moralistic advice, "To American Mothers, on whose intelligence and discretion the safety and prosperity of our republic so much depend...."[19] *...What is the profession of a Woman?* asked a distinguished educator: "Is it not to form immortal minds, and to watch, to nurse, and to rear the bodily system, so fearfully and wonderfully made, and upon the order and regulation of which, the health and well-being of the mind so greatly depends?"[20]

The relations between mother and child might hold a key to the solution of many social and moral ills, and perhaps to the future of the nation itself. Wrote Hannah Mather Crocker in her *Observations on the Real Rights of Women,* "It is woman's appropriate duty and particular privilege to...implant in the juvenile breast the first seed of virtue, the love of God, and their country, with all the other virtues that shall prepare them to shine as statesmen, soldiers, philosophers and christians."[21] Obviously, Crocker was thinking of mothers in relation to their male offspring. Lydia Sigourney, one of the leading sentimental writers of her generation, wrote similarly that woman "renders a noble service to the government that protects her, by sowing seeds of purity and peace in the hearts of those, who shall nereafter claim its honours or control its destinies." Thus sheltered from man's "stormy portion of...power or glory," woman couid not wish for a greater role in society than the guidance of future generations in the paths of righteousness.[22]

The growing prestige of motherhood derived in part from changing attitudes toward children. Historians of childhood differ in their interpretations of how parents responded to their children between 1600 and 1850, but they agree that the young were regarded as being more and more valuable during this period.[23] Childhood emerged as a distinct stage of human development, infant mortality declined, and parents enlarged their emotional investment in their progeny. Mothers, in particular, took new responsibilities for the offspring, to the point that by the late nineteenth century motherhood seemed to be woman's most consuming role. Victorian motherhood required total commitment from woman: "by definition loving, gentle, tender, self-sacrificing, devoted, limited in interests to creating a haven for her family—the mother became in time almost a parody."[24]

The pattern was well-established before 1850, as American mothers learned that they should regard the infant with most tender sentiments. Mrs. Sigourney's *Letters to Mothers* (1838), dedicated especially to new mothers, was typically sentimental:

> You are sitting with your child in your arms. So am I. And I have never been as happy before. Have you? How this new affection seems to spread a soft, fresh green over the soul. Does not the whole heart blossom thick with plants of hope, sparkling with perpetual dew drops? . . . Never before have I been so blest, as to nurture the infant, when as a germ quickened by Spring, it opens the folding-doors of its little heart, and puts forth the thought, the preference, the affection, like filmy radicles, or timid tendrils, seeking where to twine. [25]

Mrs. Sigourney stressed the value of early childhood, of the impressions obtained while the child was still innocent, "softened by the breath of a mother," and emphasized the profound religious significance of child nurture. Mothers had fearful responsibilities and their prestige rose immensely during this sentimental, moralistic, nationalistic age.

Another potential role model for American women existed from the beginning of the nineteenth century. Feminist ideology, insisting on equality between the sexes, autonomy for both, and a greatly enlarged range of activity for women, engendered a strong negative reaction in the United States. Women were not yet ready for such radical doctrines. The first great statement of feminist ideology, *A Vindication of the Rights of Woman,* had been published in 1792 by an Englishwoman, Mary Wollstonecraft. Her book was a statement of rebellion against the standards of feminine delicacy reaching their height in England at the time of its publication. Wollstonecraft herself had suffered from the restrictive notions of middle-class respectability when she attempted to support herself through teaching and writing, and she saw firsthand the defects in women's education.

Guided by her experience and by the philosophy of the Enlightenment, which viewed environment as the principal source of human culture and personality, Wollstonecraft regarded education as the solution to sexual inequality. Woman's true character, according to the *Vindication,* was formed not as a result of natural intellectual inferiority, but by what was expected of her, what she was taught. Woman could be trained to use her innate and unrealized rational capacities only if she had the chance to receive a thorough and rigorous academic education. Wollstonecraft attacked the usual women's literature of her day for its emphasis on ornamental education for women and for its defense of the double moral standard. Although the *Vindication* was an eloquent statement of certain feminist principles, it appealed to only a tiny sympathetic audience. A handful of American writers experimented with feminist ideas, but they too had little impact. Americans would require nearly fifty years to respond to Mary Wollstonecraft's appeal, years of experience, action, and ideological growth which would prepare the land for its own woman's movement.

The ideology of woman's appropriate sphere is subject to various interpretations. Did the notion of a separate sphere originate in a conspiracy against women? Since many of its leading advocates were professional men who would surely be threatened by sexual equality, the effort to assign women to a limited range of activity bears the marks of discrimination if not outright conspiracy. Circumstantial evidence is not sufficient, however, to convict the preachers and teachers who sought to guide American women in proper conduct. If a conspiracy existed, it was not explicit. More tenable is the explanation that an ideology of woman's subordination came into being during the late eighteenth and early nineteenth centuries as a response to drastic social, economic, and political changes. In a society where virtually nothing was constant or stable, women would be assigned to conserve moral and religious values, and especially to transmit these values to succeeding generations.

2

A LITTLE LEARNING

EDUCATION, a rapidly expanding enterprise between the Revolution and the Civil War, stimulated a lavish outpouring of energy and controversy in the United States during this period. What aims and means of education suited a newly inaugurated republic? What forms and institutions would serve a society in the process of modernization? How would women be instructed in the new educational framework?

The idea of educating girls beyond the rudiments would have seemed quite foreign to America's first colonial settlers. Being weaker and subordinate to men, women could not claim the same rights to education, nor could they make good use of learning if somehow they achieved it. Girls and boys in colonial New England often attended so-called dame schools, private classes taught by housewives offering primary instruction to neighborhood children. Although New England towns had legal obligations to maintain basic schools, evidence is not clear on whether girls regularly attended these public facilities. District schools often operated seasonally, with boys in school during the winter when they had little agricultural work, and girls in school during the summer. Never did young women join their brothers in the Latin grammar schools which prepared the way for attendance at college.

The problem of female literacy in colonial New England raises questions about the extent and utility of girls' schooling. Evidence from signatures on wills suggests that between the seventeenth and eighteenth centuries female literacy declined relative to that of men. Although more women could sign their names after 1670, male literacy became almost universal during the eighteenth century, while women's literacy remained stationary. This evidence indicates that in provincial circumstances a higher value was placed on instructing men than women. It does not necessarily contradict other evidence from the late colonial period of educational advances that would lead to expanded opportunities for women.

An uncertain number of young women in the middle Atlantic region obtained basic instruction in parochial schools of Dutch, German, and Quaker colonies. Here, too, the basic schools taught reading and piety; education beyond the primary levels belonged to those few young men who were preparing to go into professions. Schooling was irregular in the South, but the limited primary schools probably served girls as well as boys. Daughters of wealthy planters often enjoyed the advantage of private tutors, although their courses tended to be ornamental rather than academic. Formal education throughout the colonies was limited for all except the wealthy and the well-born.

Far more important than formal instruction in the education of ordinary folk was the pattern of everyday experience. Growing up for most boys and girls involved an apprenticeship process. Some apprenticeship was formal—children were "put out" to masters to learn a trade; most apprenticeship was simply rooted in the ways in which children learned to help around the house and do agricultural chores, graduating to increasingly significant and productive roles. Families thus assumed most of the burden of early colonial education and the curriculum was life itself. From their families most women learned subordination and domesticity, but the system permitted a few exceptional individuals to obtain abundant learning.

These patterns changed during the eighteenth century as education, under the pressure of social and economic development, became more formal, more deliberate, more institutional, "an act of will" rather than an automatic process. While a majority of young American women grew up in traditional domestic circumstances, a middle- and upper-class minority were trained to new social responsibilities. Beyond the level of reading, writing, figuring, and learning religious doctrine, as the eighteenth century advanced, elegantly bred young ladies acquired such "accomplishments" as drawing, music, fancy needlework, dancing, the French language, polite conversation, manners, and other subjects appropriate to perform in fashionable society. Those women who had more serious intellectual interests found the system inadequate. One of the early republic's most gifted women, Abigal Adams, herself unschooled in any formal sense, lamented the neglect of learning among American women:

> I can hear of the Brilliant accomplishment[s] of any of my Sex with pleasure and rejoice in that Liberality of Sentiment which acknowledges them. At the same time I regret the trifling narrow contracted Education of the Females of my own country. . . . you need not be told how much female Education is neglected, nor how fashionable it has been to ridicule Female learning.... [1]

Educational reform began in America before Independence. In his exhaustive study of colonial education, Lawrence Cremin concludes that early experimentation had a far-reaching impact: "Popularization, then, with respect to access, substance, and control, became early and decisively the single most characteristic commitment of American education."[2] Popularization was reflected in numerous curriculum reforms introduced during the second half of the eighteenth century in American schools. Collegiate studies in science, law, medicine, and modern languages, based on Enlightenment beliefs and emphasizing useful knowledge, indicated an enthusiasm for modernization and progress. New institutional forms appeared, especially in secondary education. Academies, beginning in the last quarter of the eighteenth century, offered studies suited to the needs of men who would go into business or trades instead of professions: surveying, practical mathematics, navigation, modern languages, and debating. With courses in history and political topics, they served as schools for citizenship.

Academies grew rapidly after 1800 and by the mid-nineteenth century, at the height of their influence, they numbered more than 6000 institutions. As they expanded throughout the East, into the South and West, academies became general-purpose institutions, serving local communities as day schools and attracting boarding students from some distance. Many early nineteenth-century academies were coeducational, offering useful and liberal secondary schooling to girls as well as boys. Having principally local patronage and serving the entire middle-class population, academies naturally admitted young women as did the common schools, even though some courses, such as surveying or classical languages, were not open to them. Unlike twentieth-century academies, which are generally exclusive, expensive boarding schools, many early nineteenth-century academies admitted all candidates who could afford the modest fees. Few were dominated by college preparatory programs. Thus, young women were often welcome.

Following the Revolution, Americans established a distinct rationale for women's academic education. The same enthusiastic nationalism and passion for progress which influenced education as a whole were evident in the substantial programs designed to instruct women. Benjamin Rush, the Philadelphia physician, educator, and humanitarian, took much interest in the improvement of girls' schools. In his 1787 commencement address at Brown's Academy for girls, where he served on the Board of Visitors, Rush emphasized women's duties to the nation. In contrast to the idle and "ornamental" women of England, American women had serious responsibilities and should receive preparation for active motherhood and property management. Rush was particularly concerned that women be educated for one of the primary duties of mothers, the instruction of children. To this purpose he recommended that young women be taught geography, chemistry, astronomy, and politics.

Another Philadelphian, James A. Neal, decried the meagre education given to girls and the ignorance that inevitably resulted. He insisted, in contradiction to traditional assumptions, that women could excel at studies requiring great concentration. Post-Revolutionary theorists argued that American women had grave responsibilities as republican mothers for the moral guardianship of young people, for the transmission of culture, and for the protection of republican institutions. Only through education could they be brought to realize these responsibilities and be equipped to carry them out. Education thus fitted in almost perfectly with the notions of woman's appropriate sphere that had begun to thrive in American society. Educationally, women occupied a somewhat paradoxical position: they would aid the nation to progress by conserving and protecting cultural values.

The most significant phase of American women's education before 1850 was the female seminary movement, which in its serious phase began about 1815. Five leaders, four women and one man, stand out as major influences on the seminary movement: Emma Willard, Catharine E. Beecher, Zilpah P. Grant, Mary Lyon, and Joseph Emerson—all New England Yankees. These educational reformers sought to provide for women the best instruction as was offered in academies, to approach that of men's colleges. They aimed to create institutions which would answer the demands made on American women, to be citizens of a republic and mothers of future statesmen. But they assumed that young women should be educated separately and in a different fashion from young men. The better seminaries reacted against the unsystematic and superficial operations of many early teachers of young women. Reformers tried to counteract the tendency in girls' schools to emphasize fashionable, shallow, showy accomplishments at the expense of more solid studies and character building. Wrote Catharine Beecher, one of the leading female seminary advocates: "A lady should study, not to *shine* but to *act*."[3]

The seminary movement faced four basic problems. The first difficulty was financial: girls' schools did not have the luxury of endowments or of public aid as did many boys' academies and colleges, but their financial needs were no less imperative than those of men's academies. A second and hardly less important problem was the curriculum. To become serious academic institutions, girls' schools needed to overcome prejudices against learning for women. Too many schools prospered because of their offerings of numerous superficial and ornamental studies, and reformers wanted to give increased depth to the curriculum. Third, those who hoped to give vitality and substance to women's education required experienced and trained teachers. Educated men there were, but tender young women should have members of their own sex to teach with propriety and sympathy. Finally, the educational reformers had to justify the changes which they advocated.

Emma Willard, the founder of one of the earliest seminaries, grew up in Berlin, Connecticut, in a large farm family. Her father, a political liberal, had generous notions of women's educability, and Emma Willard began to experiment in learning and teaching while a teenager. She attended a local academy and taught in local schools, then went to female seminaries at Hartford. Before opening her own school at Middlebury, Vermont, in 1814, she taught successfully at two other New England academies. During this period she experimented with curriculum and disciplinary reforms which formed the basis of a major institutional effort. Her experience at Middlebury confirmed her ideas of women's capacities for study and led her to design a major reform of education for women. In 1818, hoping to obtain public funding from the state of New York, she sent a copy of her plan to Governor DeWitt Clinton. In 1819, her *Plan for Improving Female Education* was published, the first comprehensive design for a distinct female institution of learning to be circulated in America.

To combat the "moral evils" of girls' schools in the early nineteenth century, Emma Willard proposed instruction in four major areas: (1) religious and moral training, "the true end of all education...;" (2) literary instruction, including the sciences of the mind and natural philosophy, taught in order that mothers might be better prepared to train their children; (3) domestic instruction accomplished through the students' care of their rooms and the school as a whole, exercising discipline and cooperative labor—learning by doing; (4) the ornamental branches, with "drawing and painting, elegant penmanship, music, and the grace of motion."[4]

Willard argued that a system of discrimination in education, giving distinctly inferior training to women's minds, degraded the character of their sex:

> Daughters are hurried through the routine of boarding school instruction, and at an early period introduced into the gay world; and thenceforth, their only object is amusement. Mark the different treatment, which the sons of these families receive. While their sisters are gliding through the mazes of the midnight dance, they employ the lamp, to treasure up for future use the riches of ancient wisdom; or to gather strength and expansion of mind, in exploring the wonderful paths of philosophy. When the youth of the two sexes has been spent so differently, is it strange, or is nature in fault, if more mature age has brought such a difference of character, that our sex has been considered by the other, as the pampered, wayward babies of society, who must have some rattle put into our hands, to keep us from doing mischief to ourselves or others? [5]

Her moral indignation was aroused by certain conventional attitudes, yet Emma Willard was no radical feminist. She never agitated for the emancipation of women in fields other than education and she accepted the common opinion of her time that woman's subordination was divinely ordained. Appealing for public support, she wrote: "I...hasten to observe, that the seminary here recommended, will be as different from those appropriated to the other sex as the female characters and duties are from the male."[6]

Emma Willard was disappointed in her request to the New York legislature for public funding, and in 1821 she moved to Troy, New York, where the city offered her a building. Here she inaugurated the Troy Female Seminary and served as its principal until 1838. The school became one of the most advanced and famous institutions for educating young women in the United States. Willard's curriculum was ahead of the courses offered by most girls' schools, and included algebra and geometry, history, geography, and several sciences. Her approach to geography was pedagogically progressive in its use of charts and maps. She contributed to the improvement of textbooks in the fields of geography, history, and morals. She was a great advocate of women teachers, training hundreds of young women at Troy who went out to staff the growing private and public school systems. Many other female seminaries and colleges were modeled after the Troy Seminary. In retrospect, Willard made mighty contributions toward solving the problems that faced women's education.

Catharine E. Beecher, like Emma Willard, grew up chiefly in small-town Connecticut, daughter of a father who expected great things of her. Catharine Beecher's father, Lyman, was one of the notable spokesmen for evangelical Protestantism in early nineteenth-century America and his daughter certainly derived her "mission" in education partly from his example. The young woman attended the fashionable academy of Sarah Pierce at Litchfield, Connecticut, and taught there and at New London briefly before the death of her fiancé in 1822 changed the course of her life. In the following year, she and her sister Mary opened the Hartford Female Seminary. Like Emma Willard, she sought to change the emphasis in the curriculum from fashionable subjects to more substantial courses, including Latin, philosophy, history, chemistry, and mathematics. As the school prospered, the Beecher sisters were able to add specialized instruction in some fields.

Between 1827 and 1831 the Hartford Female Seminary became one of the lighthouses of the female seminary movement. Its classes included the daughters of Hartford's best families, plus numerous young women from New England and other regions of the nation. Enjoying the patronage of the Hartford elite, Catharine Beecher was able to raise a $5000 building fund and construct a substantial Greek revival structure for the Seminary. Beecher and others considered it a model building, with its large hall seating 150 pupils at writing desks, a library, a dressing room, and nine recitation rooms. The Hartford Seminary was graded into three classes, each more advanced than preceding years. A faculty of eight plus two administrators and the principal presided over its operations. Most of the teachers had been trained by Beecher herself. As part of her scheme for reforming society by educating women, Beecher taught all students a class in mental and moral philosophy which attempted to integrate religious principles, moral duties, and social behavior, all leading to the chief aim of women's education: to develop character.

Catharine Beecher tried to carry her Seminary one step further, to establish its program on a permanent basis by raising an endowment. It was in this attempt that she ran straight into the wall of public indifference and prejudice. While the elite of Hartford could see the worth of a fine school building made of bricks and mortar, the less-tangible benefits of fine character and useful learning for their daughters appeared unworthy of generous financial support. Beecher's campaign for an endowment failed. This failure led her to retire from Hartford and join her father, who was himself seeking to rebuild his prestige. Daughter and father traveled west to Cincinnati where they attempted new educational ventures.

During the 1830s Catharine Beecher inaugurated a campaign for the improvement of education in the West and South. Through pamphlets, lectures, extensive traveling, and agitation she exposed the shocking state of American education—the two million children who had no teachers, and who, as a result, grew up without discipline or useful learning. At Cincinnati she began another female seminary—which failed— to help train teachers to fill the crying needs of the West. She pleaded for faithful and benevolent young women from New England to venture into the West to dedicate their earthly lives to training "heathen" children. Turning the movement into a full scale missionary campaign, with a central organization, agent-lecturers, local women's groups, and church auxiliaries, she hoped to provide money and motivation for young teachers to go West.

In her crusading, Catharine Beecher did not forget her commitment to female seminaries. She worked doggedly but without much success for endowed seminaries in the West, hoping that the region would train its own teachers. For a few years she was busily and successfully engaged in promoting the Milwaukee Female College (later Milwaukee-Downer College, now part of the University of Wisconsin at Milwaukee), but she retired from this work in 1856. Believing that homemaking, nursing, and teaching were woman's appropriate professions, Catharine Beecher organized courses and wrote numerous books—among the first of their kind—on "domestic economy."[7] Beyond the establishment of Hartford Female Seminary as a model school, her greatest services to the cause of women's education consisted of publicizing the needs and benefits of rigorous, professional, soundly-financed schools for young women.

The Reverend Joseph Emerson was a lesser-known although nevertheless influential advocate of female education. While he had a substantial reputation in his own time, he is remembered today largely for his impact on two women, Zilpah P. Grant and Mary Lyon. After resigning from the ministry because of ill health, Emerson in 1818 (the year Emma Willard sent her suggestions to DeWitt Clinton) opened a female seminary at Byfield, Massachusetts, where he specialized in

fundamental subjects instead of "accomplishments." Later he conducted girls' schools at Saugus, Massachusetts, and Wethersfield,
Connecticut. Like other seminary advocates, Emerson saw a close
connection between learning and religion, both in the need to instill piety
and to encourage dis-interested benevolent and religious conduct among
young people.

Emerson was one of the earliest American teachers to emphasize
pedagogy consciously in his classes for young women. He discussed
various principles of education, expounded rules for conducting schools,
lectured on "chirography," and advocated grammar as a "noble
science." As a writer of pamphlets on education in the 1820s, he
pioneered in the systematic exploration of instructional techniques. He
respected the female intellect and believed in equal treatment of the
sexes, although he felt that women occupied a "subordinate station" in
the scheme of creation, but wielded powerful influences in society
through their relations to the other sex. To his pupils, Zilpah Grant and
Mary Lyon, he communicated his enthusiasm for teaching, his concern
with instructional techniques, and his devotion to religion and discipline.

After studying and teaching with Joseph Emerson between 1820 and
1822, Zilpah Grant and Mary Lyon began their joint operations at an
academy in Londonderry, New Hampshire, establishing patterns of
graded course work, solid rather than ornamental studies, the "self-
reporting" or confessional form of discipline, and heavy emphasis on
religious and biblical studies. A dispute with the trustees led to their
resignation in 1828 and shortly Zilpah Grant and Mary Lyon took over
the Ipswich Female Seminary in Massachusetts.[8]

With Zilpah Grant as principal and Mary Lyon as her assistant, the
Ipswich Seminary flourished. Strictly controlled by these women, the
school formed a tight little community, separate from the town. Between
1828 and 1839 the students numbered from 120 to 190 each term, with
eight to ten teachers. Pupils boarded with families in the town, generally
in situations where teachers could oversee them. Their ages varied—the
youngest were about fourteen, but older pupils were sometimes in their
twenties and had years of teaching experience. The school was governed
by a rigid schedule which left no time for idleness and scarcely any choice
of activities. More than most female seminaries, Ipswich was almost
morbidly religious, akin to a Protestant nunnery.

Ipswich students and faculty alike were sustained by the conviction
that all were engaged in a terribly significant enterprise, an experiment
whose consequences would be felt in this world and the next. The

Ipswich curriculum featured basic subjects. No foreign or dead languages cluttered the course of study, calisthenics and the grace of motion substituted for dancing, and vocal rather than instrumental music was taught. Grant and her assistants taught basic science, theology, and religion. English, in the form of grammar and writing exercises, was emphasized throughout the course. Other studies, such as geography, U.S. government, and history were appropriate for future teachers and mothers.

The program at Ipswich Seminary had special value for prospective teachers. Zilpah Grant offered lectures on the conduct and management of schools, distilled from her years of experience and characterized by sound common sense rather than innovative techniques. Schools, the lectures emphasized, should be governed by the law of love, a mutual atmosphere of affection uniting teachers and pupils. Specific suggestions were provided for handling common problems and weaknesses of young children. A few of the older girls had opportunities to serve as assistant pupils or monitors, and in this capacity they listened to recitations and assisted in teaching. Especially able students sometimes remained at the Seminary after completing their course to serve as assistant teachers. Like Emma Willard and Catharine Beecher, Grant and Lyon were solving the problem of providing teachers for young women by providing training and apprenticeship. Ipswich Seminary also inaugurated a revolving scholarship fund and an employment agency for teachers to encourage them to work at "destitute" places in the West.

The Ipswich Seminary had an immediate impact on a number of other institutions. Three schools, now colleges, were patterned on Ipswich: Wheaton, Mount Holyoke, and Oberlin. Grant and Lyon helped directly in establishing Wheaton Seminary in the early 1830's, specifying duplication of regulations and courses of study. The close relationship between Oberlin's young ladies' course and Ipswich resulted from the fact that Oberlin's first lady principals had been students of Zilpah Grant and Mary Lyon. Although renowned for its coeducation, the pattern at Oberlin for women students followed principles of separation and inequality between the sexes derived from the regulations and disciplinary practices at Ipswich Seminary.

The story of Mary Lyon and the Mount Holyoke Female Seminary has a special place in the development of American women's education. More than the other seminary pioneers, Lyon was able to resolve the problems facing women's instruction and create a solid, permanent institution. Partly by her own indefatigable will, partly by taking advantage of conservative clergymen and educators, and partly by her shrewdness in enlisting hundreds of women in her cause, Mary Lyon developed the vision shared by seminary advocates of founding an endowed school capable of training teachers, with a solid course of study, a campus, and a professional faculty whose existence and appeal to a wide range of young women justified itself. In some ways Mount Holyoke climaxed the seminary movement. Its program, however, was based on that of the Ipswich Female Seminary.

Mary Lyon's views of the purpose of female education help to define the ideals of the seminary movement. In an appeal for funds oriented toward women, Lyon expressed the hopes of seminary advocates. Education ought to prepare women for their proper vocation by training wives, mothers, household managers, and school teachers:

> All our chilren — our future statesmen & rulers, and ministers & missionaries, must come inevitably under the moulding hand of the female, & must experience, through their lives, & our country & the world experience with them, the salutary or the bitter effects of this moulding influence. This is a picture of mournful reality over which many an eye has wept, & many a heart bled. 9

Female seminaries offered women a little learning, by which they might serve God and their country.

Spurred on by their missionary zeal, the promoters of female seminaries spread their institutions across the land. Mount Holyoke Seminary's institutional offspring included Western and Lake Erie Seminaries in Ohio, Monticello and Rockford Seminaries in Illinois, and Mills in California. The majority of these grew into colleges, and some survive today. One estimate of Emma Willard's influence indicates "that more than two hundred schools based upon Troy Seminary methods can...be reckoned as the fruit of her pioneer work." 10 Institutional reflections of Catharine Beecher's years of agitation cannot be calculated precisely. They numbered not only the schools she helped to found but others staffed by hundreds of young women teachers who went West under her sponsorship and the scores of institutions influenced by her writings. In addition to the many seminaries that later became full four-year colleges, the earliest women's colleges related many of their programs closely to the discipline and living arrangements pioneered by female seminaries. Both Elmira (1855) and Vassar (1865) Colleges employed women who oversaw the discipline and domestic operations, much as Beecher and Lyon had done in their seminaries. Female seminaries, like male academies, were a phase in the evolution of American secondary and higher education.

In retrospect the seminary movement's total impact was ambiguous. On the one hand they proved that women had minds capable of serious discipline, abstract thinking, and problem solving. They showed that women could teach and manage institutions successfully. Opening the way for women to enter a fairly respectable profession, teaching, they stimulated a self-confidence and a consciousness of power and mission among their teachers and pupils. On the other hand, they accepted and celebrated woman's "appropriate sphere," especially her duties as mother, teacher, missionary, and moral guardian. The seminaries, by providing education separate from and unequal to that of men, confirmed and reinforced a double standard of education, Radical women like Lucy Stone and Elizabeth Cady Stanton would later find in the limited definitions of women's learning and women's sphere fostered by the seminaries justification for a vigorous rebellion in defiance of the status quo. But for many of the young women whose minds were first challenged by these institutions, the experience was one of liberation. Hear a graduate of the Young Ladies' Course at Oberlin, patterned after the program at Ipswich Female Seminary:

> I *do* enjoy myself very much here . . . everything is perfectly reasonable and rational, and everyone seems to be happy. The course of instruction is thorough; and so far as I can judge . . . it is the only place where females are conducted through a *full* and thorough course . . . for that reason I do want much that females should have it; their minds ought to be thus disciplined; and then they will become elevated. As to the domestic department, it is bringing into the system of education a fundamental branch and establishing it upon correct principles. I feel that I never expended money for so good a purpose, as I am now expending it. . . . [11]

One of the most useful contributions of the seminary movement before 1850 centered around the attention it gave to the teaching abilities of women. All the seminary promoters campaigned zealously to make schoolteaching a major vocation for women. Yet at first they moved against a strong current that identified instruction as a profession and hence, like medicine or the ministry, not open to women. Generations earlier, in the colonial period. when education had been chiefly informal, an inherent part of the process of growing up, women had offered a variety of primary and useful instruction as a function of their domestic roles. By the early nineteenth century, when teaching had shifted from households into schoolrooms, the vocation of a teacher demanded, in theory, special qualifications of strength sufficient to apply corporal punishment and learned preparation, possessed only by men—except that women might teach the youngest boys and girls of any age. Men teachers dominated most American education before 1840.

Advocates of women teachers could take advantage of two circumstances of early nineteenth-century mass education. First, the need for teachers was growing as the country expanded and as educational standards rose. Second, the supply of qualified men could not meet the demand, whereas an increasing number of qualified women emerged from female seminaries and academies. An estimate of educational needs in 1833 assumed that 1,400,000 children were "destitute of common instruction," that a shortage of more than 30,000 teachers existed and, with the increase of school-age population, an annual increment of 10,000 teachers would be required for years. [12] Men, without permanent interest in teaching, would not fill these requirements. Wrote Thomas Gallaudet, a leading educator:

> While we should encourage our young men to enter upon this patriotic, and I had almost said, missionary field of duty . . . I believe every one must admit, that there is but little hope of attaining *the full supply* from that sex. This will always be difficult, so long as there are so many other avenues open in our country to the accumulation of property and the attaining of distinction. [13]

The answer to the teacher shortage was to employ women.

Two other facets of women's condition recommended their employment as teachers. They were by nature more attuned than men to the wants of young children. Teaching, like motherhood, derived from women's divinely appointed sphere. Governor William H. Seward of New York approved of women in the schools when he wrote:

> They are the natural guardians of the young. Their abstraction from the engrossing cares of life affords them leisure both to acquire and communicate knowledge. From them the young more willingly receive it, because the severity of discipline is relieved with greater tenderness and affection.... [14]

Educational reformers like Horace Mann declaimed rhapsodically about the natural virtues of female teachers, as for example:"there is no station, or office, or dignity, known among men—save that of the mother, only—which outranks her in importance.'' [15]

The other great advantage of women teachers was their cheapness. It became the standard argument in the late 1830s and 1840s that women would teach for less money than men. Fortunately for reformers who valued economy over most other considerations, women seemed to have few materialistic motivations: ''they are less intent and scheming for future honors or emoluments. As a class, they never look forward...to... go abroad into the world, to build up a fortune for themselves.'' [16] Educational leaders were quite explicit about the economic advantages of employing female teachers. In 1838, Connecticut paid men $14.50 per month, women $5.75. Pennsylvania, with many more men than women teachers, recorded wages of $18.50 per month for males, $11.30 for females. [17] The Ohio Superintendent of Common Schools boasted in 1839 that they ''are able to do twice as much with the same money as is done in those counties where female teachers are almost excluded. As the business of teaching is made more respectable, more females engage in it, and the wages are reduced.'' [18]

The economic argument for women teachers, along with crying needs for their services and assumptions concerning their special aptitudes for child nurture, slowly broke down resistance to their entry into classrooms. Women replaced men as teachers first in the New England states during the 1830s, and the movement spread during the 1840s and 1850s to other regions. Urban locations, where qualified women were available and school growth rates were high, employed women teachers quite rapidly. By the 1850s Brooklyn counted 103 women and 17 men teachers in its system, and Philadelphia's schools had 699 women and only 82 men teaching. [19] Rural areas and the South changed most slowly. By 1860 some states had more women than men teaching, and by the century's end women dominated classroom teaching throughout the nation. The picture for school administration, however, was totally different: here men continued to dominate almost all managerial roles.

School reformers believed that the introduction of women teachers would not only be more economical, but that the influx of females would raise the quality of instruction. At first the reformers could count on female seminary and academy graduates for their purposes. Seminary principals like Emma Willard, Catharine Beecher, Zilpah Grant, and Mary Lyon were only too willing to train and help recruit likely candidates. As early as the 1820s, reformers saw the need for additional teacher-training facilities. During the late 1830s plans were matured to provide public support for the instruction of women teachers. In Massachusetts, the state legislature agreed to match a private donation of $10,000, enabling three teacher-training institutions to open in 1839 and 1840. The first American normal school opened at Lexington, Massachusetts, in 1839, devoted exclusively to the education of common schoolteachers, setting a pattern for normal education which would dominate teacher-training in this country for almost a century.

Lexington Normal was a new kind of school, supported by taxpayers for the exclusive instruction of women. The course of study included thorough grounding in the so-called common branches or subjects "which the law requires to be taught in the district schools," and finally *"the science and art of teaching, with reference to all the above named studies."* The latter field received attention in frequent lectures and daily recitations, but most significantly in the program of the model school. Consisting of children taken from the town of Lexington, the model school was intended to be a laboratory and workshop in which future teachers might observe and themselves attempt instruction. Student-teachers received suggestions and advice from the principal, thus combining "theory and practice, precept and example." [20] Normal schools carried women's education two steps beyond the female seminaries by concentrating exclusively on teacher-training and providing public financial support for instruction. During the 1840s and 1850s the system spread throughout the East and into the West.

School reformers intended their employment of women to be advantageous to the sex. With most professions closed to them, educated women had little outlet for their skills except the classroom. Teaching was a respectable and sometimes pleasant alternative to work in textile mills or domestic service. It permitted the exercise of woman's natural maternal and affectionate impulses. And within the limits of their appropriate sphere, it gave women a great mission, an opportunity to serve their country and humanity. Few, if any, of the school reformers—most of them men—acknowledged that their plans to employ women teachers were highly exploitative.

The system emerging in the late 1830s exhibited a pattern of discrimination against women that became embedded in American public education. Women would work for half the wages of men; they would teach little children where their emotions rather than their intellectual capacities would be valued; they would put up with conditions that men, because of their opportunities elsewhere, did not tolerate. The fact is that educators, like millowners and clergymen, discovered in women a resource, a laboring force, which could be manipulated to their advantage. In attracting women into teaching, the reformers not only obtained a competent labor supply that they could not secure otherwise, but a class of workers likely to be docile, accepting of masculine domination, unlikely to threaten the system of education and the power structure erected by men.

For the women who responded to the challenge of a new profession, the opportunity to teach was ambiguous. They could not expect to earn decent wages. Even earning a living was unlikely for many woman teachers, although by "boarding around" they could have beds and meals, however inadequate these might be. For a young woman on her own, or with relatives to support, earning half or one-third of the wages offered to a male teacher was neither adequate nor satisfying. As teachers, women could achieve the prestige awarded to a noble calling, yet practically speaking they were servants of a frequently unappreciative public. Were teachers of young children not performing a traditional female task? The vocation's setting had changed from the household to the schoolroom, but child nurture remained woman's role, its low value emphasized by an inferior financial reward.

On the other hand, women's entry into schoolteaching raised issues that could not be ignored. If women were as good for the schools as the re- formers claimed, why should their compensation be so much lower than that of men teachers? If teaching was truly professional and women were so effective as teachers, why should other professions not be open to the sex? If women could function in public as instructors, why were other public roles generally forbidden to them? If women were clever enough to communicate knowledge to large groups of unenthusiastic, often hostile children, why could they not deal as intellectual peers with similarly educated men? Years later the advocates of women's rights and woman suffrage would ask questions of this kind and they would find that not only the teaching profession but the society and the political system in general were at fault. Thus women's roles as teachers contributed something—how much is impossible to say—to the growing uncertainty about sex-role definitions in mid-nineteenth century America.

Those people most affected by expanding opportunities to teach—the young women who flocked into the classrooms—seemed to find little fault with the system. Or at least they left few records of their discontent, except for some of the teachers who went West where they found conditions of life primitive and discouraging. Others complained about unsatisfactory teaching situations. But most young women teachers seem to have enjoyed and been inspired by their responsibilities. Some accepted the idea of teaching as a mission and agreed with leading educators that their work was an effort at national salvation. One catches occasional glimpses of the enthusiasm shared by these young teachers and their pupils in fragments of correspondence still surviving. [21]

A little learning for women—what did it mean? The question has no neat answer, perhaps because American women's education during the first half of the nineteenth century had so many conflicting meanings. A little learning meant some formal instruction for middle-class women, but opportunities not comparable to those of men. Their inferiority could thus be interpreted as a disability, a consequence of discrimination to be conquered. On the other hand, although it did not measure up to the standards of men's education, the quality of instruction in the best female seminaries was far ahead of any formal educational advantages open to women in colonial times. Inferior, yes; improved, decidedly yes—thus both conservatives and reformers could rejoice.

Adding to the uncertainty over benefits derived from the new education was the fact that the educators promised more than they could deliver. Learning did not necessarily lead to economic or vocational opportunities outside the realm of teaching or "scientific" domesticity. The Beechers and Willards expanded glowingly on the capacity of educated women to save the republic as well as their own and their families' souls. But the means and hope of national salvation became less and less tenable as the nation staggered toward 1861. Their expectations raised by educational reformers, middle-class women felt disappointed and deprived by the limited results of their endeavors. They experienced what Gerda Lerner has termed status deprivation, as they saw their brothers and husbands forge ahead politically and economically in a race from which they were disqualified.[22] Education had, if anything, made women's status more ambiguous than before.

Their efforts to achieve learning nevertheless had some lessons for sensitive, discontented women. One prominent feature of the education movement was its leadership by strong, active, undeviating women. If the seminary demonstrated anything, it showed that women could act and succeed in their own behalf. The examples set by Willard, Beecher, Grant, and Lyon made their students proud. A later generation, less intimidated by conventions and reacting to a more radical time, would follow these examples of female leadership in more rebellious directions.

Education gave women practical experience in leadership as well as examples to follow. Teachers were semi-public figures with a fair amount of autonomy in their classrooms, and authority over both sexes. In teaching they learned to lecture and speak in public, to exert themselves for a purpose. It is no coincidence that many of the first generation of feminists had been educated and had taught. Education also produced a set of grievances for women: a double standard in learning, limited opportunities to use their new skills and intellectual powers, and a pattern of unequal pay for the same work as performed by men.

Educational change helped to carry middle-class women toward the organized woman's movement, making middle-class, not working-class women, leaders in a new crusade. It tended to separate the lives and experience of women in the upper and middle classes from those of the working class, and left one major disability for all—the inability to vote. In this way, education contributed toward making suffrage a central issue in the woman's movement of the nineteenth century.

3

NEW BONDS OF SISTERHOOD

THE strong nineteenth-century linkage between gender and culture, separating the lives   and duties of men and women into distinct spheres of activity, threw women into the company of other women and created new bonds of sisterhood between them. Margaret Fuller recognized the emotional nature of these bonds when she wrote:

> It is so true that a woman may be in love with a woman and a man with a man. It is pleasant to be sure of it, because it is undoubtedly the same love that we shall feel when we are angels. . . . It is regulated by the same laws as that of love between persons of different sexes, only it is purely intellectual and spiritual, unprofaned by any mixture of lower instincts . . . its law is the desire of the spirit to realize a whole, which makes it seek in another being that which it finds not in itself. [1]

One immediate reaction to Fuller's description is to treat it as pathology, revealing her own homosexual leanings. Yet in the context of nineteenth-century American culture, close relationships between women, even declarations of love from intimate friends, were common and accepted. They need not be interpreted in terms of abnormal sexuality. To Fuller, the love of women for women was pure, superior to animal lusts, bringing humans to the level of the angels. Fuller revealed here the profound emotional significance which many middle-class women attributed to their friendships. In a romantic age, when sensitivity and emotion were invested with great power, interpersonal ties of sisterhood had intense value.

At least six distinct types of sisterhood flourished during the nineteenth century, all closely related, each gaining support from and nourishing the other forms. Two bonds of sisterhood were traditional: ties within families and those between close friends. The sisterhood of family members, existing through generations of mothers, daughters, sisters, and cousins, persisted despite frequent separations due to migration. The sisterhood of friends, involving close and long-term personal commitments, gained strength from nineteenth-century ideas of woman's sphere and the relevance of sentimental romanticism. Taylor and Lasch use the term "sorority" to refer to this ideal of pure friendship between women, based on shared sensitivity. [2]

New categories of sisterhood reinforced the traditional ties. As young women moved away from their homes to be instructed at female academies and seminaries, they formed close connections with classmates which often developed into permanent intimate friendships. A fourth form of sisterhood receiving unprecedented emphasis in the nineteenth century derived from the religious movement known as the Second Great Awakening. This was a sisterhood of converted women, or those seeking conversion, who thought of themselves as one in their allegiance to the Savior and who shared their anxieties and exultations of faith. Growing out of this religious drama was a fifth kind of relationship among women, binding together those who engaged in voluntary good works for religious and benevolent causes. Finally, there was another sort of sisterhood felt by women who were entering new occupations—industrial work in textiles, shoemaking, and other trades—or schoolteaching.

Abundant evidence survives to indicate the force of sisterly ties among American women in the nineteenth century. Carroll Smith-Rosenberg has surveyed a large body of personal documents such as correspondence and diaries which illuminate these highly personal yet far-reaching networks of women relatives and friends. She writes: "An intimate mother-daughter relationship lay at the heart of this female world. The diaries and letters of both mothers and daughters attest to their closeness and mutual dependency." [3] Representative of this pattern was the Pierce family of Brookline, Massachusetts. When her daughter married and moved to Maine, Mrs. Pierce wrote her frequently, giving advice, describing comings and goings in the neighborhood, summarizing sermons and lyceum lectures, listing births and deaths, maintaining a close and continuing relationship. Occasionally the mother overstepped her role, criticizing the domestic arrangements of the younger family. Such concerned mother-daughter ties were characteristic of American families at this time.

Close female family connections embraced sisters and other relatives. In Ohio, Betsey Mix Cowles and her sister Cornelia wrote one another frequently when they were apart, communicating details of their daily lives, their hopes and plans. When Cornelia died, Betsey was heartbroken, for years counted the days since her sister's death, and commemorated the anniversary of her death until her own demise in 1876.

Several notable advocates of woman's causes depended on familial ties to sustain their efforts: Angelina and Sarah Grimké worked as a team during their most creative years; and members of the Blackwell family, including Lucy Stone and Antoinette Brown Blackwell, were greatly strengthened in their feminism by their sisters and sisters-in-law. So it went: mothers, daughters, sisters, aunts, cousins, formed a female network.

Catharine Beecher illustrates another common nineteenth-century pattern, the strong dependence of woman friends on one another. Following the death of her fiancé, Beecher accommodated to her position as a single woman by cultivating a series of intimate women companions, especially during times of stress. When she taught and managed the Hartford Female Seminary, Beecher formed close attachments with some of her favorite pupils. One of these, Mary Dutton, assisted her at Hartford and Cincinnati for nearly a decade. To this friend she described a theory of the woman teacher's role as mentor and confidant:

> Next after affection to God, affection to earthly friends is the most powerful principle, and here is where a teacher's strength lies. To enlighten the understanding and to gain the affections is a teacher's business, and these duties can so well be performed that almost anything can be done with *almost any mind.* [5]

Other leaders in the female seminary movement had similar views of the critical roles that teachers might play as the friends of young women.

One of the most significant female friendships of the nineteenth-century was that of Elizabeth Cady Stanton and Susan B. Anthony. For about fifty years these two vigorous personalities had an intense, devoted relationship of interdependence which helped to catalyze the woman's movement between 1850 and 1902. In an appreciation of this extraordinary friendship, Alice Rossi has written: "The key to their effectiveness lies in the complementary nature of their skills. It can truly be said in this instance that the sum was greater than its parts, for either woman would have had far less impact on the history of women's rights than they had in combination." [6] The sisterhood of friendship was not exclusive to eminent women. Thousands of average middle-class women established long-term friendships which led to deep feelings of sisterhood and great emotional satisfaction to the friends. Female friendships accepted and sustained the nineteenth-century's definitions of femininity, providing middle-class women with a series of personal relationships quite separate from the world of men. They sustained the other, newer bonds of sisterhood prevalent at the time.

Strong ties of sisterhood developed among young women who were able to attend the new schools open to them after 1800. It is little wonder that students in female seminaries found close friends among their classmates and teachers, for companionship was one of the central aims of seminary advocates. One of the stated purposes of the Ipswich Seminary was to equip its graduates with a common set of goals, to stimulate "a mingling of the daughters from the Christian families in the higher and middle classes of society as is suited to produce a most salutary effect on each...." [7] In advertising Mount Holyoke Seminary, Mary Lyon noted the importance of "congeniality of feeling, and a mutually salutary influence between room-mates...." And in evaluating the domestic department at Mount Holyoke, in which students did virtually all the housekeeping, Lyon enumerated some of its advantages:

> 2. The promotion of social & domestic happiness. The young ladies feel at home, & on coming together are very soon acquainted with each other. Their work is all very social. One young lady remarked last spring, that she had been rather homesick, but the first working day, was an effectual remedy.
> 3. The union of interests. The wisdom of the divine appointment in the organization of families, has in this respect appeared to me peculiarly striking. In our family we have but one interest for the whole. . . . [8]

At Mount Holyoke and most other female seminaries where boarding facilities existed, the family structure served as a model for organization and discipline. Hence the concept of sisterhood was relevant indeed.

The effort in these schools to create a female environment where sisterhood might flourish was generally successful. Scores of letters preserved from early students at Ipswich and Mount Holyoke Seminaries testify to the spirit and sense of emotional unity felt by these young women. An Ipswich student wrote in 1832 to her cousin:

> The school is all I could wish & one in which I feel deeply interested. The teachers I cannot tell you how much we all love. They all love us & are

willing to make any sacrifice for our good. There is a great degree of love & friendship manifested for each other. I feel as if I needed to be here a year or more. . . . I find kind friends here, better than I ever expected to find among strangers. [9]

A Mount Holyoke graduate of the 1840s retained a strong identification with her classmates and school as she wrote to Mary Lyon:

For a few days past my thoughts have been much with you. I seem to see the gathered throng of smiling ones around the cheerful tables and in the Semi[nary] hall and to hear the light joyous foot-steps echoing through the space ways. When I picture the scenes in which I have mingled there I am with you again and my heart beats happily with the heart of the institution. [10]

When they met classmates far from home these young women retained and relived the sisterhood they had experienced within the seminary halls. An Ipswich graduate wrote Mary Lyon from Oxford, Ohio, in 1831:

I am passing this winter with our dear friend Mrs. Little. You know not the pleasure of meeting with a dear friend, *classmate* a *thousand* miles from home. It is indeed pleasant, & I have reason for gratitude. . . . The manner of passing our time here reminds us of those days we spent so happily in Ipswich where every thing went on with much system & orde:. [11]

Such warm relationships derived from schoo. experiences were by no means confined to the better institutions of New England. The correspondence of Betsey Cowles, a student and teacher in Ohio, in the late 1830s and 1840s. indicates the existence of a strong network of female affection in which the principal concern was a common interest and personal involvement in education. Emulating other schools for young women, the earliest normal schools sought to create a sense of community among their students. At the Lexington, Massachusetts, Normal School in 1842, toasts "by the young ladies" included:

The Cause of Humanity—May it find an advocate in the heart of every true Normalite. Sisters of the Normal Band. May it be said of them as of the early Christians Behold how they love one another. Normal Teachers — May they be moral ploughshares to uproot every evil that parental indulgence has sown. [12]

Earlier, the Lexington students had founded an organization for discussion and "mutual improvement and industry," holding weekly readings from "one of the young ladies." Such activities were insistent reflections of the bonds of sisterhood growing out of the expanding schools for women.

Outside the formal institutional framework of women's education there existed numerous female sisterhoods centered around intellectual concerns. Because these societies generally had brief and ephemeral life spans, they are largely unrecorded. Nevertheless, a handful of records may reflect a fairly widespread series of women's associations. At Cazenovia, New York, in 1818 a group of women announced:

> We the inhabitants of Cazenovia . . . feeling desirous to cultivate those talents, which kind nature has bestowed upon us to improve, do with united friendship and devoted hearts, dedicate ourselves to the laudable pursuit of wisdom and understanding. . . . we do agree to form a Society under the name or title of the Ladies Reasoning Assembly. . . . [13]

Their programs consisted of discussions "calculated to enlarge the ideas and improve the mind" on subjects moral and elevating, such as: "By which can a person gain the most useful information, reading or frequenting good society....decided in favor of reading." At their last recorded meeting they discussed some of the aims of women's education: "Which is the most advantageous to a body, a knowledge of domestic business and an ordinary education, or to possess the most elegant accomplishments and ignorant of all domestic affairs? Decided in favor of domestic business." [14]

Other women's intellectual societies were founded, leaving brief but earnest records. In 1834, the "Young Ladies Society for Intellectual Improvement" was formed at Austinburg, Ohio, to realize a cluster of important purposes:

> The young ladies of Austinburg being sensible that to answer the end of the Deity in forming the human family with rational faculties, these faculties should be expanded and the mind well stored with knowledge; and furthermore, that it will be for the happiness of those with whom they associate in this world and the world to come, and also for their own, to elevate the soul as much as possible while imprisoned in this first body of clay, for the purpose have convened and adopted the following con- stitution. [15]

They discussed scientific and political topics: the United States Bank, John Adams, optics, James Monroe, fashion, John Quincy Adams, anatomy, Andrew Jackson, astronomy, and slavery. As interest waned, the small sisterhood invited "the gentlemen to unite with us," and the discussions became less intellectual. Occasionally such organizations took controversial stands, as when at Warren, Massachusetts, about 1840, the Literary Society resolved that "ladies ought to mingle in politics, go to Congress, etc. etc." Often associated with an academy or female seminary, these intellectual sisterhoods reflected popular enthusiasm for learning. But like the seminaries, they were associations of women, dedicated to women's purposes, enlivening the minds and expanding the sensitivities of their organizers.

Female seminaries and intellectual sisterhoods were parts of a larger, massive religious and social organizing process of the early nineteenth-century, the Second Great Awakening. Affecting individuals as well as institutions, the Awakening created a sense of sisterhood among tens of thousands of American women who came under the influence of religious revivals. The Awakening promised much — nothing less than eternal life — yet it demanded much of its converts — a revolution in faith and attitudes and conduct. All women who sought or achieved religious conversion could feel as sisters; in fact they included for most pious women a searching, often agonizing self-scrutiny which provided a topic for frequent discourse with their fellow-seekers.

This kind of religious doubt permeated much women's correspondence of the period. Almira Eaton, a young New England woman, wrote to a friend, Weltha Brown, of her religious quest:

> O, *dear* Weltha the great theme which engrosses your attention, and which ought to employ the lips and pen of every accountable creature, is but coldly attended to by your friend Almira I have gone but few steps in the christian race, and I fear am *now* retrograding. . . . *Can* I be indifferent with Calvary before me? [16]

Once converted, each pious woman faced new responsibilities, as described by a young woman in 1837:

> I have been favored with the instructions of a pious mother . . . but never felt the power of the religion of Jesus until about two years ago. Since that period I have seen things in a new light. I have felt in some degree that I am not my own; that my time, my talents, my influence, and my all belong to Him, who has bought me with his own blood. I feel that my life should be a life of active service, and that there is need of my labors in the vineyard of the Lord. [17]

One of the chief duties of converted women was to spread the sacred message, thereby converting others. Thus sisterhood in faith tended to be activist and aggressive in responding to other women. In 1826, Mary Lyon described her exertions to foster religious concerns in her school. In addition to time spent in formal instruction, the teacher sought to reach her pupils individually: "To individual conversation on moral & religious subjects, since last week...I have conversed with several & uniformly with each young lady alone....I am inclined to think, that I never have conversed with so many individuals before in the same time." [18] Many other teachers felt similar spiritual responsibilities to the young women in their charge, and aimed to make their educational institutions religious communities as well. Not infrequently girls' schools were the scenes of religious revivals. At a typical revival in 1831 at Ipswich Seminary, forty or fifty young women "who indulged hope...met weekly...to receive religious instruction....They had also praying circles in their respective houses on Sabbath morning. Besides, the whole were divided into four or five circles who met on Friday 6 o'clock for prayer & social intercourse." Nothing was left to chance, with the result many hoped "they have found that 'pearl of great price.'" [19]

Schools were not the only or even the principal sites of revivals involving women. During the late eighteenth-century revivals in Virginia, men and women alike succumbed to the influence of violent religious emotions, experiencing the "jerks," falling insensible or rolling on the ground or exhorting and testifying to the assembled crowds. These phenomena reached a climax during the Great Revival of 1800-1801 in Kentucky frontier camp meetings. Here women were greatly affected by the bodily "exercises," rolling, jumping, falling, out of rational control. Sometimes during the meetings they addressed the multitudes while transported hysterically.

Other important changes in women's religious activities came in the cities and towns of the northeast among evangelical Presbyterians, Congregationalists, Baptists, and Methodists. Responding to the Second Great Awakening, women began to take a more active and direct part in public gatherings, apparently with more enthusiasm than their husbands and sons. One religious periodical reported: "The fact that there are twice as many female as male professors in every denomination of Christians is unquestionable." [20] As the emotionalism of religious observances increased, more women seemed to be attracted, more women than men were converted, and they seemed to be more faithful than men in performing religious duties.

Wherever new revival techniques developed, private and semi-private gatherings advanced the work of redemption, and women were regular attendants at such sessions. By 1815 women's praying societies were common in the eastern states: "In many places, 'devout and pious FEMALES' have formed themselves into praying societies and obtained in the discharge of duty—comfort to themselves, and light, and direction to others." [21] In the early 1820s women met together to pray in such diverse communities as Lyme, New Hampshire, Wilmington, Delaware, Albany, New York, and Baltimore.

The next great step in this development occurred during the New York State revivals of 1825-27 under the leadership of Charles Grandison Finney, the first modern revivalist. In the course of these enthusiastic meetings Finney developed a professional revival technique, guaranteed to produce scores of conversions. Foremost among his notorious "New Measures" of revivalism was the "promiscuous" or mixed prayer meeting in which women as well as men prayed aloud in the congregation. The dramatic results of these gatherings were suggested in an account of the Oneida County revival: "Our prayer meetings have been one of the greatest means of the conversion of souls, especially those in which brothers and sisters have prayed together. If God has honored any meetings amongst us, it has been these." [22]

Mixed praying probably grew naturally out of the earlier women's prayer circles and the mixed testimonial meetings which occurred in some localities. Female leadership in prayer apparently occurred earlier in the West than in the East, literally because there were so few who wished to pray, so few qualified to lead, and so few established institutional structures. As one frontier Presbyterian wrote, "The number of praying men was small, and our meetings were mixed up with Methodist and Baptist who encourage the practice. . . ." [23] Along with other unorthodox techniques, these joint prayer meetings produced scandal for Finney and his co-workers. Attacked by Lyman Beecher and other eastern church leaders, Finney defended the New Measures, including "promiscuous" public praying, against accusations that they encouraged immorality and lax discipline. Finney prevailed against his accusers and women continued to pray in public with men, exercising a new and affirmative role in the churches, despite St. Paul's demand that they remain silent.

Protestant Christianity, as Barbara Welter has indicated, was substantially "feminized" during the first half of the nineteenth century.

The gradual expansion of women's religious activities and influence helped to create the sense of women's sisterhood in faith. Conscious of seeking and/or achieving salvation under heightened emotional circumstances, sisters in Christ or in the church experienced increased warmth and commitment for one another. Perhaps the New Measures of Finney and other innovative revivalists enhanced women's prestige in the church and in society. Certainly the western preachers and the eastern teachers, like Mary Lyon and Catharine Beecher, encouraged women to be active instruments, not merely passive receptacles of God's will. Their sisterhood in faith helped these women to achieve an attitude of self-confidence and a sense of mission that infected many of their later activities. Surely it is no coincidence that the areas where Finney's revivals and women's religious education flourished—New England, upstate New York and northern Ohio—were early centers of women's reform work and feminism.

Encouraged by the sense of common purpose inherent in the Second Great Awakening, American Protestant women evolved another definition of sisterhood—that experienced by the many thousands of participants in organized religious enterprises having charitable, educational, missionary, and moral aims. Like their other new organized efforts, religious and benevolent societies were akin to older informal or individualistic neighborly aid. Religious benevolence in the nineteenth century was a collective process, encouraging bonds of sisterhood at all levels of organized operations, in local, regional, state, and national activities.

American religious organizations for women followed examples set in England by the evangelical movement of the eighteenth century. English women found that they could work for conversion and relief of the poor with little inconvenience and much satisfaction. Wrote Sarah Trimmer, a leader of English charities: "Working for the poor is a species of charity which forms a part of the prerogative of our sex, and gives to those who have leisure for it an opportunity of doing much good with very little trouble or expense."[24] Hannah More, an eminent English philanthropist and author of pious tracts, tales, and essays, became a model to Americans of the perfect female religious character.

A few women's benevolent institutions were founded in the eighteenth century, but the great surge of missionary societies came after 1800. The Boston Female Society for Missionary Purposes, one of the earliest of its kind, resolved in 1800 to raise funds for Congregational missions in the West. Other women's missionary organizations began operation in this decade at scattered locations. The missionary movement expanded rapidly after 1810, with local female societies joining into state organizations better to support the cause. In cities, the "domestic missionary" program inaugurated a vigorous evangelical effort to protect and extend religious influence. Formed in 1816, the Female Domestic Missionary Society for the Poor of the City of New York and its Vicinity promoted Sabbath schools, distributed Bibles and other religious publications, and aided churches in needy sections of the city.

Women's religious societies developed strong support in cities and small towns alike. The New Hampshire Missionary Society depended principally upon more than fifty local female auxiliaries for the support of its program of local preaching, foreign missions, education, Bible and tract distribution. Between 1810 and 1815, missionary advocates urged the formation of "cent a week" societies in small towns, declaring "that if people would retrench a little of their expenses, a revenue might easily be saved, which might do considerable toward extending the means of salvation."[25] The drive for missions spread into New York State where the Female Missionary Society of the Western District, organized in 1816, maintained six missionaries and raised more than $2000 in the year 1818 from forty-six towns and villages in ten counties.

Day-to-day activities of the female missionary and Bible societies reflected and supported relationships of sisterhood among members. Local societies typically "associated together once a week for that purpose of sewing and knitting; thus by their own industry, accumulating a small fund, which together with a few subscriptions from married ladies, as to be annually transmitted to the Parent Society."[26] Facing somewhat different problems, urban female Bible societies worked together to distribute the scriptures among the poor, hoping to reform and uplift them. Other causes engaged the interests of this vast national sisterhood: the distribution of tracts, helping indigent but pious young men to study for the ministry, organizing Sabbath schools to teach reading and religion to poor children, and working for the benefit and "moral and religious improvement of seamen."

In addition to supporting strictly religious causes, many women's societies provided assistance to the poor and suffering. At Baltimore in 1798, a Female Humane Association was founded to help indigent women. Similar organizations soon appeared in New York and Philadelphia. The members met periodically to discuss the unfortunate objects of their care; they accumulated small sums of money, made clothing, and occasionally brought food to the sufferers. Women's societies for relief were concentrated in the cities, but long-lived societies operated in many smaller communities such as Concord, New Hampshire, Salem, Massachusetts, and Bedford, Westchester County, New York, supplying cloth, garments, wood, or food to deserving poor families. In some cities voluntary relief organizations became so numerous as to require centralized direction. Philadelphia's Union Benevolent Association, formed in 1831, had a gentlemen's and ladies' branch. The latter embodied a notable innovation in supporting lady visitors who circulated among the poor, performing a primitive kind of social work and impressing the subjects of their charity with the "advantages of temperance, economy, cleanliness, order, regularity, and unwearied industry...."

The spread of women's benevolence was affected by several factors. It was encouraged by a cluster of large, interlocking, national religious associations: the American Board of Commissioners for Foreign Missions (1810), the American Education Society (1815), the American Bible Society (1816), the American Sunday-School Union (1824), The American Tract Society (1825), and the American Home Missionary Society (1826). The clergymen and prominent laymen who operated these national societies were anxious for female support, being well aware of the efficiency of the "sisters" at raising money and organizing àt the grass-roots level. In scores of sermons preached to local women's benevolent societies, ministers advised modest and subordinate behavior, yet they attributed great influence to women. Occasionally a clergyman would take note of the fact that women were *taking charge* in their own benevolent works:

> Charity makes its appearance with us now, in a manner to which we have hitherto been unaccustomed. Until of late years, females have encouraged charitable associations by their persuasive efforts to soften the harder hearts of men. . . . They at the present time *associate themselves,* for the purpose. Who will not say charity the most distinct and active doth not become them. [27]

As they became aware of the immediate earthly satisfactions and the more-distant heavenly rewards of religious benevolence, women with substantial social positions and leisure time enrolled in voluntary associations. Migrating from the East into the West and South, the benevolent movement soon penetrated every section. Utica, New York, was the center of vigorous female societies before 1820, and Rochester's female missionary society began in 1818 to support preaching "in feeble and destitute churches in the new settlements.'' Other towns in Ohio and Illinois, especially those settled by New Englanders, supported women's associations. Urban centers, too, in the West, such as Cincinnati, had networks of women's organizations devoted to religious purposes. The South, being less urban and more decentralized, was not so densely organized with women's societies, although where there existed centers of population, women organized benevolent groups.

In terms of sisterhood the religious movements added substantially to American women's collective identity. For one thing, they offered groups of women unprecedented prestige and significance in activities that extended the domestic definitions of their sphere. For another thing, they involved women in acting together in organized ways to help other women. Middle-class women were urged by their leaders and pastors to feel empathy for their less-fortunate sisters. Although such assistance as they offered was given patronizingly, with doses of self-righteous moralism that must have seemed offensive, the point is that women sought to transcend class boundaries, to identify with the sufferings of other women. Given the sentimental attitudes of the nineteenth century, this was not difficult to achieve, even though the benefits offered— religious conversion, moral uplift, tracts and Bibles, plus meagre food and clothing for poor women and children who could prove their ''worthiness''—might not generally appeal to wretched families. Sisterhood, then, among the middle-class givers, and between the givers and the lower-class receivers, was a major aim of religious benevolence.

Between 1800 and 1840 the women's benevolent movement had evolved from minute beginnings in a few American cities and towns into a great body of organizations numbering well into the thousands. The impulse to voluntary, collective action had affected all Americans, and women had been motivated by a sense of optimism, a faith in their moral influence and united power, to undertake campaigns that would alter their own lives in significant ways. Deriving their base in part from earlier English movements, American women seemed to carry their activities further than their counterparts in the mother country. Beginning as a moderate endeavor with relatively conservative aims, the female benevolent movement moved toward sharper goals: relief and conversion of the poor developed into efforts to improve their living habits and identify with them as sisters. Techniques, too, became less conventional: sewing and fund-raising gave way to visiting the poor, taking genteel women away from their domestic circles into the abodes of poverty. Whatever they did, whether aiding the poor or contributing to tract and Bible funds, women knew that they, as women, were doing something important.

Women in the benevolent movement served at the right hand of the clergy, contributing significantly to American philanthropy in this period. In their day the funds raised through the pennies and "mites" collected by tens of thousands of women were prodigious. To some extent these societies were equalizing influences, bringing their members together on an equal basis and seeking to lift the poor above their station. With their typical characteristics of constitution-making, elective offices, and internal political life, these organizations were miniature democratic laboratories, teaching their members self-government. They made later women reformers and social workers possible. Dorothea Dix, Clara Barton, Jane Addams, and many other leaders may be considered as direct descendants of the early nineteenth-century benevolent societies. Every variety of women's association, from the church sewing circle to the national network of women's clubs, to such current groups as the National Organization for Women, is an offspring of these early sisterhoods. The pattern of women's activities called "social feminism" by William L. O'Neill derived from organized religious benevolence.

More unconventional approaches to the problems of women also grew directly and quite immediately out of the sisterhood of benevolence. Having learned that women had a responsibility to defend the friendless and work for the regeneration of humankind, women organizers began to assert the "right" to agitate in their own behalf. Although only a minority of women ever asserted this right, those who did so could look to religious benevolence as a school for social action which they had observed or attended. Many years after female benevolent societies had first taken hold in America, a keen observer and liberal, Lydia Maria Child, could observe their consequences:

In modern times, the evangelical sects have highly approved of female prayer meetings. In the cause of missions and dissemination of tracts, they have eloquently urged upon women their prodigious influence and consequent responsibility, in the great work of regenerating a world lying in wickedness. Thus it is with those who urged women to become missionaries, and form tract societies. They have changed the household utensil into a living, energetic being; and they have no spell to turn it into a broom again.[28]

American women of the nineteenth century found another collective experience in the sisterhood of work. Occupations in industry and schoolteaching tied thousands of women into feminine communities. Of these, the most clearly defined were the sister-workers in New England textile-mill towns organ-

ized on the pattern of Lowell, Massachusetts. At Lowell, the working force
was predominantly female, worked together, lived together in company-
sponsored boardinghouses, associated together in their leisure-time activities.
When he visited the cotton-mill city in 1833,President Andrew Jackson was
more impressed by the 2500 young mill girls who paraded by his reviewing
stand than by any other feature of the industry. More than half a century later,
Lucy Larcom remembered the sense of interdependence felt by women at
Lowell:

> One great advantage which came to these many stranger girls through being
> brought together away from their own homes, was that it taught them to go out
> of themselves, and enter into the lives of others. To me, it was an incalculable
> help to find myself among so many working-girls, all of us thrown upon our
> own resources, but thrown much more upon each others' sympathies. [29]

Yet even at Lowell, where for a time conditions were relatively
favorable to the women workers, the female community was
characterized by a high degree of alienation. Lowell's mill girls seldom
felt at home in their boardinghouses. In other industrial towns a pattern of
alienation developed in the scores of early labor organizations formed by
women to protest against wages and working conditions. Unlike
sisterhoods of voluntary religious societies, the community of interest
represented in organizations of laboring women was forced on the
participants. The earliest women strikers, more than 100 in number,
probably joined male weavers in Pawtucket, Rhode Island, in 1824, to
protest wage reductions and increased working hours. The first American
strike conducted exclusively by women took place among New York City
seamstresses in 1825.

The decade after 1830 was a formative time for women's labor
organizations. Characteristic of these was the Female Society of Lynn
(Massachusetts) for the protection and promotion of Female Industry,
formed in 1833. Members of this women's group attempted to set
minimum wages for hundreds of shoe binders who worked in their
homes. "Ladies, let us be alive to our own interests and honor..."
declared a defender of the shoe binders:

> This Society was formed, if we rightly understand it, from the best of motives;
> not to usurp the rights of any, but to assert our own and firmly defend them; we
> cannot see the propriety of denying the shoe-binders that liberty which other
> females have, that of setting their own prices upon their own work. . . . [30]

These women likened themselves to Revolutionary patriot mothers, defending their rights as *"free women"* against "tyranny and oppression." At first successful, the Lynn women gradually succumbed to pressure from manufacturers who demolished the shoe binders' unity by negotiating with individuals.

Women textile workers staged sporadic strikes during the late 1820s, and throughout the 1830s and 1840s, against wage reductions and work speedups. Such strikes hit Paterson, New Jersey, Philadelphia and Manayunk, Pennsylvania, Taunton and Amesbury, Massachusetts. A walkout of young women operatives at Dover, New Hampshire, in 1828, led to a demonstration and parade which townspeople pronounced quite unfeminine and immodest. The question of female modesty could not be easily avoided in these labor disputes because industrial sisterhood brought women leaders into conflict with male factory owners. During a strike at Lowell in 1834, a young woman presided at several meetings and persuaded other workers to strike against a fifteen percent reduction in wages. A newspaper reported:

> We are told that one of the leaders mounted a pump and made a flaming Mary Wollstonecraft speech on the rights of women and the inequities of the *"monied* aristocracy," which produced a powerful effect on her auditors, and they determined "to have their own way if they died for it."[31]

But the strike was quickly broken.

Two developments of the 1840s illustrate how women's industrial organizations evolved. The Female Labor Reform Association in New England, begun in 1844, was probably the nation's most significant women's labor organization of the pre-Civil War era. Founded in Lowell as an outgrowth of that city's sisterhood of mill operatives, the Association soon established branches in Manchester, Nashua, and Dover, New Hampshire, and Waltham and Fall River, Massachusetts. It organized one of the early campaigns in favor of ten-hour-day factory legislation. It took over and for a time conducted a workers' journal, *The Voice of Industry,* and joined with male labor organizations in several conventions. And it produced America's most vigorous, talented early women's labor leader, Sarah Bagley, a speaker, organizer, editor, and reformer. In the end, however, the sisterhood of workers was no match for the power of the employers. The ten-hour movement disintegrated, as did the Female Labor Reform Association.

The second illustration of women's industrial sisterhood was the Allegheny City Cotton Mill riot of 1848. Here, in what is now Pittsburgh, women workers committed actions that eastern mill girls had never done: they engaged aggressively in full-scale industrial violence. The riot occurred after Pennsylvania enacted a ten-hour-day law which textile-mill owners attempted to circumvent. After locking workers out, a few mill owners invited the women workers to return to work under earlier conditions of a twelve-hour day. When a number of mill girls began working, large numbers of women and men screamed and threw eggs and other missiles at the submissive workers. Made up largely of women, the mob eventually gained access to the mill and damaged some of the machinery. Thus women were directly in conflict with other women. Mill operatives and workers' wives also played parts in the riot's aftermath. The employers, as in Lowell, had the last word, holding out against the workers until financial want forced them back into the mills. Thus the power of industrial sisterhood was cut off before it could take hold.

The sisterhood of industrial occupations clearly had limitations. Close bonds between women mill operatives at Lowell and a handful of factory towns organized on the boardinghouse system were results of particular circumstances: large numbers of sturdy young women from similar rural New England backgrounds, working, living, spending leisure time together. When these conditions changed, as wages were cut and working conditions deteriorated, these Yankee maids left the mills, to be replaced by immigrants of much lower prestige and self-confidence. The newcomers placed little value on the ties between women. Whereas many of the New England natives were upright middle-class girls, most of the immigrants came from downtrodden peasant and working-class backgrounds, accustomed to few privileges and expecting few. Thus the issues of survival were more critical to the newcomers than their consciousness of shared experiences as women.

Labor organizations failed to create strong bonds between working women for other reasons. Probably a major source of weakness was opposition or indifference from men. The capitalists, managers, and overseers of textile mills and other industries naturally opposed any kind of collective action by women workers in their own behalf. In the hierarchical, often patriarchal atmosphere of early nineteenth-century industrialism, mill owners had nearly total authority over employees. They could change wages and working conditions, hire and fire, and close down operations at almost any time that suited them. They had power, and the operatives, with few skills and little status, were without power. Unlike the sisterhoods of religious benevolence or female seminaries, which complemented the efforts of male leaders, sisterhoods of labor threatened the authority and economic power of corporate leaders and investors. Even the dignity and eminence of Lowell as an industrial community were ordained by the capitalists who wanted the city to be a showcase of American industry. When it suited their interests, they let the textile industry deteriorate from the high early standards of the model city on the Merrimack River.

Relationships between early men's and women's labor organizations were often strained. Skilled mechanics and craftsmen tended to see little in common with unskilled women mill workers. Yet early labor unions were strongest among skilled men who could gain advantages from witholding their work from the marketplace. Women union leaders and organizers had relatively little prestige and few roles in the tentative local and state workingmen's organizations of the 1820s, 1830s, and 1840s. Thus, where there might have been solidarity and a sense of class interests among working men and women, most men defined women as inferior. It is little wonder that women's labor organizations were generally short-lived and ineffective before the Civil War.

The occupational sisterhood of educated women gained a slight foothold during the nineteenth-century's first half. Chief among professional women bound together by their work were teachers. Graduates of female seminaries and normal schools had drilled into them a strong sense of the importance of their duties. One teacher echoed the feelings of thousands as she exulted in a new professional responsibility. Comparing schools with railroads, she sang:

> Ho the car for education
> Rise majestic through our nation
> Baring on its train the story
> Free school[s] are a nations glory.
> Roll it along through the nation...
> Hurrah Hurrah Hurrah Hurrah
> Education soon will bless our happy nation.[32]

The message traveled wherever women teachers worked. They corresponded with one another, reinforced their sense of community by exchanging visits, attending teachers' institutes, and reading a growing professional congratulatory literature.

Nineteenth-century patterns of sisterhood had a number of significant characteristics and consequences. They grew out of the segregation between middle-class men's and women's lives and were intensified by their increasing segregation. Thus, feelings of sisterhood helped many American women to think of themselves as distinct from or even in opposition to men. Sisterhood strengthened women's collective identity. By working and associating for some common purpose, whether sociability or social change, women could experience the accomplishment of group effort, in contrast to the isolation so many wives and mothers endured in individual households. Association with other women raised individual aspirations and gave women a chance to think about common topics.

To a great degree, the new bonds of sisterhood were activist, devoted to producing change in the society by supporting missionaries, helping distressed poor women, teaching school, or changing one another through religious experiences. From their active, collective enterprises, women gained a sense of power, and awareness of themselves as women, having identifiable responsibilities and needs. They were better prepared for new opportunities and still greater independence of action during the 1830s.

4

WOMEN AND REFORM

DURING the 1830s American women participated in a series of reform movements which aimed to regenerate the national society. To the reformers, no institution or attitude was too sacred to be questioned and no proposal for change too extravagant to attract support. Among the questions under discussion and agitation were the use of strong drink, cures for war and means and techniques of education, the improvement of prisons, and, most gravely, the issue of slavery. Women moved easily into becoming involved in reform, building on patterns of organization and feelings of sisterhood already established by their benevolent activities.

Nineteenth-century reform had two basic sources, one secular, the other religious. Secular reformers, deriving their principles from Enlightenment philosophy, had been most active in late eighteenth-century America. Their efforts culminated in the establishment of a republic, the United States, whose ideals and design of government derived substantially from Enlightenment beliefs. Thomas Jefferson, in one of the key statements of American reform, made Enlightenment principles part of the national creed:

> We hold these truths to be self-evident, that all men are created equal, that they are endowed by their Creator with certain unalienable Rights, that among these are Life, Liberty and the pursuit of Happiness.

Secular reform was well represented by one of the nineteenth century's most enthusiastic women radicals. Frances Wright (1795-1852), a Scotswoman, traveled to the United States in 1819 and returned in 1824 to accompany General LaFayette on his triumphal tour of the United States. Deeply opposed to slavery, she conducted a Utopian community, "Nashoba," between 1825 and 1829 as an experiment in gradual emancipation. From 1826 until 1830 she was actively involved with Robert Owen's community at New Harmony, Indiana. Beginning in 1828 a series of popular lectures in the nation's major cities, she shocked respectable Americans by giving public speeches attacking evangelical Chrisitanity, and advocating free-thinking and a number of other radical doctrines. Wright's unconventional behavior made the term "Fanny Wrightism" a common epithet during the 1830s for reference to any female conduct which observers defined as unfeminine. Far in advance of her time, she helped prepare the way for more respectable people to enter in the difficult way of a public lecturer.

Reformist drives affected the religious benevolent movement in which women played such a significant part. Instead of simply ameliorating social ills and immorality through charity and the promotion of piety, reformers began to speak and write about overturning institutions, inducing drastic changes in the behavior of men and women by altering their experiences and their environments. Faith in progress and perfectability acted like a rapidly spreading infection, as John L. Thomas has observed:

> Thus romantic perfectionism altered the course of the reform enterprise by appealing directly to the individual conscience. Its power stemmed from a millennial expectation which proved too powerful a moral explosive for the reform agencies. . . . it posited an ideal society in which this . . . individual could discover his power for good and exploit it. Such a society would tolerate neither poverty nor suffering; it would contain no condemned classes or deprived citizens, no criminals or forgotten men. [1]

Women shared the new attitudes toward social change and became involved in several important reform movements as a matter of course. What is notable about women's interests after 1825 is that much of their concern focused on the particular problems of women. The sense of sisterhood which had developed since the turn of the century now began to affect the public, organized involvements of American women. Movements for moral reform and temperance, and against slavery, appealed to women because women were the principal victims of the evils which they attacked.

A good example of the shift from benevolence to reform is the movement called moral reform, organized to eliminate prostitution and inaugurate a single moral standard governing sexual relations. Originating early in the nineteenth century as offshoots of urban domestic missionary societies were organizations for redeeming fallen women. This modest effort, led by men, encouraged prostitutes to repent, cared for them after their religious redemption, and obtained useful respectable employment for them. Typical of this class of benevolent society was the Magdalen Society of Philadelphia, founded about 1800 to care for "infamous women" until suitable positions could be found for them as domestic servants.

The Boston Penitent Females' Refuge was established in 1819 as a result of the discovery by domestic missionaries of a district of the city "composed of persons principally females, given up to the practice of every enormity.... A large number of gentlemen of piety and benevolence" joined to establish a house of refuge for the unfortunate women. The problem was of course too controversial for delicate ladies to become directly involved, but a women's auxiliary was formed in 1824 to assist the gentlemen in raising funds to support the Refuge. Women's involvement in the work changed dramatically in 1825 when, after the resignation of the male superintendent and a dispute over his replacement, the Society voted to invite a woman to supervise the house of refuge:

> Miss MARY WEBB, a Lady who, from the first formation of the Society, had taken a deep interest in its success, was unanimously elected first Superintendent of the house; and we are happy to state that she accepted. . . . With every returning month, we have had increasing reason to believe, that our deliberations on this subject were guided by Omniscient Wisdom. The appearance of the house, the improvement of the inmates in neatness, attention, and industry, bear abundant testimony to . . . MISS WEBB. . . . [2]

Two other women assisted this intrepid rescuer of her fallen sisters. Thus a sense of sisterhood refined conditions at Boston's Penitent Females' Refuge.

The radical moral reform movement, like the campaign to redeem fallen women, was begun under male leadership. John R. McDowall, a pious young Presbyterian minister, began working in New York City in 1830, where he discovered "with a thrill of horror" the notorious center of vice in the city, Five Points. The young reformer began to publish detailed accounts of his discoveries in two lurid periodicals, *McDowall's Journal* and *Magdalen Facts*.

The first moral reformers were at least as anxious to save young men from New York's prostitutes as they were to protect the virtue of women. Arthur and Lewis Tappan, great merchants and pious philanthropists, supported moral reform especially because they employed as clerks and laborers many young men who arrived in the city from rural villages and who, the merchants feared, might succumb to corruption. This emphasis changed as women took over leadership of the movement.

The New York Female Moral Reform Society, founded by women in 1834, carried on McDowall's work, supporting his mission and sponsoring an influential and widely read journal devoted to the subject. Under women's leadership the movement flourished and achieved national influence, gaining some 445 local female auxiliaries by 1839 and sponsoring a national moral reform convention in that year. The movement spread to New England, upstate New York, and as far away as Ohio by 1837. In the late 1830s the Society's journal, *The Advocate of Moral Reform,* had some 16,500 subscribers, most of them in small towns. It is interesting to note the strong rural concern for moral reform, and suggestive that the drive for a single moral standard appealed to women everywhere, not only in the cities where vice flourished.

Moral reformers supported various programs to attack the evil. In the first place, they sought to eradicate vice in the cities by harassing and ostracizing dens of iniquity, their residents, and visitors. As a corollary they would reform and convert urban prostitutes by establishing houses of refuge or retreats and halfway houses for abandoned women who wished to be redeemed. At the national level, they mounted a campaign to cleanse the entire country of the social evil, to combat obscene publications, and discountenance even the harboring of licentious thoughts. In New York State, the network of local societies worked for a law making seduction a crime, passed in 1848. The moral reformers also supported a massive education drive to induce mothers to teach their children, particularly their sons, to be aware of and avoid illicit sexual activities.

The female moral reform crusade developed an overt pro-female and anti-male stance on the issue of morality. As the movement grew, its members' feelings of sisterhood expanded and became more intense. Increasingly, women moral reformers took the offensive against men. The Female Moral Reform Society in Boston resolved not to ''turn aside to contend with obstacles or opposition…. The cause of moral reform involves principles which, if fully and perseveringly applied, will elevate woman to her proper standing in society, without moving her from her 'appropriate sphere'...."[3] Women were urged to join a fellowship of mutual protection: "Resolved, that in maintaining the *rights* of women, we will not neglect her appropriate duties, one of the principal of which duties is to guard our daughters, sisters, and female acquaintances from the delusive arts of corrupt and unprincipled men."[4] Woman's character should be "elevated" in order to protect her against "the various allurements by which the evil and designing would entangle her." Essentially, the moral reformers demanded a single moral standard applying to men and women alike: "Would men but treat their own sex, when convicted of disgraceful crime, as we treat ours under similar circumstances, the work of reformation would be comparatively easy."[5] Expectations of behavior for men would thus be raised to the level expected of women.

When finally the organized woman's rights movement appeared at midcentury, few of the thousands of women dedicated to moral reform would rally around its banner. Yet moral reform contained a major ingredient of feminism. In vigorously advocating a single moral standard, an equality between the sexes most fundamental, moral reformers came out against one of the most important traditions of feminine inferiority. Supporters of the new cause argued that because she was innocent and pure, woman was morally superior to base, animalistic man. Because of her purity, woman occupied a moral pedestal that permitted her to judge the behavior of others. This same virtue gave woman new responsibilities: within the home she should be the moral head of the household; and outside the home she should be vigilant against all evil and destructive influences. Moral reform justified an unprecedented assertion of power by women.

Women's participation in the fervent reforms of the 1830s included attacks on two favorite male activities—the consumption of alcohol and the conduct of war. Women would not become dominant in either the temperance or the peace movements until much later—with formation of the Woman's Christian Temperance Union in the 1870s, and the Women's International League for Peace and Freedom in the twentieth century. Early efforts of women against alcohol and war have not been thoroughly studied, nor have they been interpreted in feminist terms as campaigns against men. Hence what follows is somewhat speculative. Certainly; as wives and mothers, women were often the victims of destructive, improvident, alcoholic men. Early temperance writings often depicted women's terrible sufferings from the curse of drinking husbands in practically standardized accounts such as this one from the

Temperance Almanac of 1834, of a drunkard's return to his cold, wretched hovel from revels at the tavern:

> At length he comes. At the tavern he was the merry, jovial man. As soon as he crosses his own threshold, the sight of his watching, weeping, broken hearted wife, changes him into a coarse, disgusting, cross, unfeeling savage. He raves, he storms while she [attempts] . . . to soothe and calm him to repose. For all these she receives no return but the morose, unfeeling, brutal taunts and reproaches of a drunkard.[6]

Finally he beats her as she tries to protect the children against his fury. Here, then, is the formula: man the destroyer, woman the innocent protector and the moral superior.

Women had a wide range of responsibilities in the temperance movement. They should apply pressure by every possible means. As in other crusades, women could form societies to agitate the issue and help create favorable public sentiment, as long as they were properly decorous and submissive to male authority. They should read temperance publications like the *Journal of Humanity,* organ of the American Temperance Society, which published articles directed "To the Ladies," urging them not to serve the poisoned cup to anyone and to discriminate against intemperate persons. Along with pieces entitled "The Intemperate Husband," or "My Wife's Influence," they enjoyed reading accounts of the formation and significant influence of female temperance societies. They could boycott grocers and merchants who dealt in ardent spirits and patronize inns and hotels where intoxicants were forbidden. The American Temperance Society published statistics showing reduced numbers of distilleries and many fewer grocers and inns which sold liquor as a result of pressure from the temperance movement.[7]

Women could work with their husbands on occasions such as the Fourth of July, holding "Cold Water Army" demonstrations instead of traditional alcoholic Independence Day celebrations, hearing orations in favor of total abstinence in place of patriotic addresses, drinking toasts of water to their cause. As the temperance movement grew and its aims seemed to become increasingly imperative, women were urged to do still more. When appeals to their "present and future associates of the sterner sex" were ineffective, women temperance advocates formed Martha Washington societies in the 1840s and banished unregenerate males from their company:

> When any of the tee-total ladies of these associations, gives a social evening

party at her house, it *so happens,* that those nice young men who refuse to sign the pledge, who can drink or let it alone, who can govern themselves, who disdain to sign away their liberty, and whose affections for the *bottles* is greater than their regard for the *belles* of those places. . . don't get an invitation! [8]

Temperance women were sometimes accused of breaking up their own families to advance the precious goal. As early as the 1830s they agitated for some forms of prohibition through strict legal regulation or outright banning of liquor sales.

To what extent were these women anti-male? They certainly did not campaign exclusively against men drinkers. They were expected to acknowledge and meet the problems of women drinkers by extending fellowship to them as sisters fallen by the wayside. Man the drunkard, however, was seldom accorded the status of brother; he was a sinner, an enemy, an oppressor, who made a kind of slave of women. The evidence is circumstantial, but it leaves a strong impression. Like the advocates of moral reform, women who fought for temperence demanded a single standard of behavior for both sexes, that expected of women.

But, asked some men, were women not immodest who would join temperance societies and act the roles of public reformers? The answer to this question appeared simple:

If there is nothing immodest or unbecoming in a lady's renouncing openly the world, the devil, and all his works; — if in short, there is nothing immodest or unbecoming a lady's joining a *church,* then is there nothing immodest in her joining a temperance society. So far from it, there is an imperative moral *obligation* resting upon her to do so in the latter as in the former case. [9]

Yet it was not so simple. The problem led to confusion, assigning men and women coordinate responsibilities, giving the latter moral authority over the former. In their zeal, defenders of temperance marched down a dangerous path. Women had powers "nearly absolute...to suppress intemperance," announced the *Journal of Humanity.* The implications of this statement were not clear in 1830, but they would become evident in less than a decade.

Women's contributions to and interests in the peace movement of the 1830s are even less understood than their involvement with temperance. Although the pursuit of peace never had the mass appeal of temperance, it attracted a significant group of advocates. First the Quakers in the eighteenth century, then a group of clergymen after 1815 joined the movement against war. A small number of women became disciples of peace during the 1820s. In the next decade peace, like other reforms, took on a more radical coloration, as leaders raised the issue of whether any war or other form of coercion by force accorded with the loving spirit of Christianity. "Turn the other cheek": did this not mean literally no resistance to evil?

Continuing disputes separated moderate peace advocates and radicals attracted to principles of nonresistance. These debates engaged the interests of a few women, including two young Southerners, Sarah and Angelina Grimké, who became disciples of nonresistance after their brother, Thomas, published an essay on the radical doctrine. The chief advocate of nonresistance, Henry C. Wright, had some influence on the Grimkés and other women involved in the antislavery movement. By 1837 several female antislavery societies supported the radical view, and in 1838 the doctrine caused dissention within the American Peace Society, leading to a convention at Boston which organized the New England Non-Resistance Society.

Several of New England's most outspoken women abolitionists participated in this gathering, which is interesting in being one of the first reform meetings of men and women where both sexes were invited to enroll, engage in debate, and serve on committees. Some of the men were insulted by this departure from conventional practice. At one point a leading clergyman member of the conservative wing of the Peace Society was called to order by Abby Kelley, an outspoken young Quaker. "Endurance now passed its bounds...because women were to be allowed to participate in the proceedings!" [10] The aggrieved gentlemen soon withdrew. A number of women joined the Non-Resistance Society, but its total membership was small and its survival fragile. It is chiefly remembered for its involvement of Abby Kelley and other women in its formation. There is no clear evidence that anti-male attitudes influenced its women members to any great extent.

The climax of women's involvement in reform came with the antislavery movement. This great crusade was for women at once the most controversial, most political, and most effective of all the many movements of the time in directly raising questions about women's citizenship in the republic. American opposition to slavery began in the colonial period and developed slowly in the early nineteenth century. One of slavery's earliest important enemies was Benjamin Lundy, a Quaker, who founded the *Genius of Universal Emancipation* in 1821. An itinerant lecturer and organizer of abolition societies, he was the first antislavery editor to employ a regular woman correspondent, Elizabeth Margaret Chandler.

During the late 1820s and early 1830s, American abolitionists took inspiration from the British movement for total emancipation. After more than half a century of agitation, the British opponents of slavery in the West Indies organized a "bold appeal to the country," with large-scale organizing and petitioning between 1823 and 1833. One of the earliest Americans to reflect the militance of British abolitionists was William Lloyd Garrison, who joined Lundy to assist in editing the *Genius of Universal Emancipation* in 1829. Running afoul of the law because of his violent writing, Garrison began publishing his own antislavery paper, the Boston *Liberator* on January 1, 1831. The new periodical was dedicated to the immediate abolition of slavery, without compensation, colonization, or other moderate remedies. Other less-extreme reformers soon joined the ranks of the abolitionists, including the wealthy Tappan brothers, Arthur and Lewis, who sometime after 1830 converted to immediate emancipation, becoming organizers and financiers of the movement.

From its inception the antislavery movement involved women. Just as they had been attracted to other moral enterprises—moral reform, temperance, peace movements—women recognized the call for responsible commitment and action. Elizabeth Margaret Chandler, Benjamin Lundy's co-worker, appealed as early as 1829 in the *Genius of Universal Emancipation* for women to organize antislavery societies. The free-produce movement, organized to encourage consumption of products of free labor, a kind of boycott of slavery, interested a few women, particularly Quakers. American abolitionists could point with confidence to the antislavery contributions of British women. Garrison was strongly influenced by the British precedent as he challenged American women to join the new crusade:

> The ladies of Great Britain are moving the sympathies of the whole nation, in behalf of the perishing slaves in the British Colonies. We cannot believe that our ladies are less philanthropic or less influential. In their hands is the destiny of the slaves.[11]

In 1833, after a trip to England, Garrison wrote a glowing report of British female accomplishments, including the submission of antislavery petitions to Parliament signed by 800,000 women. "Cheers for the

Ladies of Great Britain!'' the editor exclaimed.[12]

Like moral reform and temperance, the slavery issue aroused women's sense of sisterhood, and, as in the other causes, man was the principal villain. Licentiousness and immoralities of every description were consequences of slavery, which set the master outside the law. What conscientious woman could feel comfortable while her black sisters in the South were without protection, liable to every imaginable vice? Along with its invitation to sexual immorality, slavery destroyed the ties which women valued above all others — the bonds of family. Deprived of the love, companionship, and protection of husbands, liable to have their children torn from their arms, slave women appeared to suffer a fate worse than death.

Slavery's assault on womanhood was amply described in the antislavery literature produced between 1830 and 1860. Theodore Dwight Weld's comprehensive anthology of evidence, *American Slavery As It Is,* elicited numerous shocking details concerning women's degradation under slavery. One of Weld's witnesses described a liason between a master and his Methodist slave girl:

> He proposed a criminal intercourse with her. She would not comply. He left her and sent for the overseer, and told him to have her flogged. It was done. Not long after he renewed his proposal. She again refused. She was again whipped. He then told her he intended to whip her till she should yield. The girl, seeing that her case was hopeless, her back smarting with the scourging she had received, and dreading another repetition, gave herself up to be the victim of his brutal lusts. [13]

Weld's chronicle of debasement described many circumstances despoiling the virtue of slave women. Illegitimacy, immodesty, nakedness, promiscuity, all these and other sins and indignities constantly affected these pathetic creatures. Slavery also had a marked impact on the white mistresses, turning otherwise pleasant, humane, white women into monsters of cruelty, encouraging indolence among this pampered class, and forcing these genteel ladies into accepting lewdness from their husbands and sons.

The impact of this attack on slavery is difficult to evaluate. Delicate, innocent women were not supposed to know about or certainly to acknowledge the existence of circumstances described in the antislavery literature. Nevertheless, in countless appeals made to women on behalf of ''the injured children of Africa,'' women were urged to ''rise in the moral power of womanhood; and give utterance to the voice of outraged mercy, and insulted justice," to show their "abhorrence of the soul-degrading sin of slavery," and listen to "the sighs, the groans, the death-like struggles of scourged sisters at the South." [14] In emotional rhetoric such as this, overt references to sexual realities of adultery or promiscuity were unnecessary. Moral outrage and indignation reflected the attitudes of decent women without the need for explicit statement. An Ohio woman stated the appeal of antislavery in proper Victorian terms:

> We have forgotten the thousand naked women writhing beneath the scorching sun & the still more torturing lash, we have not remembered those who were the spoilers prey until not a vestige of that delicacy wh[ich] is the sanctity & glory of woman is left. [15]

Thus the proper northern lady could identify with the black female slave of the South. Despite a gulf of color and culture, both shared a common womanhood, a sense of sisterhood.

Encouragement came from several sources in urging the formation of women's antislavery societies. Garrison recommended that women organize, and in February, 1832, a female antislavery society composed of black women was founded at Salem, Massachusetts. Other societies followed in eastern New England, and the most famous of women's groups, the Boston Female Anti-Slavery Society, was formed in October, 1832. As women's interests became more serious, the *Liberator* published many statements written by women to persons of their own sex, urging more feminine support for the antislavery movement. One correspondent, years ahead of her time, demanded:

> Now can you, with these and many other incontrovertible evidences of the greatness of your moral and intellectual capacities, grant for a single day that doctrine to be true, that inferiority is stamped upon the fair sex by the hand of nature? [16]

A dedicated spokeswoman for the Dorchester Female Anti-Slavery Society asserted, "There is no being neutral on the subject, either for slavery or against it." A voice from Providence, Rhode Island, declared: "If our gospel teachers will not lead us, we must lead them! Should we not blush . . . inasmuch as our sisters are in bonds, and we have not so much as lifted a hand to save them?" [17]

Women's antislavery organizations received support from other sources. The New England movement was given vigorous encouragement by an influential spokeswoman, Harriet Martineau, the eminent English author and social observer who toured the United States between 1834 and 1836. Lamenting the subservience of many American women, Martineau strongly favored all forms of women's antislavery work, arguing that the sexes should act equally in any moral enterprise. She despised the evangelical clergy who would exploit women for their own purposes and turn against those who insisted upon making their own decisions when embracing abolitionism or some other great cause. Once she was aware of the courage and liberality of women abolitionists, she openly espoused their work, declared her allegiance to Garrison, and was shortly ostracized by most leading Americans. The Garrisonians naturally appreciated her espousal of their work and considered her "new and grand thoughts of the nature, sphere, duties, and rights of woman..." to be beneficial in leading toward a broader appreciation of women's rights and duties. [18]

In the West, where attitudes towards woman's "appropriate sphere" were slightly more advanced than eastern views, leading abolitionists welcomed female support. The Ohio Anti-Slavery Society hailed its women members as "dear sisters & coworkers in the most glorious cause that has ever claimed the attention of the philanthropist & christian." [19] Answering objections against women's appearing in "so public a cause," a leading Ohio abolitionist wrote:

> "In Christ Jesus there is neither male nor female." That is, in moral enterprises, moral worth and intellect are the standard. A mind whether deposited in a male or female body is equally valuable for all moral and intellectual purposes. Indeed there is no station in life but what may be filled as ably and as beneficially by woman as by man. The difference is made principally by education. Abolition is opening a new field for female effort. I pray you sieze [sic] with avidity the opportunity thus offered to redeem your character and name from unjust reproach. [20]

This man's views had ominous portents for the defenders of female inequality.

The mid-1830s were vital in the growth of issues which would lead eventually to the organized women's movement. As moral reformers, temperance workers, advocates of peace, and abolitionists, women came into direct confrontation with significant male traditions and behavior patterns. But abolition was the key reform. Between 1834 and 1838, thousands of American women found roles to play in their own antislavery societies, later in organizations of men and women. Their activism carried them into state and national politics — unprecedented situations for women in the 1830s. During these few years, women abolitionists took a vigorous part in America's social and political dialogue, becoming themselves the subjects of intense controversy.

5

A NETWORK OF FEMALE SOCIETIES

WOMEN'S entry into the antislavery movement was consistent with earlier patterns of their participation in religious movements. In seeking acceptable means to resolve the slavery issue, which were positive, specific, assertive, yet noncontroversial, they could rely on two sets of precedents. First, they had American models in the thousands of local societies which met, sewed, prayed, raised money for missions, distributed tracts, and performed relief work and educational services for religious organizations. Second, they could look to the immediate examples set by British women abolitionists. As the movement developed, American women followed both these precedents, working as individuals and forming hundreds of female antislavery societies.

Two notable early contributions by American women to the cause resulted from the conscientious scruples of two New Englanders, Lydia Maria Child and Prudence Crandall. These women, both self-supporting, respectable professionals, found that their advocacy of human rights practically destroyed their careers. Child, a widely known author of historical romances, guidebooks and manuals, popular history, and editor of a favorite children's magazine, *The Juvenile Miscellany,* had been regarded as one of New England's principal woman writers and first women of letters. As a result of her conversion to abolitionism, she felt compelled to write a work which drastically changed her fortunes: *An Appeal in Favor of That Class of Americans Called Africans* (1833). She anticipated a negative response, although she may not have realized how serious it would be:

By publishing this book I have put my mite into the treasury. The expectation of displeasing all classes has not been unaccompanied with pain. But it has been strongly impressed upon my mind that it was a duty to fulfill this task; and earthly considerations should never stifle the voice of conscience. [1]

The *Appeal* was one of the earliest antislavery tracts by an American woman. It demonstrated in incident after incident the degrading and sinful consequences of slavery as they affected all persons involved with the institution. Child pointed out the baselessness of prejudice against color and defended the principle of racial equality. She favored abolition over colonization and urged her readers to follow the example set by British women in exerting their energies against slavery. As a result of her indiscretion in publishing the *Appeal*, "the most popular as well as the most useful of our female writers" lost her following and gained only "ridicule and censure." [2] Sarah Josepha Hale, eminent female editor of *Godey's Lady's Book* magazine and guardian of genteel taste, later summarized Child's blunder in becoming involved in "the agitation of political questions":

> Seventeen years ago she consecrated her powers to this work. The result has been, that her fine genius, her soul's wealth has been wasted in the struggle which party politicians have used for their own selfish purposes. Had Mrs. Child...written for this mission of peace [colonization of Negroes in Africa] as she has poured her heart out in a cause only tending to strife, what blessed memorials of these long years, would now be found to repay her disinterested exertions! [3]

Thus could a conservative woman writer dismiss the efforts of a libertarian.

Although Child's embrace of the antislavery cause reduced her general popularity, abolitionists were enthusiastic over the development. A correspondent of the *Liberator* wrote: "I hope it [the *Appeal*] will be the means of rousing those of her *own sex* to a proper attention to this subject. With a few notable exceptions, they have been shamefully indifferent to the wrongs of our colored people." [4] Later "A few ladies of Salem and Lynn, Massachusetts" paid tribute to the fallen author: "The course which you have pursued, in openly and fearlessly advocating a most righteous, but unpopular cause, may have driven from you some old friends, but it has secured to you many new ones. . . ." [5] Child continued to publish antislavery articles and essays, and for a time during the 1840s edited the *National Anti-Slavery Standard*.

The year 1833 also witnessed the beginning of another important controversy over women's antislavery roles. Early in the year Miss

Prudence Crandall, mistress of the select school for young ladies at Canterbury, Connecticut, announced her intention of opening the school to "young colored Ladies and Misses." She had been invited to the village two years earlier specifically to provide schooling for young ladies of Canterbury. When a black girl applied for admission, Crandall, a Quaker with abolitionist leanings, struggled with her conscience but finally determined to admit the girl. Thereupon most of the other students were withdrawn. Not knowing how else to survive, Crandall reopened the school in April 1833, as a school for black girls. There followed a year of persecution for the school mistress and her pupils.

At first the town fathers tried to enforce an old state vagrancy law against the little girls, but friendly abolitionists provided bond. Leading townsmen then went to the Connecticut legislature and secured a law to prohibit the private instruction of out-of-state blacks. Crandall was tried three times and jailed once under this law, but her conviction was finally reversed on appeal. Begging the antislavery movement for help, she received aid from many prominent humanitarians and reformers including Garrison, the Tappan brothers, and other leaders. After being boycotted by town merchants, having her well filled with manure, finding her school set on fire and partly destroyed by vandals, the young teacher finally capitulated, taking her "young colored Ladies and Misses" away from Canterbury forever. More than half a century later, when she was recalled as a gallant heroine rather than an irresponsible incendiary, the state of Connecticut voted her an annuity.

Female antislavery societies were organized in many areas of the northeastern and middle Atlantic states between 1832 and 1835. One of the most prominent, early, and long-lived of these organizations was the Philadelphia Female Anti-Slavery Society, whose records provide a continuous account of its activities, interests, and development. Philadelphia's Quakers had a distinct antislavery tradition, and in the 1830s a few Quaker women became fervently devoted to the cause of abolition and not afraid, as women, to express their beliefs. Quakers, after all, believed in a degree of equality and freedom of expression for both men and women. During one of the first meetings of the American Anti-Slavery Society at Philadelphia in 1833, Mrs. Lucretia Mott and three other women were present. When the assembly entered into a discussion of the Declaration of Sentiments, Mott suggested that the document's wording (composed by William Lloyd Garrison) be changed. It was so changed, establishing a controversial and far-reaching precedent for women's participation in the antislavery movement.

Only three days after the American Society's adjournment, Mrs. Mott and a few other Philadelphia women responded to the recommendations that "ladies of the land" found antislavery societies and "publish tracts and addresses calculated to wake up a slumbering nation," issued by the American Anti-Slavery Society. After hearing addresses from Garrisonians Samuel J. May and Nathaniel Southard, fourteen women, including Lucretia Mott and two others who had attended the national meetings, formed a committee to draft the constitution of a female antislavery society. The gentle Quakers faced several critical problems from the very beginning of their antislavery work. They were naturally regarded with suspicion in a city with strong Southern business connections and much racial prejudice. As Friends, they had to be wary of taking outspoken, controversial stands on any public issue, especially one which might create popular excitement.

The Philadelphia Female Anti-Slavery Society began its career with great propriety. At first men assisted and spoke at meetings, addressing members on such sordid topics as treatment of the slaves, punishment of those held in bondage, and the moral issues involved with slavery. Women could act in their own societies as managers, accountants, and debaters, but public speeches on important subjects still demanded a man's intellect and experience. In its first year the Society purchased and distributed early periodicals and tracts of the American Anti-Slavery Society, including Lydia Maria Child's *Appeal in Favor of That Class of Americans Called Africans*. The Philadelphia women later gave substantial outright financial support to Garrison's struggling *Liberator*. In addition to subsidizing such publications, they contributed to the treasuries of the local and national antislavery organizations. The Philadelphia Female Anti-Slavery Society also published a few antislavery tracts of its own, such as an "Address to the Women of Pennsylvania," in 1836.

In order to support its many good works, the women abolitionists of Philadelphia had to devise some effective method of raising money. At first members contributed their petty cash, saved perhaps from household funds, or derived from income of their own property. Beginning in 1836 the Philadelphia Society conducted annual fairs or sales which became major sources of operating funds.

At one time or another the Phildelphia Female Society contributed to the support of an antislavery agent — male — who toured the area, lecturing, distributing literature, and arousing public interest. Along with most antislavery organizations, the Society joined in the great abolition petition campaigns, pleading with Congress to abolish slavery in the District of Columbia, or seeking some other antislavery aim.

In two of its more important activities the Female Society followed closely the traditions of benevolence and charity established by earlier Philadelphia women's organizations. Dedicated to improving the condition of Philadelphia's free black population, the abolitionists maintained at least one school for these people and in 1836 arranged for scientific lectures for them. The school aimed at teaching its pupils good Quaker virtues — mildness, humility, good morals — which were also good attitudes for Negroes in a hostile environment. One of the most interesting programs inaugurated by the Philadelphia Female Anti-Slavery Society was a system of roving visitors to blacks in the city. The Society

> proposed to divide the city into sections, appointing two visitors for each section, whose duty it should be to seek out all colored persons residing therein, whose circumstances render them proper objects of their attention, and endeavor to impart to them that instruction and assistance which they may need, and which the visitors have in their power to bestow. [6]

Here, in somewhat primitive form, was a program of social work, much like that inaugurated earlier by benevolent organizations to aid the poor and suffering. But these abolitionists, instead of giving attention to "deserving poor," were assisting a generally despised and ignored group of people.

Besides its local work, the Philadelphia Female Society played an important role in the growing national female antislavery network. Lucretia Mott, for many years the Society's corresponding secretary, kept in touch with other organizations in the United States and Great Britain. Such correspondence was helpful to the morale of all these women's organizations. Keeping in periodic correspondence with each other, the female network continually revived their sense of sisterhood in a great enterprise, as well as exchanging points of view on new techniques of agitation.

The Philadelphia Female Anti-Slavery Society included among its members some of the most prominent women in the entire abolitionist ranks. Mary Grew and Sarah Pugh, both leading abolitionists, later became lifelong feminists, as did others in the group. Two sisters, Sarah and Angelina Grimké, joined the Philadelphia Society and later became noted speakers on the slavery question. The leading member of the organization and one of its founders, Lucretia Mott, was in her own right one of the most remarkable women of her age. These women, and many others now forgotten, carried on the day-to-day work of the Society, visiting Negro families, making articles for sale, supporting and distributing antislavery tracts and periodicals, circulating petitions — all the tasks, great and small, which combined to foster and spread the movement against slavery.

Philadelphia's antislavery women tried to conduct themselves so as not to offend the city's leaders or population in general. They deplored mob violence and apparently inspired less of it than some antislavery organizations. But their programs naturally created hostility. According to a late annual report of the Society, all Philadelphia churches excepting one were closed to its meetings. Along with other reformist groups, the Philadelphia Female Anti-Slavery Society occasionally faced forceful opposition. During the 1838 Anti-Slavery Convention of American Women, an unruly mob roamed Philadelphia's streets, threatening many women abolitionists and destroying property. Such violence was directed at the abolitionists in general, not toward the Philadelphia women in particular.

Although it faced consistent opposition, the Philadelphia Female Anti-Slavery Society also received critical encouragement from male abolitionists and its sister organizations. In 1836 the Society enjoyed hearing from James Forten, Jr., a prominent black abolitionist of Philadelphia:

> I rejoice to see you engaged in this mighty cause; it befits you; it is your province; your aid and influence is [sic] greatly to be desired in this hour of peril; it never was, never can be insignificant. Examine the records of history and you will find that woman has been called upon in the severest trials of public emergency. That your efforts will stimulate the men to renewed exertion I have not the slightest doubt. . . . It has often been said by anti-abolitionists that the females have no right to interfere with the question of slavery or petition for its overthrow; that they had better be at home attending to their domestic affairs, etc. What a gross error — what an anti-christian spirit this bespeaks. Were not the holy commands, "Remember them that are in bonds, as bound with them," and "Do unto others as ye would they should do unto you," intended for woman to obey as well as man? Most assuredly they were. [7]

Slavery was a moral issue, thus it fitted into definitions of woman's "sphere," and her moral duties were no less demanding than man's responsibilities. Later in the same year Charles C. Burleigh, an associate of the most prominent antislavery leaders and a well-known lecturer on abolition, spoke before the Philadelphia Female Anti-Slavery Society on "The right of females to plead the cause of the oppressed, the duty of all to contribute to their aid in so righteous a cause, and urging us to avail ourselves of our 'noble privilege to do good.' " [8] It must have been a comfort to these women, oppressed by doubts and constantly under attack from opponents, to hear such encouraging words.

Depending on their circumstances, women's antislavery organizations had different programs. Yet they varied not too far from the model of Philadelphia, except that the majority were situated in villages rather than cities. At New York City, the ladies' society was founded in 1835 after a speech from the noted British abolitionist, George Thompson. The Ladies' New York City Anti-Slavery Society based its organization on the churches of the city. Its orthodox religious roots required its leaders to be particularly circumspect in their conduct, so as not to offend the Protestant clergy and conservative laymen. The "Ladies' Anti-Slavery Sewing Society" was a working auxiliary of this organization. Along with other female societies, the New York organization held fairs and took part in the petition campaign.

Another situation, similar to that of Philadelphia, provided women with an opportunity for teaching and social work among former slaves. Cincinnati, like Philadelphia, had a large black population existing in wretched living conditions. Following the Lane Seminary rebellion in 1834, when most of the theological students resigned from school in protest against a ban on discussions of slavery, a vigorous antislavery and Negro-assistance crusade developed in the "Queen" city. After the Lane Seminary abolitionist debates the students formed a "large and efficient organization for elevating the colored people in Cincinnati,"including a lyceum, a circulating library, and schools, among them a "Select Female School," for "raising" young black women. [9] Women were obviously needed to work with black members of their own sex, but because no female abolitionists lived in Cincinnati, the Lane rebels appealed for feminine assistance from elsewhere. The Tappan brothers in New York responded to the call, offering to pay expenses of any volunteers who would journey to the West. Several pious young abolitionist women responded.

From their arrival in Cincinatti, "the sisters," as they were called, took over many of the most arduous labors in the schools. Their roles involved far more than commonplace schoolteaching, however. They became religious missionaries, social workers, reformers, and intimate friends of the people they attempted to help. One of the teachers described her duties in some detail:

> I have not yet been able to win any of them to Christ. Still they are leaving off bad habits, forming good ones, and are twisting themselves most closely around my heart. The temperance effort has been glorious in its results and promises to do much towards urging this degraded and ignorant population up the inclined plane. I fear sometimes that our hopes are too sanguine, for observation teaches us the coloured people are not good to keep promises. Nearly every scholar of mine is decidedly in favor of waging war on king alcohol. . . . They want I should set their names to the pledge. Some of them that are so young they can scarcely say temperance society. [10]

Despite their somewhat patronizing and biased attitudes toward blacks, the "sisters" apparently established rapport with their clients. One of the Lane students wrote, "The sisters are doing nobly. They are everywhere recieved [sic] with open arms. they visit, eat, and sleep with their people and are exerting a powerful influence in correcting their domestic habits." [11]

From the first their efforts faced an uphill battle. Bad habits resisted change, few of the students saw any value in school, and when the young reformers stirred up a revival, no clergyman was ready to accept the converted souls. Funds were always scarce, although limited support came to the schools from women in Pittsburgh and other places. Abolitionist-sponsored schools operated in Cincinnati for about two years, from mid-1834 until the summer of 1836. The lack of financial support and a hostile environment were probably major factors in their abandonment, as the Lane students left Cincinnati and the "sisters" apparently followed.

Women continued to be attracted to employment in Ohio's Negro schools. Scores of young women traveled to the new college at Oberlin to attend the first collegiate institution open to their sex. And Oberlin College became a center for recruitment of female reformers. Many were inspired to teach or help in the establishment of schools for blacks in Ohio. Leaders in the cause of Negro education appealed for financial help from women's antislavery societies in Ohio:

> The need of money for . . . schools is as great as this. Out of the sixteen female teachers of colored schools that I have known, not more than three have received money enough of the colored people, to pay their board. Many of

them have boarded themselves and lived on the plainest, cheapest fare, that their expenses might be as small as possible. [12]

Despite hardships, the teachers persevered. The motivations for lifting these "ignorant and degraded" people from "their ignorance on religious subjects" were the very highest: nothing less than their eternal spiritual welfare. Many Ohio towns and villages had such schools, taught generally by women. While she was a student at Oberlin College, Lucy Stone taught sucessfully in Negro schools in the village, and was paid partly by her pupils, partly by abolitionists. Schoolteaching among blacks seemed to combine two acceptable roles for women in the second quarter of the nineteenth century, those of teacher and missionary. Yet prejudice against blacks and their white advocates made their teachers controversial and often outcast figures.

Women who opposed slavery were subjected to conflicting impulses. On the one hand they were driven by conscience to work for abolition and for the "elevation" of an unfortunate group of people, yet at the same time they found opposition to activities that would have been respectable had the beneficiaries possessed white skins. They discovered one service, however, which gained widespread acceptance and produced tangible benefits for the cause: raising money by means of fairs. The antislavery fair, already mentioned as one of the programs sponsored by the Philadelphia Female Anti-Slavery Society, probably grew out of similar fund-raising techniques used by British women's organizations and by earlier American women's benevolent societies. The typical fair or bazaar was a sale of "fancy and useful articles," most often handmade by members of sewing circles (needlework was a highly acceptable female avocation), or manufactured and contributed by interested friends. Many fairs were held in conjunction with major antislavery meetings, or arranged to coincide with Christmas, to take advantage of holiday customers. The most elaborate fairs included entertainment and in some cases, speechmaking, to which admission was charged.

The earliest recorded antislavery fair took place at Boston late in the year 1834, under the leadership of Lydia Maria Child. According to the *Liberator,* the fair received contributions from a number of women's antislavery societies in New England and netted some $300 in proceeds. "Use your needles in the cause of bleeding humanity," the *Liberator* urged. Two years later the Massachusetts Anti-Slavery Fair had expanded greatly and sold manufactured as well as handmade goods. In 1840 more than thirty-five different female societies contributed objects with an estimated value of $450, including needlework, jewelry, ornaments, hats, straw-work, food, and countless other items. Its managers reported as follows:

> The attendance of visitors was numerous and constant. Boston seemed pleased with the fair and showed that it was so by the amount of its purchases. The hall was open four days, and the receipts averaged $500 per day—in all *Two Thousand & one Dollars*. It would be difficult to describe the satisfaction of the friends in making this gift of the season to the Cause of Freedom. It has been suffering for funds & and is so still. [13]

By the late 1830s women's fairs had become major fundraising projects for the entire antislavery movement. The Philadelphia Female Society obtained total net profits of more than $28,000 from fairs, more than four-fifths of its collections from all sources. The fair system migrated at least as far as Ohio, and for years a National Anti-Slavery Bazaar was held at Boston with contributions from many organizations. In New England the proceeds of women's fairs helped sustain the *Liberator* and supported agents of the Massachusetts Anti-Slavery Society. From Lynn, Massachusetts, in 1837, Abby Kelley, an outspoken young Quaker, sent $200 for the Massachusetts Anti-Slavery Society and attempted later in that year of financial depression to raise $500 more. The Boston Female Anti-Slavery Society made a practice of pledging $1000 annually to the Massachusetts Society and sent smaller sums to Garrison personally. [14]

Antislavery fairs had social consequences for their participants that transcended money-raising. They provided meaningful opportunities for women to work for the cause, even for those who were uncomfortable in assertive roles. To leaders and followers alike they gave satisfaction and prestige from the performance of important services to the movement. They provided experience in leadership and management that were otherwise not easily available to women. Most significantly for many women, they institutionalized and warranted close, long-term relationships of sisterhood. The fair system tied together female antislavery societies, depending for its success upon detailed correspondence, an interchange of ideas and "fancy and useful articles," and a sense of community among women. From this system of women cooperating in a network of organizations, the participants could gain a consciousness of power, the reward of accomplishment.

Women's antislavery societies varied in size, membership, leadership, and location. A few societies such as those of Boston and

Philadelphia chose nationally recognized officers. Most groups, like the small network of female antislavery societies in Ashtabula County, Ohio, were little-known outside the immediate area. Nevertheless they had important functions in keeping abolitionism alive and influential. Depending upon the interests of their members, different societies had varied conceptions of their duties to the cause. Like most other women's organizations of the time, antislavery groups attracted pious women who believed in circumscribed notions of woman's "sphere." In a few cases, because of the influence of leaders of both sexes, antislavery societies were radical, unafraid of public disapproval. The more radical groups met criticism with strength and unyielding determination.

The most notorious women abolitionists were probably those of Boston. A number of members of the Boston Female Anti-Slavery Society took an advanced view of woman's role in the struggle, a point which they proved in October, 1835. The season would go down in the annals as one of the most violent eras of the antislavery movement, with mobbings in New York state, Vermont, Massachusetts, and elsewhere. The Boston Female Society had invited George Thompson, a highly controversial British abolitionist, to address its meeting, creating such a violent public reaction that no public hall could be found. Postponed to a later date at the Anti-Slavery Society rooms, the Boston women's meeting attracted a large and noisy mob. The meeting opened conventionally with "some appropriate passages of scripture," but it was constantly interrupted with loud cries, peering faces, and disorder from the outside. Boston's Major Lyman appeared and implored the women to disband in order to "avoid a scene of bloodshed and confusion." After discussing their civil liberties, the Society voted to adjourn and left the building through a great and disorderly crowd. Not finding Thompson, their intended victim, the mob captured and manhandled the *Liberator*'s editor, William Lloyd Garrison, who was finally lodged in the city jail for his own safety. The Boston mob became notorious as the "gentlemen of property and standing" who behaved as undisciplined rabble. Led by their aristocratic chief, Maria Weston Chapman, Boston's women abolitionists were not intimidated.

One of the major contributions of women to the antislavery movement was their work in the petition campaign, an important effort to make slavery into a national political issue. Quakers had sent antislavery petitions to Congress from 1790 onward, but only with the rise of radical abolitionism in the 1830s did petitioning become a massive weapon against slavery. By 1837 the petition movement was organized as a systematic national enterprise, with regional and local offices and thousands of volunteer workers to circulate the forms sent out from a central headquarters. In 1838, when the campaign decentralized, antislavery petitions flooded the House of Representatives. In response to this onslaught, Congress passed an annual set of "gag" resolutions to prevent discussion of the petitions and of the slavery issue.

At first women's petitioning was local, with hundreds of signatures obtained in a few communities. As the process became more highly organized and more urgent, women went from house to house, tramping the streets in winter and summer, adding thousands of names to their lists. In Boston, the Female Anti-Slavery Society considered petitioning to be a critical duty:

> Let every woman into whose hands this page falls, INSTANTLY . . . with pen and ink-horn in hand, and armed with affectionate, but unconquerable determination, go from door to door "among her own people" that every one of them may have an opportunity of affixing her name to these . . . memorials. [15]

According to the *Liberator,* New England's women sent twice as many petitions to Congress as did the men. Their response elsewhere was similarly gratifying.

Petitioning might be uncomfortable and trying, but the antislavery women pursued their task with devotion. One of the New York City volunteers wrote:

> There is so much aristocracy here, so much walking in Broadway to exhibit the butterfly fashions, that we can seldom gain access to the consciences of the women. I have left many houses ashamed of my sex. . . . [16]

Sarah Pugh, a prominent member of the Philadelphia Female Anti-Slavery Society, expressed mixed feelings about the petition effort:

> I never undertook anything that was so entirely distasteful to me; but as it is in many things, the anticipation was more than the reality. In our aristocratic district we were generally civilly received, and heard, and as civilly refused with few words. [17]

As an organized campaign of publicity, petitioning naturally brought criticism of women. They were declared to be "unsexing" themselves: "By argument and ridicule, by conscious expostulation and unblushing rudeness, from pulpit, press and parlor," female petitions were "most zealously assailed, as entirely unbecoming our sex, and we are gravely and fairly told that the whole subject is beyond our province." [18]

Both Northern and Southern Congressmen were upset by the

number of petitions from women asking for abolition of slavery and the slave trade in the District of Columbia, prohibition of slavery in the Territories, or action on some other subject relating to the cause. Women — "sensitive females of shrinking modesty," of "domestic peace and quiet," of "more delicate physical organization" — had no business meddling with public concerns. [19] Representative Howard of Maryland defended conventional views:

> I think that those females should have a sufficient field for the exercise of their influence in the discharge of their duties to their fathers, their husbands, or their children, cheering the domestic circle and shedding over it the mild radiance of the social virtues, instead of rushing into the fierce struggles of political life. I feel sorry at this departure from their proper sphere. . . . [20]

John Quincy Adams, defender of the right of petition, would not accept such limits for his constituents:

> Why does it follow that women are fitted for nothing but the cares of domestic life. . . ? The mere departure of woman from the duties of the domestic circle, far from being a reproach to her, is a virtue of the highest order, when it is done from purity of motive, by appropriate means, and the purpose good. [21]

The argument was familiar, involving the interplay of moral and political issues, domestic and public life. Discussing the subject among themselves, arguing with husbands, sons, or brothers, even organizing societies dedicated to opposing slavery might be acceptable. But registering public disapproval of the institution in the nation's legislative halls injected women into political life, which was most unfeminine. The argument of Mary Grew, a leading Philadelphia abolitionist, that it was proper for women's "generous sympathies of human nature to flow out, unchecked, at the sight or sound of human suffering," could hardly apply to political action. [22]

Petitioning sponsored by local women's societies suggested some form of national petition system to be established by a national female antislavery organization, a wholly new departure from earlier practices. While controlling their own local societies, women had generally been "auxiliary" to and dominated by male organizations on the regional and national levels. In the antislavery movement, too, women's groups were "auxiliary" to men's societies, but by 1835 extensive correspondence and cooperative efforts among many local female organizations had formed bonds of sisterhood and interests between them. As the petition campaign increased in scope and intensity, female antislavery societies in Boston, New York, and Philadelphia began to discuss the desirability of forming a national women's executive committee. The idea apparently originated in Boston, but both the New York and Philadelphia societies responded enthusiastically to the suggestion.

The first Anti-Slavery Convention of American Women met in New York City in May, 1837. Its elected officers formed an honor role of the most prominent female abolitionists, and its discussions dealt at length with women's tasks in the movement. Observers at this meeting noted how women had matured in their public roles during the brief period of their participation in the antislavery movement. Much discussion dealt with petitioning. Lydia Maria Child proposed a distinct, highly organized women's petition network like that established by the American Anti-Slavery Society. By having central petition offices in three major centers of women's antislavery activity — Boston, New York, and Philadelphia — they hoped to secure a million signatures on petitions.

In addition to debating procedures and techniques, the women raised more basic questions about their place in the entire reform movement. They approved of discussion and agitation of the slavery issue by women, despite its controversial and political nature. The debate went much further, however, in asserting woman's rights: "Resolved, that as certain rights and duties are common to all moral beings, the time has come for woman to move in that sphere which Providence has assigned her, and no longer remain satisfied in the circumscribed limits which corrupt custom and a perverted application of Scripture have encircled her." [23] Not all of those in attendance at the Convention were willing to go this far, and debate on this resolution was the most heated of the entire meeting. Conservatives offered qualifying amendments while radicals defended their assertion of equality. It was finally approved, but without unanimity. National women's conventions met again in 1838 and 1839, helping to clarify the position of women in the antislavery movement.

Although they were a minority of the total number of American abolitionists, women's contributions to the cause were out of proportion to their numbers. Their financial support aided such areas as Philadelphia and Boston in becoming and continuing as primary centers of abolitionism. In petitioning, women were far more active than men, as evidenced by the vast number of female signatures on antislavery petitions in comparison to their numbers in the antislavery crusade. Thus, in a curious fashion, women did more than their share to make abolition into a political issue — one in which they could have no legitimate direct voice. Antislavery politics, and ultimately, emancipation, would probably have occurred without the organized assistance of women, but their involvement in the movement was inevitable. Had they not participated, emancipation would have come more slowly.

Women's antislavery agitation had a major impact on the emerging question of woman's rights, for the female abolition societies were direct ancestors of the equal rights movement. Abolitionism brought women into a public arena of controversy, setting precedents for political movements to be undertaken by women. The slavery issue raised more direct questions about the status of women than previous benevolent and reform work had done. Involved in the antislavery agitation were issues of human rights and limits on freedom, principles which might apply to the condition of women as well as to that of slaves. The full implications of this analogy between slaves and women were not recognized until after 1840, but hesitant steps were taken in this direction as a result of women's antislavery work.

More directly, women's antislavery societies gave inspiration and experience to many of the earliest advocates of woman's rights. Lucretia Mott, Maria Weston Chapman, Abby Kelley, the Grimké sisters, and later, Susan B. Anthony and Lucy Stone, along with countless other, lesser figures, had experience in women's antislavery societies. They learned the techniques of organizing and doing business; they found that women could withstand violence and public hostility as well as more subtle forms of opposition. They gained an awareness of their own strength, a recognition that leadership was not an exclusive property of the male sex. They also discovered a power that had been only tentatively explored and incompletely understood in earlier women's activities — the power of collective female engagement. They called each other "sister."

Another important development coming out of female antislavery activities occurred somewhat earlier. In the summer of 1836 the Agency Committee of the American Anti-Slavery Society proposed that women be hired as antislavery agents — speakers and propagandists. The Committee "*Voted* that in our view it is expedient to appoint females & compensate them to perform such services as are appropriate." [24] By this action the Society engaged the first professional women reformers of any American organization. Although it seemed innocent enough, the decision broke precedent, marking a significant advance in women's roles in social reform. It opened the lecturing field to two women, Angelina and Sarah Grimké, the first of scores of women to be lecturers on reform. And it raised profound questions about the rights and duties of women in society.

6

RIGHTS AND DUTIES OF MORAL BEINGS

THE Grimké sisters did not appear as likely candidates for conversion to immediate abolitionism. Members of one of the first families of Charleston, South Carolina, daughters of Judge John Faucheraud Grimké, planter, lawyer, jurist, and former officer in the American Revolution, the sisters should have been firm pillars of the Southern way of life. But something in their experience had made them rebels. Both Sarah and Angelina had gone through long soul-wrenching religious struggles which led them away from the fashionable Episcopal church and eventually into the ascetic Society of Friends. Born in 1792, Sarah had been a somewhat lonely, introspective child. Eager for learning, she was frustrated in her efforts to gain an education equivalent to the studies naturally offered her brothers. Twelve years old when Angelina was born in 1805, Sarah became a surrogate mother of the younger child, supervising much of her rearing. This close tie between the sisters was to have a profound impact on their emotional lives and their careers as reformers.

How did two Southern gentlewomen become abolitionists? No final answer to this question is possible. However, some of the influences of their childhood and youth predisposed them to understand the plight of slaves. Like many Southern girls and women, the Grimkés were hostile toward slavery and felt an empathy, especially toward female slaves—unprotected by the familial relations which they themselves valued so highly. The sisters grew up when doubts about slavery could still be openly expressed in the South, when a vocal minority could discuss the institution's lamentable consequences. Moreover, being sensitive and offended by the inhumanity of slavery, they developed an early abhorrence of servitude and did what they could to ease the lives of slaves closest to them. One brother, Thomas Smith Grimké, had strong humanitarian and reformist interests which attracted Sarah and Angelina. Extremely religious and sensitive, these women who should have defended the South and its "peculiar institution" were just the kinds of personalities who would be susceptible to the "conversion" experience which some abolitionists believed was essential to rid the South of slavery.

As adults, the two women migrated to Philadelphia and lived as converts to the Society of Friends in that city's closely knit Quaker community. But their lives never became integrated into the inbred society of their Quaker associates. Perplexed by religious doubts and problems, Sarah failed to gain satisfaction from her faith, and Angelina searched for a vocation in charitable work and schoolteaching, but remained unfulfilled. After 1834, the antislavery movement began to influence Philadelphia's women, and Angelina Grimké, remembering her earlier sympathy for the downtrodden, was attracted to this appealing cause. She attended her first antislavery lecture early in 1835 and probably joined the Philadelphia Female Anti-Slavery Society in April, 1835. Later that year she wrote William Lloyd Garrison a fervent letter of support which the editor published in the *Liberator,* embarrassing Angelina, astonishing Sarah, and offending the conservative Quakers. Stimulated by criticism, Angelina Grimké became more active in the Philadelphia Female Anti-Slavery Society and began corresponding with other women abolitionists. Suppressed for years, her old rebelliousness had been reawakened.

Disturbed for some time by the emptiness of her life, Angelina Grimké committed herself fully to the cause of abolition in the summer of 1836. Her first major contribution to the movement was a pamphlet entitled an *Appeal to the Christian Women of the South* (New York, 1836), which outlined the degradation of slavery and pleaded for Southern women to take a religious position against it. She was enthusiastic about her new vocation as she wrote to Sarah: "O Sister I feel as if I could not only give up friends but life itself for the slave if it is called for, I feel as if I could go anywhere to serve him, even down to the South. . . ." [1] At about the same time, Sarah had reached a crisis in her religious struggle when she attempted to speak out in Quaker meeting but was rebuffed by one of the leading male Friends. She too was ready for a drastic change in her pattern of life. Thus, both sisters responded favorably to an invitation from the American Anti-Slavery Society in New York, asking the Grimkés to "meet with Christian women in sewing circles and private parlors," for discussions of slavery. [2]

In November, 1836, Sarah and Angelina Grimké joined a group of newly recruited antislavery agents in New York City for a series of indoctrination meetings. They were great additions to the antislavery crusade because, as Southerners and former slaveholders, they knew of slavery firsthand and they opposed it vigorously. The sisters were deeply impressed by the arguments and discussions that developed during the intense agents' meetings. During the proceedings, the Grimkés were invited "to state such facts representing slavery as they may choose," and evidently they did so.

After the exhilarating and exhausting experience of the agents' meetings, the Grimké sisters had to develop an approach to antislavery agitation. Despite prejudices against women's public speaking, the sisters agreed to hold a meeting in a Baptist church, and they faced their first audience in December, 1836. From this time until March, 1837, they lectured in the New York City vicinity, and despite the novelty, their modesty and simplicity engendered little opposition. In theory, their meetings were not "promiscuous"—open to both sexes—but in practice it seemed difficult to exclude men. Once a man was escorted from the hall by a clergyman, and when on another occasion a male listener stayed for the lecture, Angelina did not find "his presence at all embarrassing & went on just as tho' he was not there."[3] Their winter meetings were generally successful, despite the fact that they were women speaking in public. They were a great deal more familiar with the institution of slavery than most antislavery agents. In addition, the sisters, especially Angelina, were becoming skilled lecturers.

The Grimkés were particularly influenced by two abolitionists during this period. They met Theodore Dwight Weld at the agents' indoctrination meetings and were immediately impressed by him. Weld was the leading antislavery lecturer and organizer, a master of the subject of abolition, with several years of experience as an agitator in Ohio and New York State. Angelina described one of his speeches as a "moral and intellectual feast," and was thrilled when he called her "my dear sister."[4] Weld reassured the Grimkés when they doubted their abilities to go forward as public speakers, calling for their "testimony, *testimony*, TESTIMONY."[5]

A somewhat different influence came from another antislavery agent, Henry C. Wright. An ex-minister and radical pacifist, Wright believed that one reform could not be divorced from another. Domination in all its forms needed to be fought—including the tyranny of men over women. During the winter and spring of 1837 this radical reformer met occasionally with the Grimké sisters for discussions of peace, defects of the orthodox clergy as reformers, and the rights and duties of women. As Quakers, pacifists, and rebellious women, the Grimkés sympathized with his radical views, although they did not always agree with them. Nevertheless, he encouraged their thinking on the subject of women's roles as reformers. Both Weld and Wright strongly supported "the abilities & the dutys of woman...to preach...."

In May, 1837, the Grimké sisters came into greater prominence during the first women's antislavery convention. Both women prepared strong resolutions for the meetings. Sarah denounced the sexual immorality of slavery, a disturbing feature of the "peculiar institution" especially repellent to women. Angelina declared that "certain rights and duties are common to all moral beings," thus it was time for woman to throw off her shackles and "plead the cause of the oppressed in our land. . . ." The resolution produced a spirited debate. Even more radical than her resolution on woman's duties was Angelina Grimké's *Appeal to the Women of the Nominally Free States*, published by the women's convention. Here she wrote:

> Are we aliens, because we are women? Are we bereft of citizenship because we are the *mothers, wives* and daughters of a mighty people? Have *women* no country—no interest staked in public weal—no liabilities in common peril—no partnership in a nation's guilt and shame? [6]

Women had equal responsibilities with men in moral and political concerns. Already the Grimkés were rebels far in advance of most of their co-workers in their attitudes toward restraints on woman's freedom.

Following the Anti-Slavery Convention of American Women the Grimké sisters traveled to Massachusetts where they had previously agreed to give a series of lectures. They found audiences more eager to hear than any they had addressed earlier. Angelina noticed the different attitudes prevailing in Massachusetts: "We feel ourselves surrounded by an elastic atmosphere which yields to the stroke of the wings of effort & sends up the soaring spirit still higher & swifter in its upward flight. In New York we were allowed to sit down & do nothing—here invitations to labor press in from all sides." [7] The Boston Female Anti-Slavery Society, which brought the Grimkés to Massachusetts, was a bastion of radicalism. Maria Weston Chapman, its leading member, was powerful and unflinching. "Are we FREE!" she wrote, "it is because we have burst our manacles in the effort to undo those that weigh so heavily on (the slave)." [8] In a circular letter urging all New England women to support the Grimkés, the Boston Female Society declared of women's mission:

It is of paramount importance, that both man and women should understand [women's] true position and mighty responsibilities to this and to coming generations. In all spiritual things, their functions are identical. . . both for all the duties growing out of that spiritual equality here, and for communion with their maker during their immortal life hereafter. . . . [9]

Immediately after their arrival in Boston, the Grimkés began holding private meetings with "brothers and sisters" where they often conversed about women's duties and women's rights. In one discussion they "found a very general sentiment prevailing that it was time our fetters were broken. . . ." Angelina felt that they were pleading "not the cause of the slave only . . . but the cause of woman as a responsible, moral being. . . . What an untrodden path we have entered upon!" [10] The sisters delivered their first public lecture before a crowded meeting of the Boston Anti-Slavery Society early in June. Later in the month they began a tour of eastern Massachusetts through portions of Essex, Middlesex, and Worcester counties. Their friend, Henry C. Wright, then engaged in promoting abolitionism among children, agreed to arrange their schedules and plan for their lectures in various towns.

As their notoriety increased, the sisters attracted larger audiences of both sexes, curious to see these strange Southern females who unsexed themselves by speaking in public. At Lynn the Grimkés addressed their *"first large mixed audience"* of about a thousand persons. Of the meeting Angelina wrote: "Great openness to hear & ease in speaking." At a second Lynn meeting many persons were turned away and nearly a hundred stood at the door. Occasionally the significance of the lectures dawned on members of the audience. After hearing the sisters at Lynn and watching the interest they aroused, a gentleman "hastened away," declaring, "This will never do. . . . Next thing they will be in Congress." [11] Aware that their speeches to men and women were a significant, controversial departure from common practice, the Grimkés thought it "wonderful" that they were able to speak to "mixed audiences."

Traveling throughout the summer, the sisters met many difficulties in trying to adhere to a rigorous schedule. Clergymen often refused to read announcements of their lectures, and in some towns they were not allowed to speak in churches. Their application to address the students at Ipswich Female Seminary was denied. In other places they found a positive response to their work. At Salem they spoke several times, once to a mixed audience of some six hundred Quakers. "Their addresses

seemed to move Salem as it had never been moved before," reported the
Liberator. At Amesbury they arranged to debate with two young men,
recent visitors in the South. Taking the negative on the question "Does
the Bible sanction American slavery?" the sisters demolished their
opponents, according to a friendly observer. Two days later the same four
argued the question of whether Northern laborers were more degraded
than Southern slaves. Pointing out that slavery meant concubinage and
illegitimate offspring, that slaves lived as chattels without wages,
without legal protection, contractual or property rights, and that they
were forbidden education, the sisters again scored impressively.
Although not typical of their meetings, these debates suggest the great
impression which the Grimkés made in Massachusetts.

They addressed their largest audience, fifteen hundred persons,
including many Lowell mill girls, at Lowell, and at the village of
Pepperell, where the meetinghouse was closed to them, Angelina
lectured in a barn. At Concord, where they spoke three times, Angelina
wrote, "I have been nowhere where the aristocracy came out so generally
& seemed to be so pleased. We had more invitations than we could
accept. . . ." [12] At the end of September they attended state and county
antislavery meetings in Worcester where the right of women to speak in
public was vindicated, despite serious opposition. Scheduled to address
the general public, the sisters attracted a large, curious, and restless
audience. Angelina was not pleased:

> It was an unsatisfactory meeting to me, the excessive crowd comprised of so
> many who came out of *mere* curiosity, produced a feeling of unsettlement, so
> that it seemed like the rolling waves of the sea, & yet it was remarkably still as
> to the *outward,* except when a bench broke down in the house, or a wagon on
> the outside, &c. [13]

The sisters lectured through the month of October, although they were ill
and fatigued, but Angelina's health broke down entirely at the end of this
month and they retired from the field.

At first the Grimké sisters determined not to become involved in
general discussions of women's problems, except to defend their own
right of free speech and assert the duty of women to oppose slavery. The
woman question could not be ignored, however. Startling enough was the
fact that the Grimké s discussed controversial issues in public; even more
shocking was the fact that their audiences included men. Strong
opposition to the sisters' lectures came immediately from individual
ministers, but it was not long before the church as a body took action.

Meeting at Brookfield on June 27, 1837 the Congregational General Association of Massachusetts published an annual pastoral letter which attacked much of the antislavery activity then taking place. Singling out the "dangers which at present seem to threaten the Female Character with widespread and permanent injury," namely the public appearance of women as lecturers and reformers, the ministers asserted:

The appropriate duties and influence of women are clearly stated in the New Testament. Those duties and that influence are unobtrusive and private, but the sources of mighty power. But when [woman] assumes the place and tone of man as a public reformer, our care and protection of her seem unnecessary, we put ourselves in self-defense against her, she yields the power which God has given her for protection, and her character becomes unnatural. We cannot, therefore, but regret the mistaken conduct of those who encourage females to bear an obtrusive and ostentatious part in measures for reform and countenance any of that sex who so far forget themselves as to itinerate in the character of public lecturers and teachers. [14]

These strictures on women's preaching were supported by most Massachusetts clergymen. Basing their arguments on the scriptural "appropriate sphere" of the sex, several prominent ministers published sermons denouncing public speaking by women. According to the Reverend Parsons Cooke, the prohibition against women's speaking in church applied not only to religious meetings but to all public gatherings:

Even if it were true, that some woman in an assembly had more talents than all the men present, the excess of her talents, so far from making a reason why she should display them, would make it a still stronger case of usurping authority over the man. [15]

Reverend Cooke singled out Fanny Wright, the notorious female infidel, as a woman of talent who had overstepped her sphere. Woman's inferiority was thus complete: such ability as she had must remain hidden, so that universal and biblical tradition would not be upset. Other conservative ministers, like the Reverend Hubbard Winslow, defended the divine "law of female subjection," and specifically denounced women abolitionists. Although not mentioned by name, the Grimké sisters' lectures were the most prominent violations of "modesty, deference, delicacy, and sweet charity . . ." in Massachusetts in 1837.

The question of women's speaking involved not only scriptural interpretations or conventional practices, but a fundamental civil right for which all abolitionists had been contending. William Lloyd Garrison, Theodore Dwight Weld, even John Quincy Adams in the House of Representatives had expended great energy to vindicate the right of free speech. Would the same men defend the same right when women were the speakers? As it developed, the controversy over lectures by the Grimké sisters became a major issue *within* the antislavery movement as well as outside it. Leading antislavery men urged the sisters not to speak to audiences of both sexes. John Greenleaf Whittier wrote from New York cautioning the sisters against raising the issue of woman's rights at the expense of abolition. Theodore Weld also advised them against discussing "lesser questions" than slavery.

Sarah and Angelina were unprepared for such influential and serious opposition from their friends. Deeply perplexed, Angelina wrote to Weld:

> Was it right for us to come to Massachusetts? I expected to meet with trials, *personal* trials & I (vainly perhaps) *think* I could have born *them,* but all this unsettlement and complaint among the friends of the cause is so unexpected that I dont know how to bear it. [16]

Some critics assumed that as members of the Society of Friends, which permitted women to preach, the sisters were simply carrying out a denominational practice, Angelina responded: "WE do not stand on Quaker ground, but on Bible ground and *moral right*.What we claim for ourselves, we claim for *every* woman whom God has called and qualified with gifts and graces." [17] After lengthy discussions with her radical friend, Henry C. Wright, Angelina concluded that God had made no original distinction between man and woman. Both had equal "dominion over the fish of the sea & over the fowl of the air...."

> If woman stands on a *lower* platform of *human* rights than man, then of course her *duties must be of a lower grade*. But if she stand side by side with man.... upon *her* rest *all* the responsibilities, toil & duties which press upon *him*. [18]

Sarah, too, responded to criticism. In a long letter to the Reverend Amos A. Phelps, general agent of the Massachusetts Anti-Slavery Society, she insisted that prejudiced clergymen had misinterpreted Saint Paul and had "thereby deprived women of those rights with which God invested them as moral & responsible beings. The clergy have done an infinite injury to woman. . . ." If, in pleading the wrongs of slavery, they also became involved in a controversy over the rights of woman, it was not their fault: "God has unexpectedly placed us in the fore-front of the battle which is to be waged against the rights & duties & responsibilities of woman, [and] it would ill become us to shrink from such a contest." In the end Sarah rested her case for freedom of speech on the "fundamental principle that man & woman are created equal"; if it was right for the clergy to speak to "promiscuous" audiences, then it should be right for women to do the same. [19]

Despite the growing furor over the woman's rights issue, the Grimkés attempted to concentrate on slavery in public lectures and discussions. Speaking privately, however, the sisters were not so reticent. On the way to a lecture in Franklin, Massachusetts, Angelina nearly converted a traveling companion to her opinions:

I threw out my views on women's preaching in the course of the ride & verily believe I convinced him, for he said he had no idea so much could be adduced from the Bible to sustain the [stand] I had taken, & remarked this will be quite new to the people & I believe they will be glad to hear these things. . . . [20]

For a time Sarah and Angelina considered the possibility of starting a newspaper devoted to the rights of woman, but they concluded that Garrison's *Liberator* would serve their purpose, as that paper devoted more and more attention to the new issue.

During the summer of 1837, both Angelina and Sarah Grimké published essays dealing with the woman's rights issue. Angelina wrote a series of public letters in answer to an *Essay on Slavery and Abolitionism With Reference to the Duty of American Females, Addressed to Miss A.D.[sic] Grimke* (Philadelphia, 1837), by Catharine Beecher, the educator. Beecher had been especially distressed by women who spoke in public and participated actively in antislavery agitation. "Woman is to win everything by peace and love," she wrote, "but this is to be all accomplished in the domestic and social circle." Female influence depended upon "woman's retaining her place as dependent and defenceless, and making no claims, and maintaining no right. . . ." God's law defined distinctions between the sexes: "It is the grand feature of the Divine economy, that there should be different stations of superiority and subordination, and it is impossible to annihilate this beneficent and immutable law." [21] In this "Divine economy," man was naturally superior, but when she exercised her domestic influence, woman might wield great power.

Angelina Grimké began answering Beecher's *Essay* immediately after her arrival in Massachusetts. Using the same moral argument asserted in her personal correspondence, Angelina insisted that women had the same duties to eradicate sin as men, and cited examples of various biblical women who preached and prophesied in public. Concerning the right of petition, Angelina thought it little enough to grant to women: "If their numbers are counted to swell the number of Representatives in our State and National Legislatures, the *very least* that can be done is to give them the right of petition in all cases whatsoever. . . ." [22] The doctrine had dramatic political implications:

> Now, I believe it is woman's right to have a voice in all laws and regulations by which she is to be *governed*, whether in Church or State, and that the present arrangements of society, on these points, are a *violation of human rights, a rank usurpation of power*. . . . If Ecclesiastical and Civil governments are ordained of God, then I contend that woman has just as much right to sit in solemn counsel in Conventions, Conferences, Associations and General Assemblies, as man—just as much right to sit upon the throne of England, or in the Presidential chair of the United States. [23]

Equality thus meant full civil and religious participation—radical doctrine indeed! Angelina did not explore the details of her discovery, but the principle was clear: once full equality was asserted it could lead to full partnership. Angelina had found "the Anti-Slavery cause to be the high school of morals in our land," the school of "*human rights*. . . ."

Sarah Grimké wrote a more significant exploration of woman's rights in a series of fifteen letters to the *New England Spectator*. At the outset she claimed total dependence on the Bible, arguing that most commentators had misconceived "the simple truths revealed in the Scripture...." According to her reading of the sacred text, the word *man* was simply a generic term, God created woman to be man's equal. "God... is our King and our Judge, and to him alone is woman bound to be in subjection...." But because fallen man was full of the "lust of domination," he used woman "as a means to promote his selfish gratification...but never has he desired to elevate her to that rank she was created to fill." Woman, like the slave, was a victim of man's wickedness. Replying directly to the Massachusetts clergy, she insisted that woman should lead in all reform work, for "She is fulfilling one of the important duties laid upon her as an accountable being...." [24]

Arguing in favor of the "Ministry of Women," Sarah Grimké defended female preaching. Women had "unquestionably" been gospel ministers in the primitive Christian church, and the concentration of clerical influence in male hands was another instance of masculine corruption and exploitation. Moreover, when battling against sin, women should attack "moral pollution" of every sort, including those offenses which "false delicacy" led most females to shun and overlook. Custom, along with religious doctrine, led women away from their true rights and duties. Writing from her own experience, Sarah declared that women's education was "miserably deficient; that they are taught to regard marriage as the one thing needful, the only avenue to distinction; hence to attract the notice and win the attention of men, by their charms is the chief business of fashionable girls." [25] Under this debasing influence women became "pretty toys . . . mere instruments of pleasure," dressed and adorned fashionably but empty within. As slavish victims of man's "passion for supremacy," women had no independent right to their own persons or property, and, if married, they had all the duties of servitude but none of the rights which should derive from their God-given equality. When employed in jobs similar to those performed by men, women were universally paid less than—sometimes not even half as much as—their brothers.

Sarah Grimké, like her sister, stood on the firm ground of moral equality: *"Whatsoever it is Morally Right for a Man to Do, It is Morally Right for a Woman to Do."* Woman's role in reform movements would be of critical importance: "the great moral reformations now on the wheel are only practical Christianity; and if the ministry is not prepared to labor with us in these righteous causes, let us press forward, and they will follow on to know the Lord." [26] Yet women must realize their important duties, their true rights:

O, my sisters, suffer me to entreat you to assert your privileges, and to perform your duties as moral beings. Be not dismayed at the ridicule of man; it is a weapon worthy only of little minds, and is employed by those who feel that they cannot convince our judgement. [27]

Sarah Grimkés *Letters* marked a new departure in the development of the woman's rights issue. Taking the offensive against her persecutors, this formerly timid Quaker women condemned man for his debasement of woman's true nature, identifying him as woman's enemy. She faced the issue squarely, attacking the ancient principle of hierarchical government, of clerical, aristocratic, or masculine domination from the liberal ground of equality, with arguments similar to those of other humanitarians. In the end she arrived at a surprisingly militant statement of feminist grievances and aims, the first such statement to be published by an American woman. Gerda Lerner and other writers have noted the landmark role of the Grimkés' writings in the development of American feminist thought. Lerner observes about the sisters' argument:

> Its strongly religious derivation made it particularly adapted to the American scene. Considering that it appeared ten years before the Seneca Falls Convention and seven years before Margaret Fuller's *Woman in the Nineteenth Century,* the outraged reaction with which so many of even the most radical reformers greeted it, is quite understandable. [28]

Although the Grimké sisters' publications concerning woman's rights did not achieve an immense circulation, their *Letters* were apparently read and enjoyed in the sisterhood of abolitionists. In the rural town of West Brookfield, Massachusetts, a young schoolteacher, Lucy Stone, was fascinated by the Grimkés' lecture tour and the controversy it aroused. Commenting on Sarah's *Letters,* Lucy Stone wrote to her brother: "If you could read them and she says nothing but what she proves, I guess that you would not think that I was to [o] obstreperous. I tell you they are first rate, and they only help to confirm the resolutions I had made before, to call no man master." [29] A decade later Stone became one of the pioneers of the woman's movement. To Ohio, six hundred miles to the westward, the example of the Grimké sisters penetrated. Elizabeth Robinson, a young Quaker from Mount Pleasant, was delighted with their triumphs:

> What cause for rejoicing & surely light is being elicited from sources the most unexpected when such advocates of *Humane Rights* as Angelina E. and Sarah M. Grimke are raised up. . . . Angelina's last letters . . . contained so many truths, exposed so many inconsistencies which have been acted and reacted till woman . . . considered *[sic]* as an inferior being not by man alone but even views herself in that light and acts accordingly. [30]

Thus the sisters' efforts clarified the new issue and provided a rallying point for sympathetic people everywhere.

The Grimké influence was strongest in Massachusetts. Although many persons who heard them speak were attracted more by curiosity and had little interest in woman's rights or slavery, a few listened and were moved. Anne Warren Weston, a pillar of the Boston Female Anti-Slavery Society and member of a dedicated antislavery family, supported the new views on the rights and duties of women. Reflecting the arguments of Sarah Grimké, Weston refuted her critics by appealing to scriptural interpretation. How could the advocates of equality carry their point? Perhaps the Grimkés' "heroic and noble career" offered an example to the believers in woman's rights, for the sisters' "eloquence, devotedness, & zeal in the cause of the Slave is equalled only by their piety, delicacy and accurate sense of all that constitutes truly feminine decorum." [31]

The existing network of women's organizations and relationships helped to spread the Grimké sisters' influence. Some of these connections were personal, as when Anne Warren Weston visited a friend in Groton, Massachusetts, just before the sisters spoke there: "I explained away all St. Paul's verses that are 'hard to be understood,' and charged [Sarah Rugg, member of the Groton Female Anti-Slavery Society] *now* to hold on to her ground." Sarah Rugg became a fervent admirer and advocate of the Grimkés:

> Sarahs [sic] writings are doing wonders, some few females here have Emancipated themselves & are beginning to stand erect, to the great astonishment of the aristocratic spectators. When our Sisters were here you know how they were treated, even by abolitionist, they were only allowed to breathe once, this one breath was not lost entirely, some felt the purifying influence. . . . [32]

A wider audience was exposed to the sisters' activities through frequent reports in the *Liberator*. That paper also published responses of organizations such as that of the Providence Ladies Anti-Slavery Society: "We deed the self-denying labors of the Misses GRIMKE worthy of all praise. . . . We totally disapprove of the late 'Clerical Protests,' regarding them as injudicious and unchristian." [33] Altogether the evidence suggests a widespread excitement among women's organizations and individual women as a result of controversies over woman's rights initiated by the Grimkés.

Outside of New England many women took notice of the sisters' lectures. The Philadelphia Female Anti-Slavery Society, of which the Grimkés were "valued members," voted to "encourage them to perseverance in the work. . . ." Some women were perplexed by the difficult issue of free speech. Juliana Tappan, a leading member of the Ladies' New York City Anti-Slavery Society, recorded her uncertainty as to whether the sisters' membership in the Society of Friends justified their addressing *"gentlemen* as well as ladies'':

> If it is forbidden in Scripture, as many contend, it is wrong whether Quakers or not. Is it not very difficult to draw the boundary line? On the one hand, we are in danger of servile submission to the opinions of the other sex, & on the other hand, in perhaps equal danger of losing that modesty, & instinctive delicacy of feeling, which our Creator has given as a safeguard, to protect us. . . . [34]

Miss Tappan's perplexity undoubtedly represented the feelings of many women who could not easily determine whether their pious friends, the Grimkés, had overstepped the bounds of propriety.

Among abolitionists of the "other sex," the sisters' lectures were even more controversial. Orthodox and evangelical clergymen generally disapproved of their speaking to mixed or "promiscuous" audiences. Many evangelical laymen, such as the wealthy Tappan brothers of New York, or the Quaker, John Greenleaf Whittier, feared that the sisters endangered the cause of abolition by mixing in a new issue, woman's rights. Other prominent leaders in the American Anti-Slavery Society, however, supported the sisters' speaking, including Henry B. Stanton, and Elizur Wright, Jr. William Lloyd Garrison encouraged them and opened the *Liberator's* pages for discussions of the issue. In his prospectus of the *Liberator* for 1838, the editor declared:"As our object is *universal* emancipation, to redeem woman as well as man from a servile to an equal condition,—we shall go for the RIGHTS OF WOMAN to their utmost extent." [35] Henry C. Wright gave direct and, for a time, day-to-day support to the Grimkés, urging them to speak in public, encouraging them to take advanced views on the woman's rights issue, and consulting with them as they prepared their publications concerning the rights and duties of women as reformers.

Cold autumn weather, overwork, and illness had driven the sisters from the lecture field in October, 1837. Not until January, 1838, were they able to emerge from retirement to witness a debate sponsored by the Boston Lyceum on the equality of the sexes. Even the opponents of women admitted their intellectual and moral equality, but argued against them on the basis of "delicacy" and physical inferiority. Amasa Walker, a thorough abolitionist and defender of women, asserted that "women had always been found on the side of humanity and religion, foremost in every good work; and the nearer they approximated to an equality of rights with men, the better it would be for society." [36] A *Liberator* correspondent noted the importance of organized reform in bringing about change: "There is nothing like agitation. Free discussion will finally break all fetters, and put down all usurpation " The Lyceum voted against equality of the sexes, but Angelina Grimké's hopes for the woman question were "elevated" by the discussion. Although their regular lectures were finished, the sisters' influence was still alive.

After some three months of rest, Angelina Grimké had a remarkable opportunity to speak before a special committee of the Massachusetts legislature convened to examine the question of antislavery petitions. It was suggested to her, "half in fun and half in earnest," that she might defend abolitionism before the committee, but after interpreting the proposal as a joke, she concluded that she owed it to the cause to speak out. On a February day, unaccompanied by Sarah who was ill, she faced a crowded hall in the State House for nearly two hours. At several points she remembered that both she and her audience were moved to tears by the awful realities of slavery. Two days later Angelina addressed an even larger and predominantly male audience on the expediency, safety, and results of immediate emancipation. To Theodore Weld she wrote,"I was suffered to speak without the least interruption for two hours to the densest and most quiet crowd I ever spoke before. . . . If I am any judge of the effect produced," she estimated, "I think it was good." [37] Following a third speech, some days later, her political speaking was done.

Although her addresses to the legislators dealt primarily with slavery and abolition, Angelina presented a strong defense of women's petitioning and participation in other antislavery efforts, asserting the rights of 17,000 women who had signed petitions to the Massachusetts legislature:

> I hold, Mr. Chairman, that American women have to do with this subject not only because it is moral and religious, but because it is political, inasmuch as we are citizens of this republic, and as such, our honor, happiness, and well being, are bound up in its politics, government, & laws. [38]

Her radicalism on the woman's rights issue was undiminished, and she hoped that her lectures before the legislators would help to bring "manumission of the slave and the elevation of women. . . ." Undoubtedly these proceedings had "an important bearing on the Woman Question," for notices in the press both praised and attacked the Grimkés and their defense of woman's rights. More than forty years later, Lydia Maria Child could recall Angelina Grimké's appearance at the

State House, "her pale countenance and trembling limbs," and the way in which, despite her fears, "her words flowed forth, free, forcible, and well-arranged." [39]

Not long after Angelina's appearance before the legislature, the sisters presented a series of six lectures on slavery under the sponsorship of the Boston Female Anti-Slavery Society. By this time widely known, they attracted immense crowds to the Odeon Hall. According to one listener, "Every part of the building was crowded, every aisle filled. Estimated number 2000 to 3000 at each meeting. There was great attention & silence, & the addresses were intensely interesting." [40] Sarah, who spoke at one meeting, described the occasion with great feeling. Her address on the history of American slavery was critical of the North's attitude and caused several disturbances in the audience. Angelina addressed five large gatherings during March and April, creating great interest. On April 23, 1838, the Grimkés left Massachusetts, having finished their stormy careers as agitators. Never again would they be so influential.

Angelina left Boston to be married. Her correspondence with Theodore Weld had blossomed into romance, and the two abolitionists, having buried their differences over the woman's rights question, were married in Philadelphia in a simple, unconventional ceremony during which both parties resolved to avoid relationships of power or obedience to the other. Most conservative abolitionists were happy about this union, believing it would remove a major obstacle—the Grimké sisters—from the smooth operations of their enterprise. Radicals such as Henry C. Wright were disappointed at the marriage, predicting that it would end the sisters' active roles in reform. Following their marriage, Mr. and Mrs. Weld, along with the spinster Sarah, set up housekeeping and soon began to work on *Slavery As It Is,* an immense compilation of documented testimony against slavery, eyewitness accounts of the institution, chiefly from slave-holders, published in 1839. With strong attachments to both sides in the growing disputes among abolitionists—the New York group and the Garrisonians—Weld and the sisters were deeply disturbed by arguments over woman's rights and other issues. They resolved to take no part in the controversy. Having been such public characters, the sisters felt the necessity of proving their capacity to keep house and perform in their "domestic sphere." Following the birth of Angelina's first child in December, 1839, she suffered from a variety of gynecological ailments and remained in constant discomfort and frequent pain. Although they retained an interest in woman's rights and other reforms, Angelina Weld and Sarah Grimké were no longer able to contribute, except occasionally, to the social reform movement.

The Grimké sisters had, however, made a major contribution in articulating an approach to woman's rights. Several circumstances led to their success in Massachusetts. First there was the environment. The state had been a major center of women's educational and benevolent activities, and many of its women were accustomed to act as sisters in organized groups for a variety of purposes. Massachusetts women were later involved in reform work—moral reform, temperance, peace, and abolitionist movements. Leading individual women—members of the Weston family, Abby Kelley, and others—were among the nation's most vigorous abolitionists. The Grimkés' chief sponsor here, the Boston Female Anti-Slavery Society, already had advanced notions about women's roles in reform, having faced the Boston mob and contributed significantly toward the support of abolition in the area. Finally, Massachusetts was the home of several universal reformers or "ultra-ists," such as William Lloyd Garrison and Henry C. Wright, who supported radical views of woman's rights and free speech. Already possessing a strong feeling of sisterhood, Massachusetts women were ready to listen and be aroused. As Angelina Grimké put it, the environment was "elastic."

The Grimké sisters themselves constituted a second major factor in explaining their success. Wherever they might have gone in the summer of 1837, they would have created controversy, for their attitudes toward the rights and duties of moral beings were already far advanced. As Southern women, converts to abolitionism, they were among the most influential and attractive of all antislavery lecturers. Rebellious and articulate, they would probably have faced opposition from orthodox clergymen almost anywhere in the United States. Having themselves experienced personal emancipation from slavery and repression, the sisters were prepared to be radical, with the zeal of converted souls in pursuing their cause.

Third, the particular evolution of the woman's rights issue in this environment helped to provoke contention between these zealous protagonists and a highly influential body of opposition. On several occasions, as when the "clerical bull" of the Congregational clergy attacked them, or when they debated the slavery issue with young men, or when Angelina spoke before the state legislators, the drama of their situation was intense. Their encounters with influential opponents stimulated the sisters to increase their efforts, even to court martyrdom. Conflict between the Grimkés and orthodox clergymen represented a larger controversy in the Congregational denomination, between Calvinism and two other wings of the church, Unitarianism and Finneyite revivalism. Thus the ministers correctly identified the sisters as disorganizers who threatened the structure of orthodoxy and the power of its clergy. When ministers denied their pulpits to the Grimkés, they were seeking to retain moral authority over their congregations—an effort at which they were clearly failing. This power struggle had its ideological implications also: it was an encounter between a radical egalitarian definition of freedom and a traditional view of society structured as a hierarchy wherein men, women, children, slaves and servants, the rich and the poor, occupied strictly defined positions.

Finally, a fourth factor adding to the significance of women's rights and duties as reformers was the controversy within the antislavery movement over this issue. Paradoxically, a substantial group of people organized to liberate a major class of human beings—slaves—from bondage could not agree whether another major class—women—should participate as equals in the liberation movement. The paradox was not lost on the Grimkés and their supporters. In asserting the right of freedom of speech and the duty of participation by women—rights and duties of moral beings—the sisters, as Sarah put it, had ignited a spark: "We greatly hope . . ." she wrote, "that the spark we have been permitted to kindle on the Woman question will never go out." [41] Her hope was abundantly realized.

7

THE WOMAN QUESTION

THE "woman question," as Sarah Grimké and thousands of abolitionists termed the controversy over woman's rights, became a major issue within the antislavery movement between 1837 and 1840. It was not the only issue dividing the movement, however. Abolitionists faced an economic crisis resulting from the depression of 1837, setbacks in their evangelical campaign against slavery because of bitter religious divisions, and debates over carrying the crusade directly into politics. On one side of the controversy over woman's rights were the organized clergy, chiefly orthodox, and a large body of abolitionists offended by the boldness of the Grimkés and their defenders. On the other side were Garrisonian abolitionists, consisting of a somewhat heterogeneous group of religious liberals, including some Quakers, Unitarians, Universalists, Perfectionists, and others. In keeping with their practices during the Grimké sisters' lecture tour, opponents of woman's rights attempted to exclude women themselves from debates over the issue, as if they had no business being concerned with their social roles. The Garrisonians, in contrast, encouraged women to enroll in the debate, bringing a number of powerful women agitators into prominence.

For about two years the contention over woman's activities in abolitionist organizations remained centered in Massachusetts. In the fall of 1837 there occurred some hint of what was to come as Boston's radical women, encouraged by the Grimké example, asserted themselves. The Boston Female Anti-Slavery Society's annual report, *Right and Wrong in Boston, Number Three,* prepared by Maria Weston Chapman, contained a bitter criticism of the orthodox clergy of Massachusetts. Using basic arguments stressed by the Grimké sisters, Chapman insisted that women, as moral beings, had the duty of entering into their true sphere of action by opposing slavery and speaking freely against it whenever opportunity arose. Chapman's report immediately stirred up ill feelings. Several members of the Female Anti-Slavery Society insisted upon adding a "minority report" as an appendix to *Right and Wrong*. Chapman and her supporters were furious, and, although the Society weathered this first crisis, it represented an open breach between radical and conservative members that was never fully healed.

Fundamentally, the Female Anti-Slavery Society controversy involved two differing conceptions of women's roles in reform. Chapman and the Garrisonians stood for an aggressive, strong, and self-actuated woman's movement in which participants were as free as men to carry on whatever activities their consciences might dictate: "Both sexes are ultimately to stand upon the dead level of humanity, equal in rights, in dominion, in honor, in dignity, in renown." [1] Conservative members of the Society were fearful of overstepping conventional limits of female modesty and propriety, preferring to work quietly and subserviently, guided by men. For members of their sex to presume to criticize the clergy seemed terribly bold and disorderly to these less-radical women. Although the phrase seems not to have appeared in their debate, autonomy for women was the determining question.

The scene of controversy over woman's rights shifted briefly in May, 1838, to Philadelphia, where the second Anti-Slavery Convention of American Women met under auspicious circumstances. The cause seemed at this point to be prospering. Women's antislavery work — fund-raising, petitioning Congress, circulating literature, and arousing interest in the issue — appeared to be on the increase. Moreover, the Convention was to inaugurate a great new auditorium, Pennsylvania Hall, dedicated to "Free Discussion, Virtue, Liberty and Independence," which had been financed by abolitionists and other reformers as a headquarters for the discussion of some great issues which could not be spoken of openly in the churches and other public halls. The mood was enthusiastic and full of hope. "The crisis *has* come when it would be a sin for woman to stay at home and remain silent," wrote one eager participant. [2]

Every prominent woman abolitionist attended this meeting, and many of the most notable leaders spoke out. Angelina Grimké Weld declared: "Each one present has a work to do, be his or her situation what it may, however limited their means or insignificant their supposed influence. The great men of this country will not do this work. . . ." Lucretia Mott lamented that "many of the members considered it improper for women to address promiscuous assemblies. She hoped that such false notions of delicacy and propriety would not long obtain in this enlightened country.'' Maria Weston Chapman and Abby Kelley delivered their first addresses to ''promiscuous'' audiences of women and men. Among the questions discussed were the need for women to dissolve their connections with pro-slavery churches and the importance of petitioning Congress.

The Convention adopted an ''address'' which asserted women's right to engage in antislavery agitation:

> May not the ''ornament of a meek and quiet spirit'' exist with an upright mind and an enlightened intellect? Must woman necessarily be less gentle because her heart is open to the claims of humanity, or less modest because she feels for the degradation of her enslaved sisters, and would stretch forth her hand for their rescue? [3]

The rhetoric was sentimental, echoing the phrases associated with concepts of women's ''sphere,'' but its force was strong with the sense of outraged sisterhood. The scene in and around Pennsylvania Hall was highly dramatic as a howling disorderly mob outside attempted to shout down the women's meetings within. When they adjourned, the mob threatened them with bodily harm and completed its work by setting fire to the building. By morning the once-proud temple of virtue and free discussion was a smoldering ruin. If this outcome suggested what was in store for radical women, it made little impression on many of them. The delegates from Massachusetts returned from Philadelphia buoyed up by their experience and encouraged in the pursuit of their rights.

The issue reappeared at the end of May, 1838, during the fifth annual New England Anti-Slavery Convention, where a storm was almost immediately precipitated by Oliver Johnson, one of Garrison's devoted followers, who resolved that ''all persons present, or who may be present at subsequent meetings, whether men or women, who agree with us in sentiment on the subject of slavery, be invited to become members and participate in the proceedings of this Convention.'' And a number of women's names were added to the membership roll. With Garrisonians in control of the Convention, there was little difficulty in admitting the women, but the orthodox clergy were quite displeased. Eight ministers wished to ''have their names expunged from the roll of the Convention, in consequence of the permission given to women to participate in its proceedings. . . .'' [4]

The Convention added injury to insult by appointing Abby Kelley to a committee which was instructed to prepare a memorial beseeching the clergy of New England "to bear their testimony against the sin of slavery, and to open their mouths in behalf of its crushed and bleeding victims." Debate waxed over this challenge to clerical pretensions, and according to one report, "Miss Kelley rose and defended herself and cause most *manfully,* though with great modesty and dignity, and carried her point by acclamation." [5] The woman question was also argued during debates on petitioning: "Petition is the only mode of access which the women of this country have to Congress, and to shut against them this door is to blot them out of a civil existence." Still unready to submit, the ministers had the last word:

> The undersigned [are] of the opinion that the action of the New England Anti-Slavery Convention . . . inviting women to vote, debate, and aid generally as members of this body . . . is injuring to the cause of the slave, by connecting it with a subject foreign to it. . . . [6]

This was to be the line of argument: the orthodox would insist that by bringing women into the meetings to speak and act with men, the Garrison faction was introducing a new issue, woman's rights, which had no connection with abolition. By raising this unnecessary question, the antislavery movement would alienate a substantial body of faithful brethren who conscientiously opposed the public activity of women. Garrison and his supporters defended women's freedom of speech and pointed out that the Constitution of the American Anti-Slavery Society invited all *persons* who would subscribe to its publications and contribute to its treasury to join its ranks. The Constitution made no distinction between the sexes. Indeed, according to Garrison, it was the clergy, and not dedicated abolitionists, who raised the issue by creating such a disturbance when provisions of the original Constitution were asserted.

The controversy developed quickly and brought expressions of opinion from outside New England. John Greenleaf Whittier wrote in the *Pennsylvania Freeman* that the debate concerning women had "nothing to do with the professed objects of the Convention; and a discussion of the merits of animal magnetism, or of the Mormon Bible, would have been quite as appropriate." Disturbed by criticism from an old friend, the Garrisonians rose to the defense of woman's rights. A correspondent of the *Liberator* argued that the issue involved freedom of speech: "Shall we, when a woman responds aye or no to a proposition which may have come before us, or rises, under a conviction of duty, to express her opinion, or to pour out the feelings of her soul in relation to the unutterable horrors of slavery, APPLY THE GAG?'' [7] Applying the gag to women might be subjecting *them* to a form of slavery. "Aequalitas" put the question directly to Whittier:

Who, in our Anti-Slavery meetings, conventions and periodicals, are guilty of introducing this question? *Those* only who would not suffer a women to obey the dictates of her own conscience. Friend Whittier, art thou ready for the question? Shall women be left at liberty and be treated as *persons*? Yea or nay? [8]

Opponents of women felt persecuted and insisted that their rights of conscience were violated by permitting women to take part in "promiscuous meetings." But the right of conscience was a double-edged weapon, requiring the ministers to deny rights of conscience to women who would speak and to men who wished to hear them. There might even be occasions when ministers themselves sought instruction from experts on slavery such as the Grimké sisters. Those who denied the operation of a basic principle such as human equality also threatened the entire antislavery enterprise, which depended on a belief in God-given equality. Opponents of women attached great significance to the resolution of the New England Anti-Slavery Convention, declaring that it "covers the whole ground of female rights. . . . And the effect of the resolution . . . is to commit the Convention in favor of . . . [woman's rights in general]." [9] Defenders of women responded that they did not mean to settle the problem of woman's situation in society, but to protect women's roles in reform.

In contending over womens rights as reformers, the two sides clearly touched a basic issue not easily separable from the question of slavery itself. If all blacks were human and deserved to have their humanity and their freedom acknowledged, why were all whites not human, women as well as men? The position taken by Garrison and his followers represented a substantial commitment to justice and human freedom. Seeing consistency and unity among all reforms, the radical reformers would not advocate the emancipation of one segment of humanity and deny freedom to another group. The Garrisonians understood the analogy between slaves and women. Aileen Kraditor, in an exposition of Garrison's ideology and practice, has written of his commitment to free discussion: "To Garrison, universal reform was a means to universal freedom, and freedom of discussion was a means to universal reform. Freedom was thus both a means and an end. . . . And obviously freedom of discussion *on all questions* implied freedom of discussion *for all persons. . . .* '' [10]

During the first half of 1839 opponents of woman's rights attempted to gain control of the antislavery movement in Massachusetts. The Garrisonians discerned a ''plot,'' as clergymen attempted to reassert their pastoral rights, regain control of public opinion on moral questions, and reestablish their position of social leadership. The drive for a new antislavery organization had begun in the fall of 1837 and apparently gained strength following the New England Anti-Slavery Convention of 1838, when Garrison had shown his power. Led by Amos A. Phelps and Charles Torrey, both orthodox ministers and seceders from the Convention, the movement soon gained enthusiastic clerical support. Evidently its friends hoped to ''pack'' the annual meeting of the Massachusetts Anti-Slavery Society in 1839 by sending solid male delegations from local societies opposed to the woman's rights heresy. As expected, the annual meeting which convened on January 23, 1839, was a stormy occasion. Maria Chapman wrote: ''It preserved its original heterogeneous character, being composed of old and young, men and women: of every sect, party, condition, and color, all filled with the most absorbing interest.'' [11]

The woman question took a prominent part in the annual meeting's discussions. To the clergy the *Liberator* had been objectionable ''ever since it began the inculcation of its views on Women's rights. . . .'' [12] The Garrisonians were anxious to proclaim their own righteousness, insisting that the woman question had been settled by organizations such as the Eastern Pennsylvania Anti-Slavery Society, which admitted women to its proceedings without objection. The Reverend Samuel J. May, a Unitarian, paid tribute to women's writing for the cause, their toil, their financial support, their fearlessness in encountering persecution. The woman question was not simply a firebrand thrown by Garrison into the antislavery struggle. It had arisen inevitably because of the Grimké sisters who ''were, through the good providence of God, led to embrace the anti-slavery cause.'' May introduced a historical precedent into the debate: ''Be it known to you, that the Convention at Philadelphia, in 1833, which formed the American Anti-Slavery Society, settled this question, for themselves at least, without hesitation. And three women addressed that body, greatly to its edification.'' [13]

Although they retained control of the Massachusetts Anti-Slavery

Society through this disorderly meeting, the Garrisonians were on the defensive. Professor William Smyth of Bowdoin College would not under any circumstances sanction woman's equality by continuing his membership in a Garrison-dominated organization. A New Hampshire gentleman wrote, "I think the principles contended for in this matter, if carried out, would strike a death-blow at the purest and loveliest social condition of man, & ruin the broadest & wisest foundations of human virtue & happiness." [14] Thus the double standard was asserted to prevent woman's equality in humanitarian activities. Woman's domestic status was sacred, universal, unchanging, and women who departed so widely from tradition as to speak in public were immoral or worse. The conservatives certainly had no interest in hearing from women themselves concerning this issue.

After failing to control the Massachusetts Anti-Slavery Society, the anti-Garrisonians set out to take over local societies throughout Massachusetts. The Reverend Alanson St. Clair lectured in Bristol and Barnstable Counties, urging local antislavery groups to reject membership in the Massachusetts state society and become auxiliaries of the American Anti-Slavery Society. The Reverend Orange Scott, a prominent Methodist, urged, "There *must be* a new organization in this State, and I believe we are about ripe for it. I think I can pledge *nine tenths* of the Methodist influence in the State for a new State society." [15] One of the cardinal principles of the new society would be a strict avoidance of the woman question, or "petticoat government" as one gentleman termed it. In February, 1839, the *Massachusetts Abolitionist* began publication as a rival of the *Liberator* opposed to woman's rights.

The woman question emerged into the forefront of controversy during the month of May, 1839, when two important meetings of abolitionists concentrated their discussions on the rights of women to participate equally with men in the antislavery struggle. At the annual meeting of the American Anti-Slavery Society in New York, the Garrisonians collided openly with the executive committee of the national organization. Several Massachusetts societies sent women delegates, including Abby Kelley, who represented Millbury. The question "which excited the most discussion, assumed the gravest aspect, and caused the most division . . . ." concerned the admission of women as delegates to the national meeting. Again the two sides argued over whether to admit only men or to allow all persons to take part. Virtually all the New England ministers opposed women's participation, as did such prominent abolitionists as James G. Birney and Lewis

Tappan. Other leading antislavery men favored enrolling women as full members, including several who were not Garrison's followers. After one and a half days of argument, a vote was taken admitting women.

The issue was not fully settled by the vote. The Reverend Amos A. Phelps resolved, "that in adopting the resolution admitting women to sit as delegates, that it was not thereby intended by the Society that they should speak, act on committees, fill offices, etc." In reply, Gerrit Smith of New York State defended the right of any societies to choose persons, men or women, as their delegates, without interference by the national body:

> There may be a collision betwixt the Parent Society and its auxiliaries. If some prefer to send up here, as their delegates, your Chapmans, your Kellys [sic], and your Barneys, have we the right to object? If a woman can do my work best, I wish to be at liberty to select a woman. [16]

Eliza Barney, a Quaker woman from Nantucket, and Abby Kelley also discussed the issue "very briefly, with excellent propriety, and to great acceptance." Barney was appointed to a committee on correspondence and Kelley joined the committee on publications. A protest signed by 122 persons against women's participation was read in the meeting and printed in the report of its proceedings.

Opponents of women feared that tying the new issue to abolition would offend many current and potential supporters of the antislavery cause. Women's participation would bring "*unnecessary* reproach and embarrassment to the cause of the enslaved . . ." by enlisting "the influence of the Anti-Slavery Society in favor of the dogma of *women's entire equality with men as to rights.* . . ." Anti-women delegates accused those who sympathized with women of being sectarian! Virtually all religious periodicals opposed debate on the issue, although they contributed vigorously to such debate. The New York *Evangelist* commented on the American Anti-Slavery Society's vote: "It is scarcely necessary to say, that if the Society must wear an aspect as utterly offensive to all men of sound judgement, and *adhere* to a principle so dishonorable to the dignity, character and influence of women, it cannot be expected that judicious men will give it their sanction." [17]

"Judicious men" received another shock a few weeks later. At the anniversary of the New England Anti-Slavery Society, many of the same men met to discuss participation of women in the antislavery movement. The proposal of Amos A. Phelps that gentlemen alone be invited to enroll was heartily rejected by the Garrison-controlled meeting, and two prominent women, Lydia Maria Child and Maria Weston Chapman, were appointed to the business committee. As before, the orthodox ministers were outraged and protested against this violation of biblical authority, to no avail. Garrison defended his course of action, saying that the opponents of women, not their defenders, were the chief agitators of the woman question. Amidst cries of "sectarianism" from both sides, the New England Anti-Slavery Society split wide open.

The long drive for a new antislavery organization in Massachusetts ended with the formal establishment of the Massachusetts Abolition Society on May 29, by seceders from the New England Society. Although it was the most immediate complaint of the clergymen and orthodox laymen, the woman question was one of several issues—Garrisonian "heresies"—which had upset the new organization's leaders. In order to avoid its possible domination by radicals, the Abolition Society defined its membership and provided a representative system in its business meetings, thus preventing "the believers in the doctrine of 'Woman's Rights' as it is termed, from embarrassing the society with that question." [18] Outside New England the new organization received a mixed response. The executive committee of the American Anti-Slavery Society approved its admission as an auxiliary as soon as it applied. Other abolitionists found fault with both sides and regretted the formation of a new society. Gerrit Smith wrote to Amos A. Phelps: ". . . it seems to me that you & your friends make a needless ado about 'Womans rights.'" [19] Further away, west of the Hudson River, the "eastern controversy" was scarcely known, except by the most prominent abolitionists.

From its beginnings in the summer and fall of 1837, the issue of woman's rights had infected the Boston Female Anti-Slavery Society. The controversy was suppressed until a quarterly meeting of the Society in January, 1839, when the effort to shift its loyalty away from Garrison began in earnest. Opponents of the editor talked at length against the *Liberator* and opposed maintaining subscriptions, but a large majority of the membership voted in favor of the paper. Later in the year it appeared that the anti-Garrisonians were gaining control and would change the Society's allegiance. The struggle for control reached a climax during the regular quarterly meeting early in April. The meeting was crowded with new members, many of whom, so the Garrisonians believed, had been rounded up from orthodox churches in order to "pack" the organization. Maria Weston Chapman led the radical forces, speaking

again and again—she "roared like a *female bull!*"—exclaimed one of
her critics. But the roaring did little good as the Society voted to
contribute its funds to the American Anti-Slavery Society instead of the
Massachusetts State Society.

Undaunted, the supporters of Garrison, led by Maria Weston
Chapman, set out to organize the largest Massachusetts antislavery fair
yet. Thus in 1839 there were two antislavery fairs in Boston, one
conducted by the "regular" or orthodox members of the Female Society,
the other by Chapman and the Garrisonians, called the "fair of
individuals." Chapman and her cohorts were far more capable than the
timid orthodox ladies, and conducted the most successful event of its kind
down to that time, raising $1500 for the Massachusetts Anti-Slavery
Society. Never before had the women of this region produced such a
selection of useful and beautiful articles.

Meetings of the Boston Female Anti-Slavery Society continued to
be bothered by factional controversy. At the annual meeting in 1839, the
chief point of dispute was the selection of officers—whether to continue
with orthodox leadership which sympathized with the anti-woman's
rights forces in Massachusetts. An election confirmed the Society's
adherence to orthodoxy and moderation, but Garrisonian members
claimed the election had been rigged and denied its validity.
"Communications," "contradictions," "corrections," and "certifi-
cates" followed upon one another in the *Liberator* and the entire story
was later gathered together for a special "extra" edition of the paper.
Debates in the Female Society did not touch directly on the woman
question, but the issue of woman's roles underlay the larger dispute.
Chapman and the Garrisonians bitterly opposed the dependent outlook of
orthodoxy.

Maria Weston Chapman unleashed a new tempest of charges and
counter-charges with her publication of *Right and Wrong in
Massachusetts* in the summer of 1839. Telling the "true story" of anti-
Garrisonian plotting since 1837, the new *Right and Wrong* contained a
detailed exposé of the treachery committed by orthodox clergymen in
their efforts to undermine Garrison. The plot against sound abolitionism
arose from the attitudes of narrow-minded, self-interested reformers who
would exclude women from their societies: "In the horror of their great
darkness on the subject of '*woman's* rights,' they trampled on *human*
rights, and the rights of *membership,* in the persons of those women
whom they would exclude." [20] The basic "foundation principle of
inalienable *human* rights" admitted of no exceptions grounded upon

orthodox religious prejudices, and in excluding women from full participation in antislavery societies, the ministers sinned against freedom.

Chapman, like her mentor Garrison, was no mean or trivial antagonist. In deploring woman's entry into agitation, the clergy probably had her specifically in mind. Although they intended at first to ignore her accusations, the clerical abolitionists finally replied. Amos A. Phelps called *Right and Wrong: "a tissue of misstatements, or misrepresentations and perversions of facts; and of falsehood,"* and threatened to reply to it, exposing the "real plotters." A heated exchange of accusations and counter-accusations took place between the Reverend Charles Torrey and Chapman. Many friends were mightily pleased by this history of antislavery troubles. One woman wrote: "I think it will do much good. . . . I think every one who reads it prayerfully and candidly will see the inconsistency of the disorganizers of the true friends of the slave." [21] Chapman was plainly out of her "sphere" with the publication of *Right and Wrong,* and she brought a sympathetic reaction and a thrill of excitement from other women who rejected the domineering attitudes of orthodoxy. She helped to inspire and free the minds of some New England women.

During 1839 the woman question entered into still another realm of public discourse in Massachusetts. Early in the year some women of Lynn, Dorchester, and other communities presented petitions to the Massachusetts House of Representatives, praying for the repeal of all state laws which discriminated in any way against black persons, particularly against the ban on intermarriage between people of different races. At first the petitions, signed by more than 1400 women, met with scorn and ridicule. In March the Committee on the Judiciary presented a report on the petitions which was heavy with sarcasm and mock seriousness:

> No light cause should draw the matrons and maidens of Massachusetts from the retirement of the homes they bless with their virtues and adorn by their graces. Their appropriate sphere has heretofore been in the domestic circle where there is still space ample enough for the exercise of the gentle charities which make life happy.

Yet a particularly "pressing social or moral evil" might require "the necessity for the interposition of their powerful influence to resist oppression."

The Committee believed that many petitioners were ignorant of the moral implications of their requests for legalized racial intermarriage. Admittedly some were serious in their claims:

> It was represented, on the presentation of their petition . . . that they were accomplished politicians in petticoats, deeply skilled in jurisprudence, and desirous of vindicating alike the rights of men and women. Infinitely more was claimed for them, than they could possibly have desired to assert for themselves.

Thus the politicians could dismiss women's petitions by treating them with sarcasm. This coarse attack on their integrity infuriated the Garrisonians, who held a mass meeting to denounce reports of the legislative committees. Garrison attacked the law banning marriage between the races as a "bold, deliberate, and profligate abolition of the marriage institution," and declared that the citizens of the state were "virtually guilty of shameful immorality and brutal oppression." [22] Decency and the womanhood of Massachusetts had been slandered and outraged.

In April the state House of Representatives heard a lengthy and spirited debate on the issue of women's petitions. George Bradburn, an antislavery member of the House from Nantucket, attacked the report on petitions against the intermarriage law. He dealt with the issue of woman's rights, asking specifically whether the legislature was qualified to discuss woman's "appropriate sphere," her virtue, or her modesty. Lydia Maria Child joined the contest, sending a personal petition to the House, which denounced the ban on intermarriage as "an unjustifiable interference with domestic institutions. . . . " She felt insulted by the way women's petitions had been treated by the Legislature:

> Lastly, your petitioner, as a free-born woman, sharing moral and intellectual advantages with all the sons and daughters of this intelligent Commonwealth, begs leave . . . to protest against the contemptuous treatment offered to her sisters in Lynn. To sustain this protest she appeals to no law of "chivalry. ..|she prefers a plain appeal to the respect due from the representatives of a free and enlightened people to the decorous expression of any conscientious views and opinions from any member of the community. [23]

When women had business with the government they were persons — citizens, not slaves.

Arguments over the virtue of women petitioners illuminate one of the complexities which advocates of women faced at this time. In being concerned publicly with questions of marriage, racial mixture, and sex, they were on dangerous ground, for although everyone knew something about sexual relations, women, being "delicate," were not supposed to admit any such knowledge. Hence petitions from hundreds of women relating to the choice of marital partners or the legitimacy of offspring were doubtful at the least. Just as speaking out in "promiscuous" meetings of men and women suggested immorality if the speaker were a woman, so petitioning on a forbidden subject raised serious doubts concerning the virtue of the petitioners. Thus the attitude of the Massachusetts legislature, its scorn toward the women who signed petitions against the law banning racial intermarriage, had considerable significance to women abolitionists. It magnified the importance of the right to petition in behalf of their injured and debased sisters. Their campaign was not immediately successful, but the effort to repeal the ban on intermarriage finally achieved its objective in 1843.

In 1839 the third and last women's antislavery convention met at Philadelphia, this time under protest from the mayor who was concerned about the probability of violence. Because they had been refused any meeting place, women abolitionists had to gather in an abandoned and roofless riding school, but their high spirits were not diminished by the handicap. After 1840 the most militant women were accepted as equals in the American Anti-Slavery Society, eliminating the need for separate women's conventions. Lydia Maria Child, who generally opposed the women's conventions, felt they had helped women: "For the freedom of women, they have probably done something; but in every other point of view, I think their influence has been very slight." [24] Philadelphia's antislavery women also emphasized the role of these meetings in raising their consciousness:

> By the concentration of our efforts in this way, we not only advance the cause of . . . the slave, but . . . the fettered mind of woman, is fast releasing itself from the thralldom in which long existing custom has bound it and by the exercise of her talents in the cause of the oppressed — her intelligence as well as moral being is rising into new life....[25]

Most women who attended them agreed that these conventions of women combined exhilaration and liberation, with a strong sense of sisterhood, and an awareness of braving the prejudice of the world outside.

The year 1839 also witnessed the emergence of a new and powerful personality in the female antislavery network: Abby Kelley began her career as a public lecturer. Already an active, tenacious opponent of slavery, Kelley had been so impressed with the Grimké sisters' influential lecture tour that in 1838 she resolved to follow their example. After months of study and reflection, she began lecturing on slavery in Connecticut — a state relatively untouched by antislavery agitation, and inhospitable to a woman lecturer. Kelley endured intense persecution which seemed only to harden her resolution "to arouse her sisters to action in the cause of the down-trodden slave." In the town of Norfolk she was shunned, evaded, and not allowed to speak. Attempting to stay at the hotel, she was told: "They believe you to be a bad woman; the vilest woman of New York could I presume be received as soon as you" [26] Other experiences were less disturbing.

What was the impact of Kelley's lectures in Connecticut? She herself was not too hopeful of their results. After holding 65 meetings during a two-month period, she had made little headway against the apathy and prejudice which prevailed. Little true antislavery enthusiasm could be evoked, although she had obtained the opportunity to speak in most communities. Discussing the opposition to public speaking by women, she wrote:

> Of course, there is at first, a strong prejudice against women's talking in company, if the company shall happen to be called a *meeting,* but it soon vanishes. . . . In the several county meetings, and one state meeting that I attended, women participated. In some of these, the aid of woman's voice was officially solicited. [27]

Thus Abby Kelley began a lecturing career of more than twenty years, unmatched by any other woman in the antislavery movement. She served as a living, practicing demonstration of woman's rights.

In 1840 the woman question was transformed from a local and regional issue into a dispute which affected the national antislavery movement. The same pattern of disputes which had split the Massachusetts Anti-Slavery Society in 1839 now threatened to divide the American Anti-Slavery Society. In March, 1840, Lydia Maria Child wrote for the *Liberator* a blistering attack on Lewis Tappan and James G. Birney, accusing them of previously condoning public speaking by women in "promiscuous" assemblies. Now, having acquired religious scruples, Tappan wished "to have a New Society formed, unless the American Society rescinds its vote to allow women a participation in its meetings." [28] Tappan denied Child's accusations, but he could not assent to public speaking and unlimited participation by women in the antislavery enterprise.

Prospects for the annual meeting of the American Society in 1840 seemed more perilous than the previous year's meeting, when the woman question had been so divisive. To counteract the power of the Society's executive committee, Henry C. Wright urged the Garrisonians to "induce as many as possible to come on from Mass. R.I. & Conn. who will stand by the *true & right* — women as well as men." [29] Garrison's opponents were also planning and plotting to capture the national organization. Garrison's scheme to control the American Society was familiar — he planned to "pack" the New York meeting with delegates of radical stamp who would vote as a group. To encourage an ample attendance of their partisans, the Garrisonians chartered a steamship to carry the delegates from Providence to New York City, thus reducing the fare and expenses of the trip. Some 450 persons, including about 100 women, took advantage of the special accommodations. This floating "mass of *ultraism*" constituted the "moral and religious *elite* of New England abolitionism," Garrison declared. He later admitted that "It was our anti-slavery boat-load that saved our Society from falling into the hands of the new-organizers." The New Yorkers also engaged in "packing" the meeting, but unlike New England's moral elite, they operated "by the most dishonorable means." [30]

With both sides packing the annual meeting, the American Anti-Slavery Society attracted more than 1000 delegates. Francis Jackson, a prominent Garrisonian, served as chairman, and shortly appointed a business committee which included Lydia Maria Child. Lewis Tappan objected:

> When the time came (as I was on this Com) I arose, moved, as Mrs. Child was not present that her better half (who was present) should be substituted, but the society put on Abby Kelley. . . . Soon I asked to be excused from serving upon this com. & begged leave to [state] my reasons — 1. Putting women on business com. is unconstitutional — 2. Was throwing a firebrand into the ranks — 3. Was contrary to the usages of the civilized world. — 4. Tends to destroy efficient female anti-slavery action. It produced a spirited debate. [31]

Thus the annual meeting split apart over the question of admitting women to full and complete participation as equals with men in doing the business of the antislavery movement.

The "spirited debate" which followed Abby Kelley's nomination was by now predictable in its outcome. Nowhere in the East had orthodox people been able to tolerate women's acting in concert with men. Lewis Tappan called for the formation of a new antislavery society, and some 300 persons, including virtually the entire executive committee, departed from the American Anti-Slavery Society, leaving the Garrisonians and the women in thorough control. There is no doubt that the large Massachusetts delegation and its women's votes contributed to Garrison's triumph. Of the 449 Massachusetts delegates — nearly half of the total number attending the annual meeting — 97 were women. Thus Garrison's margin of victory of just over a hundred votes was largely provided by his female adherents. Three prominent antislavery women — Lucretia Mott, Lydia Maria Child, and Maria Weston Chapman — broke all precedents and accepted appointments to the new executive committee of the American Anti-Slavery Society, now thoroughly committed to supporting woman's rights as reformers.

The new divisions within the antislavery movement set off another round of accusations in the religious press. Much of the debate centered around women's roles in reform. The Boston *Christian Witness* pointed out that about 150 "females" had voted with Garrison, having been brought to New York for that purpose:

> So, it may truly be said that Mr. Garrison succeeded in his design of obtaining the endorsement of the American Society for his "Woman's Rights" crusade, first, by the votes of the Massachusetts delegation — and second, *by the votes of a company of women, trained and disciplined for the accomplishment of this very object.*

The *Witness* attacked the radical *"onslaught upon the institutions of Society, the proprieties of civilized life, and the inflexible morality of the Decalogue,"* and declared that few women would follow the radicals "in unsexing themselves and mingling in boisterous debate with men in churches and public halls." [32]   The Reverend E.R. Tyler in the *Connecticut Observer* asserted that Garrison and his followers aimed to *"destroy the Churches of Christ, and set every minister of the Gospel adrift."* Tyler explained the radical success: *"Massachusetts abounds with a population, which is ready at any time, to sustain anything which is opposed to orthodox Christianity, and which rails against the clergy."* [33]   Thus the church was endangered by a handful of obstreperous women.

Relatively untroubled by religious barriers, the defenders of women could argue on the basis of a principle that showed up the inconsistency of orthodox reformers:

> What else than a *pro-slavery* spirit, is that which refuses to labor in behalf of the oppressed by the side of any human being, merely on account of her sex? Wherein does such a spirit differ from that which dooms millions of the human race to chains and slavery on account of their complexion? Abolitionism *in its purity* can no more live in a soul which fosters this spirit, than in the heart of the slaveholder himself. [34]

Human rights, as the Grimké sisters had argued in 1837, were indivisible. This flaw of many religious abolitionists — their unwillingness to accept the full implications of antislavery ideology — probably contributed to the alienation of several active and prominent workers in the cause, moderates like Theodore Weld, Henry B. Stanton, and Elizur Wright Jr., who believed in and applied the principles of equality to blacks and to women.

Following the division, Garrison's American Anti-Slavery Society carried on its business with relative tranquility, passing resolutions against the "American Church" as a pro-slavery instrument. The minority, having seceded, formed a new organization, the American and Foreign Anti-Slavery Society, "controlled, financed, and directed largely by Lewis Tappan." It was the sort of businesslike, disciplined, and highly evangelical society of which Tappan, the merchant, had long dreamed. By avoiding strong criticism of the churches, cultivating orthodox ministers, remaining neutral in politics, and above all, steering clear of that awful threat to Christian civilization, the woman question, the new society solved many of the difficulties of pious abolitionists. But the mild appeals and "moral suasion" of the new society made little impression on the great mass of public opinion.

The collapse of the old American Anti-Slavery Society had little impact on abolitionism as a whole, which had already moved in new directions. In Ohio, where a strong antislavery movement flourished, the woman question stirred up little interest:

> We have never made a question of it at our annual meetings, for the plain reason, that women's rights have never been denied. They have always been taken for granted, as on a level with those of men, and the manner and extent of their exercise have been left to the woman's own notions of propriety. [35]

Some Ohioans admired the *Liberator* for its independence and outspoken position on woman's rights. Susan Wattles, a former Oberlin abolitionist, wrote to Garrison: "Women must know what their rights are. . . . I rejoice that there is one paper which dares advocate such an unpopular doctrine. . . ." [36] Ohio had not been "Garrisonized" — this would come later in the decade — but pockets of radical sympathy already existed here and in New York State.

Between the introduction of debates over woman's rights by the Grimké sisters in 1837 and the breakup of the American Anti-Slavery Society in 1840, arguments concerning the woman question had gone on at great length. Although they tended to be repetitious, adding little to the ideology laid down by the Grimkés, these arguments had kept the woman's rights issue alive. By their very repetition, they established the woman question as a legitimate social problem. Aside from achieving a prominent place in debates over the conduct of reform movements or religious doctrine, however, the controversy had little impact on the general public. The decade of the 1840s would spread the issues of woman's rights and responsibilities away from the East and aid in the formation of a distinct woman's movement.

8

A DECADE OF AGITATION

THE decade of the 1840s is often overlooked by students of American feminism. Between the time when woman's rights were articulated and explored by the Grimké sisters and others during the late 1830s and the Seneca Falls Convention of 1848, the issue appeared to lie dormant. One writer has called this era "The Fallow Decade": "The forties had to lie fallow till the young rebels then springing up here and there had matured sufficiently to make an impression on their century." [1] Neither Elizabeth Cady Stanton nor Susan B. Anthony promoted woman's rights before 1848, hence the decade is virtually ignored in the movement's official *History of Woman Suffrage.* Nevertheless, the 1840s were rich in accomplishments. Rather than calling it the fallow decade, observers might well call it a decade of agitation.

One event of the period is seldom forgotten. The World's Anti-Slavery Convention at London in 1840 was the scene of another fierce debate over the woman question. The World's Convention had been suggested by Americans as a means of encouraging unity and dramatizing the international crusade against slavery. The idea appealed to British antislavery leaders, but a lengthy dispute then occurred over who would be acceptable as delegates. Naturally, American radicals interpreted a call to "the friends of the slave in every nation and of every clime," in their own way, as an appeal to "the EQUAL BROTHER-HOOD of the entire HUMAN FAMILY, without distinction of color, sex, or clime." [2] The Massachusetts Anti-Slavery Society appointed several women delegates, as did other organizations. Learning of the appointment of women, the British hosts revised their invitations to read "gentlemen only." Lewis Tappan was pleased by restrictions against women and so was Sarah Grimké: "We were not aware of any intentions to send women, but we have greatly regretted it since we heard

113

of it & hope the Lord will preserve them from presenting themselves there in the character of delegates." [3]

From Philadelphia went Lucretia Mott and four others, while New England sent three women delegates. It was evident upon their arrival that the women would not be seated in the Convention, but they and a handful of advocates were prepared to protest their rejection. Reaching England some two weeks before the Convention's opening, Lucretia Mott was immediately thrown into the agitation over seating women. Not impressed by appeals from British leaders to accept a decision against them, Mott and other Americans attempted to show "the inconsistency of excluding Women Delegates" all to no avail—"our appeals made in vain." For the next week Mott discussed the question of admitting women to the Convention at every opportunity. A black male delegate from Jamaica "thought it would lower the dignity of the Convention and bring ridicule on the whole thing if ladies were admitted—he was told that similar reasons were urged in Pennsylvania for the exclusion of colored people from our meetings." [4] The comparison inevitably arose: were black men superior to white women? Should common usage be ignored in admitting blacks to meetings of men only, while women were excluded?

On June 12 about five hundred delegates were present for the opening of the World Anti-Slavery Convention. Following a brief address from Thomas Clarkson, eighty-one years old and one of the grand old men of British abolitionism, some procedural business was disposed of. Then Wendell Phillips of Massachusetts arose to urge that the Convention itself determine credentials of its delegates and ask that the roll "include the names of all persons bearing credentials from any anti-slavery society." He wished to determine the status of the women who had been sent as delegates from American organizations which admitted women to membership on an equal basis with men. Were the societies themselves to determine their representatives, or would this be decided by a British committee?

A spirited discussion followed Phillips's motion. The radicals charged their British hosts with inconsistency in rejecting women delegates at a meeting dedicated to the principle of human equality. A number of Americans joined with the majority of the British, insisting that most true friends of the slave in the United States did not admit women to equal participation in their organizations. After a day was consumed in discussing the merits of women delegates, the members voted "That this convention, upon a question arising as to the admission of females appointed as delegates from America to take their seats in this body, resolve to decide this question in the negative." [5] Relieved at having disposed of the woman question, the Convention went on to its business, discussing the slave trade, West Indian emancipation, American slavery, the duty of withholding Christian fellowship from slaveholders, color prejudice, and the use of free produce.

Suddenly, in the midst of its proceedings, the Convention was interrupted by a new attack on its policy toward women. On June 17, William Lloyd Garrison reached London with his party consisting of the black abolitionist and orator, Charles L. Remond, and two other New England men. Because of the Convention's rejection of women, Garrison and his companions refused to take part in its proceedings but took seats in the gallery near the women to observe the action. That he aroused much curiosity is evident from an account written by one of his party: "The first day we sat *alone* in the gallery; but, on the second day, the people, wishing to see how we looked, came and went the whole day." Lady Byron visited the four delegates, taking a special interest in the black man, Remond. Several British abolitionists were impressed by the Garrisonians' demonstration. William Ashurst, a wealthy and enthusiastic reformer, supported the radical stand, believing that "to keep truth before the minds eye, is the sure way ultimately to establish it to the understanding." Dr. John Bowring, a member of Parliament and delegate to the World Convention, found the woman question of "singular interest." The rejected women "made a *deep* if not a wide impression, and have created apostles if as yet they have not multitudes of followers." [6]

While Garrison watched the proceedings from his distant seat, several radical spokesmen in the Convention offered a protest against women's exclusion. It was attacked vigorously and quickly laid on the table, and a proposal to include it with the official minutes was quashed as the radicals cried "gag." The Convention took no further action on the issue. Certainly the divisions within the American antislavery movement had played a part in the British committee's action. Having been warned by conservatives in the United States about the disruption resulting from woman's rights, British leaders resolved to exclude women. Sectarianism within the Society of Friends also affected the situation. As a member of the Hicksite Friends of America, Lucretia Mott, the leading woman delegate, was shunned by Britain's Orthodox Friends.

After their rejection as delegates the American women, led by Lucretia Mott, negotiated to meet with their British sisters, but they could not agree on plans and had to be content with informal gatherings. Despite their rejection by the Convention, the Americans found that they had given British women an unusual opportunity to observe the proceedings:

> We were willing to be mere lookers on & listeners from without, as, by so doing we should be the means of many more women having an invitation to sit as spectators—which we found was accounted a very high privilege, in this land by their women, who had hitherto, most submissively gone forth into all the streets, lanes, highways & bye paths to get signers to petitions, & had been lauded long & loud, for this drudgery, but who had not been *permitted* even to *sit* with their brethren, nor indeed much by themselves in public meetings.[7]

Mott and other advocates of woman's rights were active outside the Convention. Their notoriety made them interesting figures in Britain at this time and they traveled widely, meeting many of the kingdom's most important reformers. Mott's travels through the country had an effect somewhat akin to that of the Grimké's in the United States, of sparking interest in a new issue—woman's rights. At Muswell Hill, the home of William Ashurst, she discussed Sarah Grimké's essay, *Letters on the Equality of the Sexes*. She met Elizabeth Fry, the prison reformer, and she had repeated conversations with Anne Knight, a vigorous abolitionist who later became one of the first leaders of the British woman suffrage campaign. With Lady Byron she had "much conversation on housekeeping—neglect of families—woman's sphere etc.—very pleasant visit." After a visit to Harriet Martineau and a busy week of sightseeing in London, taking "leave of our loved friends, with full hearts," Lucretia and James Mott embarked from Liverpool for New York aboard the ship *Patrick Henry*.[8]

American advocacy of woman's rights evidently left a residue of interest in Great Britain. The great Irish patriot Daniel O'Connell, after initially denying the argument in women's favor, came to agree that the London Convention should not have deprived legally chosen women delegates of their places:

> Mind has no sex; and . . . it is the basis of the present Convention, to seek success by peaceable, moral and intellectual means alone. . . . Our warfare is not military. . . . We rely entirely on reason and persuasion common to both sexes, and on the emotions of benevolence and charity, which are more lovely and permanent amongst women, than amongst men. [9]

Other prominent British men, like William Howitt, a liberal member of the Society of Friends, and Thomas Clarkson, an antislavery pioneer, sympathized with American women.

The new idea took root, too, among British women. Anne Knight lauded the "new & grand principle launched in our little island & shipwrecked as it were in its birth," and believed that men could not much longer "deny the equality of talent as well as worth of their wives sisters daughters." Women were "not the same beings as fifty years ago," content to "sit by the fire and spin"; they were called upon to engage in important benevolent and reform movements, to grapple with "the dreadful monster *slavery*," and they could not wait for men to lead the way, for "the men are gone to sleep." [10] Elizabeth Pease, a Friend and dedicated abolitionist, was strengthened in her adherence to the radical view of woman's rights by the visits of Garrison and the Motts. New interest was aroused in the pioneering work of the Grimké sisters in asserting woman's rights. Out of this experience would come for women in Britain a new consciousness of their independent power, their capacities to act, and their need for an enlarged sphere of action.

The London Convention was a great experience for other American women delegates. The four women who accompanied Lucretia Mott from Philadelphia were naturally offended, but not discouraged, by their failure to be seated in London. Mary Grew, a leader in the Philadelphia Female Anti-Slavery Society, and later a woman suffragist, drafted a report to her organization that was enthusiastic about the "adherence to the right" of America's radical abolitionists:

> In their eyes, the anti-slavery platform was large enough to admit the lovers of truth & freedom of every nation, or sect, or sex, or color; and it was not because they were faithless to their principles in the hour of conflict, or lukewarm in their defense, that the genius of liberty was on *any* occasion dishonored there. Their positions were logically & eloquently sustained, and they deserve the gratitude of the friends of universal freedom. . . . [11]

Sarah Pugh, another leading member of the Philadelphia Female Society, believed that women had achieved important results by appearing at the World Anti-Slavery Convention: "The poor rejected delegates have been anything but the despised. The women there . . . thanked us most heartily for coming; they would not have been admitted even as visitors had we not come. . . ." [12] The rejected American women returned across the Atlantic with their heads held high.

The London Convention of 1840 has a special place in the history of the woman's movement. Many years later Elizabeth Cady Stanton wrote:

"The movement for women's suffrage, both in England and America, may be dated from this World's Anti-Slavery Convention." [13] In 1840, as the bride of an American delegate, Henry B. Stanton, Mrs. Stanton sat in the audience "behind the bar" at the World Convention with other American women. Staying at the same lodgings with the Motts, Garrison, and other pro-woman's rights people, the young bride was exposed to a strong dose of radical sentiment. Elizabeth Stanton was fascinated by her new friend:

> I have had much conversation with Lucretia Mott and think her a peerless woman. She has a clear head and a warm heart. Her views are so many of them so new and strange that my [?] finds great delight in her society. The Quakers here have not all received her cordially; they fear her heretical notions.

Mott argued "that all the friends of freedom for woman must rally round the *Garrison standard*." Years later Stanton recalled: "I shall never forget the look of recognition she gave me when she saw by my remarks that I fully comprehended the problems of woman's rights. . . . Mrs. Mott was to me an entire new revelation of womanhood." [14]

The two friends were busy traveling until just before the Motts' return to America. For a week they were often together in London. Mott recorded one active day:

> Visited Infant School with E. C. Stanton—not equal to our expectation & hopes—felt much for the poor little children...E. Stanton would like to remove them in Omnibuses to Hyde Park to romp & play—talk with her on increase of poor &c—from there to British Museum...found ourselves among the curiosities....[15]

They had abundant opportunity to discuss the questions of social reform which absorbed their interests. Stanton later asserted that plans for the first woman's rights convention were launched in London, although Mott's recollection was slightly different. Another encounter between these two women led to the meeting at Seneca Falls to discuss the rights of woman and the need for a suffrage movement.

Returning to the United States, the advocates of women witnessed a curious spectacle: the participation of women in a presidential election campaign. The contest of 1840, pitting "Tippecanoe and Tyler Too" against Martin Van Buren, was the most massive popular election campaign before 1860, engaging not only American men but thousands of women as well. Some of the young women from Oberlin College rode in a campaign procession in a "cart drawn by 35 yoke oxen, containing about 100 women." At Dayton, Ohio, an estimated 10,000 women waved white handkerchiefs as their hero, William Henry Harrison, rode by. In Richmond, Virginia, the great Daniel Webster spoke to an audience of women in Harrison's behalf, complimenting their accomplishments and influence as mothers. The irony of women's political exertions was not lost on the advocates of woman's rights. Describing a Whig rally in Massachusetts, one of the radicals wrote:

> Truly the "Sphere of woman" must be made of [rubber] of the most elastic description it so well accommodates the never ending inconsistencies of this . . . generation! When she can be used as the tool of man for the accomplishment of his ambitions or sectarian designs . . . her sphere is just where she can be used . . . but if she ventures to act on her own account as an independent immortal for the attainment of some great good to the race & straightway she is relegated to the kitchen & the nursery as the only places where she can properly appear! [16]

Other observers read the evidence differently: ". . . the late political campaign has effected a most surprising revolution in [woman's] favor. . . . . it is too late to roll back the car of reform, which has been moving on for sometime past with most surprising velocity." [17]

During 1840 the affairs of the Boston Female Anti-Slavery Society were resolved, as the Garrisonians fought bitterly to regain control of this valuable organization. Complaining that Garrison's heresies threatened the foundations of social order, conservative ladies formed the Boston Female Emancipation Society, auxiliary to the Massachusetts Abolition Society. Its old members reestablished the Female Anti-Slavery Society and from this time forward were firmly united with Garrisonian abolitionism, providing important organizational and financial support to the *Liberator* and other abolitionist enterprises. The Boston Female Society's fair at Christmas, 1840, raised about $2000 and "exceeded in richness and splendor any former exhibition of this kind. . . . The number and variety of curious and beautiful articles were greater than we have ever before witnessed on similar occasions. Many of these were wrought by female members of the Mass. Anti-Slavery Society, others were given by its friends." [18] Events of the year seemed to invigorate the radicals everywhere.

Women antislavery lecturers ceased to be exceptional during the 1840s, although they remained controversial. Of a number of militant women, the most outstanding was Abby Kelley. Throughout the decade she traveled nearly every year for weeks, even months at a time. New England in 1840, 1841, and 1844, New York in 1842 and 1843, Pennsylvania in 1844 and 1845, and Ohio in 1845-46 were aroused by her energetic efforts. The year 1840 found her in Connecticut facing terrible opposition:

> She was compared to Fanny Wright called a *man woman*, one who had done more to injure the abolition cause than any one else &c. &c. She in her turn... said there was no Abolitionism here, intolerant, persecuting, cold hearted, that she would shake off the dust from her feet when she left.

Alice Welch Cowles, the lady principal at Oberlin College, met Kelley on a visit in Connecticut and found her fascinating: "On many points, I sympathized deeply with Miss K. She is devoted to the slave, to the whole human family. She is very intelligent. Her conversation, was elevated, and excellent in every respect, except when she reproved those with whom she was conversing." [19]

As her fame spread, demands for her services came from many areas of the Northeast. Characteristic of these appeals was this one from western New York:

> I want Abby Kelley — in Western New York — she is the only woman who speaks in public and we must have her. . . . she will do more good than any 3 lecturers the land can produce. 1st She would bring this mooted question [woman's rights] to an issue. [20]

When she made an intensive tour of upstate New York in 1843 she brought new life to the female antislavery movement here, preaching "comeouterism," urging her listeners to renounce allegiance to churches, government, and other institutions that sanctioned slavery. In the village of Seneca Falls she stirred up an antislavery revival, denouncing the churches and calling on the ministers to defend themselves. Kelley helped the women of Seneca Falls to form an antislavery sewing circle and convinced them to hold a fair. Five years later this village was the site of America's first woman's rights convention.

Moving on to eastern Pennsylvania in 1844, Abby Kelley awakened interest in her cause and raised money for the Garrisonian abolitionists. A friendly observer praised her "excellent meetings" for "getting the soil in good order & sewing the good seed. How sad to think that the most efficient of all will have so little time among us" [21] The next year she was in Ohio, giving new spirit to the weak Garrisonian organization there, the Western Anti-Slavery Society. She was instrumental in securing the establishment of the *Anti-Slavery Bugle*, Ohio's first radical antislavery newspaper. Promoting it continuously, she sought subscribers and financial support, as in the fall of 1845: "A letter from Abby last evening contains 87 new subscribers, & nearly $200 in pledges, all of which were obtained at their last two meetings in the lower part of the State." [22] Kelley's impact in Ohio was roughly comparable to that of the Grimké sisters in Massachusetts eight years earlier. Experience only seemed to make her bolder, less submissive, as when she spoke to the Quakers at Mount Pleasant, Ohio:

The orthodox Quakers . . . carried Abby Kelley out of their Meeting of a Sunday for speaking in their meeting in behalf of the slaves she all the way kept addressing them they even attempted to carry [her] out of the yard but the crowd being so dense they could not force her through and had to listen to her the younger Friends think it a great outrage. [23]

In December, 1845, Abby Kelley married Stephen S. Foster, one of the most denunciatory of all the radical abolitionists, and from that time onward they were united in spreading radical doctrines. The two abolitionists made visits to Oberlin College in 1846 that greatly upset the piety and order of that evangelical campus. Since the college was noted as a center of reform, Abby Foster was anxious to preach her "disorganizing" doctrines there. She described their first visit during a religious revival: "They had got up a revival of their superstitions before we got there, and so had a good excuse for crowding out our discussions, yet we succeeded in obtaining three hearings in which we showed their connexion with and support of slavery through the government and the Church." The Oberlin *Evangelist* was indignant at their attack on organized religion and one member of the college faculty complained that they talked of what should *not* be done about slavery, not what *should* be done. A few students were highly encouraged by this radical preaching. Lucy Stone, then an Oberlin student, was delighted at the discussion provoked by the Fosters: ". . . you set a ball in motion, that is still rolling, and it *will* roll, for there are a few, who are *pushing* it, and who will *contrive* to do so.'' [24] The radical couple returned to Oberlin in the fall at the request of some students and held a discussion of disunion — the separation of nonslave states from the slavocracy — with President Asa Mahan of the college.

Abby Kelley Foster seldom lectured on woman's rights, although she often expressed opinions on the disputed topic. In 1840 she attempted to stimulate a published debate on the woman question with the editor of the *Connecticut Observer*. She took a typical radical position: "Whatsoever ways and means are right for men to adopt in reforming the world, are right also for women to adopt in pursuing the same object.'' The editor attacked her views as being unscriptural and declined to publish any additional communications on the subject. She continually advocated women's involvement in reform: "*One* woman is worth *two* men, any day, in a moral movement.''[25] She possessed a clear perception of man's moral weakness and a prejudice in woman's favor:

> Woman can do more than man for the extension of righteousness. Not that they are naturally better or wiser but because they have not, from the customs of society, been so much perverted. The temptations, the tolerated tricks and falsehoods of trade and politics into which the boy is baptised and in which the heart when it comes to manhood becomes petrified more than half and in some instances entirely unfits [sic] it for the work of purifying the world. Women are not so situated as to be so entirely corrupted and hence their moral perception is much clearer. [26]

One admirer and fellow-abolitionist called Abby Foster "*The Woman* of the age.'' Another declared: "Abby still continues more worth seeing than Queen Victoria.'' [27] Her career as an agitator and public figure embodied the rights of woman and exercised a powerful influence over other women. Combining a high degree of personal appeal in intimate social circumstances such as parlors and dining rooms with unusual gifts as a public speaker, Foster could be highly persuasive. Evidently some women already disposed toward reform were unable to resist her. Even those who despised her and felt threatened by her radicalism were affected. Wherever she went the issue of woman's rights arose. It is surely no coincidence that the areas where she was active — central New England, upstate New York, eastern Pennsylvania, northern Ohio — became sources of the organized woman's rights movement during the 1850s.

Throughout her career as a public lecturer, Abby Kelly Foster acted as a magnet to talent for the radical cause, encouraging many women to speak out, to write, to edit newspapers, and to engage in agitating and organizing for the cause of abolition. Her accomplishments in bringing others into the field were important for woman's rights since several of her converts became early leaders in the feminist movement. On her first lecture tour through New York State, Abby Kelley Foster induced Paulina Wright, of Utica, to join her temporarily as an assistant and companion. After her first efforts at public speaking, Foster described her associate as being "Bold as a lion for the truth." Following her husband's death in 1845, Wright studied female anatomy and physiology and began lecturing to women on these subjects. She gained much notoriety for her use of a female mannequin to illustrate her discussions. The close friendship between Abby Foster and Paulina Wright continued during the following years, having a direct impact on the organization of the woman's rights movement. Married in 1849 to Thomas Davis, Paulina Wright Davis became the principal organizer of the woman's rights convention held at Worcester, Massachusetts, in 1850.

In 1844, Abby Kelley Foster recruited another young upstate New York woman as a lecturer — Jane Elizabeth Hitchcock. Under her instruction, Hitchcock learned to address the public, becoming quite an eloquent extemporaneous ·speaker. Traveling with Foster in New England and Pennsylvania, she settled at Salem, Ohio, where she married another abolitionist, Benjamin S. Jones. Describing her active life and influence as an abolitionist in 1845, Jane Elizabeth Jones wrote to Boston:

> B.S. Jones & myself hold meetings every week in the surrounding country, sometimes 3, 4, 5, or 6 sessions as the case may be, & attend to the paper between times. The cry for meetings comes up from every quarter, & the friends not infrequently make themselves a journey of 50 or 100 miles in order to get us to their respective places & back again. [28]

In 1848 she published *The Young Abolitionists*, an antislavery tract for children consisting of cheerful conversations designed to illustrate the evils of slavery and the good being accomplished by abolitionists. Jane Elizabeth Jones served prominently in the first Ohio woman's rights convention in 1850 at Salem.

During her tour of Ohio, Abby Kelley Foster influenced other women. Betsey M. Cowles of Austinburg had been involved in an early antislavery organization in Ohio, but had lost interest in the cause until her conversion by Foster to Garrisonism in 1846. She became an avid

Liberator reader, a speaker in meetings, an active member of the Western Anti-Slavery Society, an agent and correspondent of the *Anti-Slavery Bugle*. In 1847 and 1848, Cowles was a principal organizer of abolition fairs held to raise money for the movement in Ohio. She helped to set up several local women's antislavery societies in the Western Reserve. She was a great admirer of Abby and Stephen Foster, a well-known and influential personality in northern Ohio, who, Abby hoped, would be "drawn to the field, as a more active laborer, for reform." [29] Although she never became a regular lecturer, Betsey Cowles took an interest in the rights of woman. An educator of some distinction, she was quite aware of discrimination against her sex in the schools. In the summer of 1850 she served as the president of the first Ohio Women's Convention, held at Salem. She participated in other early Ohio meetings for the advancement of women and joined the executive committee of the Ohio Woman's Rights Association, formed in 1852.

Abby Kelley Foster's example and influence were critical for one of the most zealous American feminists, Lucy Stone, who probably met Foster some time in the early 1840s when the latter lectured in West Brookfield, Massachusetts. Entering Oberlin College against her father's wishes in 1843, Lucy Stone almost immediately became one of the most radical young women there. Unlike the majority of students, she was a great admirer of Garrison and the radical abolitionists, praising their *"moral grandeur"*. She was ready and eager to listen to Abby and Stephen Foster when they appeared at Oberlin in 1846 to denounce the corruption of the clergy and the national government. Following their visit, Lucy Stone began preparing herself to take up a vocation as an antislavery lecturer: "I have made myself rather odious here by discussing at a public soc. extemporaneously, and making gestures, and also for an essay on woman's province, and calling it wide as the universe of God." [30] She also published an article in the *Anti-Slavery Bugle* condemning the Oberlin church for holding fellowship with clergymen who accepted slavery and "men-thieves." A year later Lucy Stone refused to prepare an essay for commencement because the faculty would not, on the grounds of propriety, allow her to read her own words to an audience of men and women.

Abby Foster pleaded with Lucy Stone to go into the field as a lecturer, and the latter resolved to do so, much against her family's wishes. "You know how it will make much talk in our quarter of the world," her father wrote. But Foster's example had freed Stone from her fear of ridicule and hostility from opponents. From a time before her graduation, she was urged to travel for both the Massachusetts and the Western Anti-Slavery Societies. In 1848, Abby Foster "beset" Lucy Stone "to go lecturing this summer I told her I did not know how, but I was willing to try she wrote immediately to Mrs. Chapman. . . ." [31] The novice shortly received an appointment from the Massachusetts Society and became a successful agitator. At New Bedford, "Lucy Stone did remarkably well, and very much interested the N.B. folks. She is doing, directly & indirectly, a very good work." In the next year the Philadelphia Female Anti-Slavery Society sought to employ her. Thus Lucy Stone's long career as an advocate of women was launched.

A powerful influence was exercised by another eminent woman abolitionist during the 1840s. Lucretia Mott, the veteran of antislavery women in America, was more overtly interested in the question of woman's rights than most of her antislavery sisters. In this decade she devoted much of her time to lecturing, speaking on religious topics, in the slave's behalf, and for woman's rights. Like most radicals at this time, Mott grew more and more impatient with the constraints of traditions, creeds, and denominations. Returning from the World Anti-Slavery Convention, she quickly threw herself into an arduous series of lecture tours which occurred throughout the decade. She spoke often at Friends' meetings, but also addressed the general public on questions of religion and reform. One tour took her to the legislatures of Delaware, New Jersey, and Pennsylvania "where a patient & respectful audience was granted while [she] plead the cause of the oppressed." [32] Corresponding with Elizabeth Cady Stanton, she urged her young friend to be free of the outworn creeds and dogmas of theology and sectarianism.

In the fall of 1841, Lucretia Mott spoke at Marlboro Chapel in Boston on reforms of the day, the breaking down of distinctions between men and classes of men, reducing the influence of forms and ceremonies, and increasing the moral power of women. "I long for the time," she declared, "when my sisters will rise, and occupy the sphere to which they are called by their high nature and destiny." No longer would they be the playthings of men, satisfied with trivial social or intellectual pursuits. "The tendency of truth on this subject, is to equalize the sexes." [33] In 1842, on a visit to Friends' meetings in Maryland and Virginia to urge her sisters and brothers to accept abolitionism, Mott stopped in Washington, D.C., where in a public meeting she endorsed "woman's duties and responsibilities." Here she also had a cordial discussion of the slavery issue with President John Tyler.

One of her purposes at this time was to arouse the consciences of

Quakers concerning slavery and stir up the extremely conservative leadership in many Friends' meetings. In Philadelphia she brought Stephen S. Foster to speak in Quaker meetings. On another occasion, after an orthodox Friends' wedding ceremony, "she rose from the wedding company — commenced speaking . . . she went on without attending to what had passed, the audience most profoundly attentive — very many moved to tears . . . by her appeals on behalf of universal righteousness — a very large part of the mtg. were indignant at the conduct of the presiding elder. . . ." [34] Controversy with rigid leaders in her religious society whose "high handed measures" threatened liberals and actually disowned several stalwart abolitionists alienated her increasingly from the Society of Friends. Lucretia Mott remained a staunch Garrisonian in her abolitionist sympathies, however.

Toward the end of the decade, Lucretia Mott became more outspoken than ever concerning woman's rights. In 1847, she addressed the yearly meeting of Hicksite Friends in Ohio on the rights and duties of women, claiming that, as woman was equally accountable with man as a moral being, she should have an equal education and go forward in all reform efforts. In 1849, she delivered a major address in Philadelphia, answering a speech of Richard Henry Dana, Sr., who urged that women retain the innocence and subordination which were so vital to the sex. Defending a greatly expanded public role for women, Mott declared that her sisters would not lose their "beautiful mind and retiring modesty" by being active in the world. Beyond obtaining sanction for their equality as moral beings, women needed greater legal protection, expanded property rights, and more independence after marriage. And this expansion of their equality was claimed as a right, nor a favor:

> Let woman then go on — not asking favors, but claiming as right, the removal of all hindrances to her elevation in the scale of being — let her receive encouragement for the proper cultivation of all her powers, so that she may enter profitably into the active business of life; employing her own hands, in ministering to her necessities, strengthening her physical being by proper exercise, and observance of the laws of health. [35]

The example set by Lucretia Mott, more than that of other radical women, served as a beacon in the long struggle for woman's rights during the second half of the nineteenth century and the first two decades of the twentieth. By acting out and insisting upon the right to speak in public, despite the force of religious and public hostility, and by discussing openly the principles of sexual equality, Mott assisted in keeping the woman question alive. Because she was a Quaker, other Quakers listened to her, although few agreed with her views, and because she was well-known, many non-Quakers listened and were affected. Like Abby Kelley Foster, Lucretia Mott carried the message of woman's rights into new geographical territory during her lecture tours. Her efforts provided an important connection between the first hesitant assertion of woman's rights in the antislavery movement during the 1830s and the organized crusade for equality which began about 1850. When, in 1848, favorable circumstances made a woman's rights convention possible, she was the leading participant in the meetings at Seneca Falls.

Several male abolitionists had a significant influence on the agitation over woman's rights during the 1840s. William Lloyd Garrison, Parker Pillsbury, Henry C. Wright, Stephen S. Foster, Oliver Johnson, and other radicals were involved either directly or indirectly with the woman question. Without their support the movement for equality would have been significantly handicapped. They stood behind and joined with the women who met in the first conventions and published the first daring assertions of their equal rights with men. Generally their support was indirect, yet when the occasion arose they advocated woman's cause directly. For example, one of the most loyal and amiable Garrisonians, the Reverend Samuel J. May, the same Unitarian minister who had defended Prudence Crandall in 1834, preached an influential sermon on "The Rights and Condition of Women," at Syracuse, New York, in 1845.

Reformist agitation took on other dimensions during the 1840s, emphasizing the possibilities of women's involvement in public concerns. The antislavery movement, for example, spread deeply into the Middle West during the decade. A series of local and county female abolitionist organizations were formed in Michigan to raise money for publications and advertise the cause in other ways. In 1846, a state Ladies Antislavery Association was reportedly established in Illinois with plans to organize local female societies throughout the state. In Wisconsin, the Female Anti-Slavery Society of Prairieville published its constitution as a model for other women's societies, and in 1845 held its first anniversary meeting with speeches from several "gentlemen from abroad." An "Address to the Ladies by a member of the Milwaukee Female Anti-Slavery Society" proclaimed in 1844 woman's involvement with the sin of slavery because of its gross violation of motherhood and female virtue. Women, free and slave, possessed ties of sisterhood.

The radical abolitionists' decade of agitation greatly expanded interest in woman's rights. It would be impossible to judge accurately what portion of the American population became interested in the issue. Nevertheless, hundreds of letters preserved in antislavery manuscript collections testify to the widespread stirrings of interest. The issue was being publicized in antislavery newspapers such as the *Liberator, National Anti-Slavery Standard, Anti-Slavery Bugle,* the *Signal of Liberty*\ in Michigan, and *American Freeman* further West. An anonymous correspondent, writing to the *Signal of Liberty* in 1846 on the "Condition of Females," laid out a few "particular wrongs endured by my sex." She complained of the lack of dignity or rewards offered women for successful performance in occupations and noted especially the unequal rates of pay for men and women performing the same tasks. Another writer in this paper, discussing "Woman's Sphere," attributed her lowly condition to customs, laws, and inadequate training, and argued in favor of equality. The Wisconsin *Free Democrat* reported early in 1850 on a lecture given in that state by Giles B. Stebbins, a Garrisonian abolitionist, on "the true position, influence and duties of woman. Mr. Stebbins used no flattery, but told a plain, unvarnished tale of what woman is as he has seen her, and of what he thinks she ought to be. He anticipates for woman 'in the good times coming' an equality of rights and duties."[36]

Extensive attention to relationships between the antislavery movement and woman's rights during the 1840s kept the new issue before the American public. Urged to remember their black sisters toiling beneath the lash in the South, northern women could not forget their own inequality in an oppressive, sex-role-divided system. But the outstanding emphasis of abolitionist agitators during the 1840s was positive. They convinced their listeners of women's collective power to achieve reform, to overturn arbitrary social arrangements and antiquated customs. The examples set by these forceful women had an abiding influence on others who would follow them and organize the movement for woman's rights.

9

AN EXPANDING DEBATE

DURING the 1840s discussions of the status of woman and the limitations of her "sphere" increasingly circulated in the literature and popular media of communications. In their extreme forms, two attitudes were represented. Defenders of woman's domesticity and moral authority insisted that she should be subordinate to man and confined in her duties, but that in faithful housekeeping, motherhood, and moral guardianship, woman had immense influence. Opposing this conventional outlook, a minority of radicals claimed that woman should be free to choose where and how to exercise her talents. Woman, like man, ought not to be limited by outmoded custom in her intellectual, social, occupational, or political opportunities.

Chief among conservative authorities in her influence was Catharine E. Beecher. In 1841, Beecher published her *Treatise on Domestic Economy*, championing domestic reform. The *Treatise* was one of many how-to-do-it or admonitory manuals appearing after 1830, but it was the first to advocate the transformation of housekeeping into a science — Woman's Profession — deserving close study and high prestige. Thus, the author was one of the precursors of home economics as a distinct and respectable field of study. The *Treatise* was reprinted nearly every year for fifteen years and reworked into other books, making Beecher's name a household word throughout the country.

The author proposed a number of changes to improve woman's domestic life. She provided directions for better housekeeping (but no recipes — Beecher's *Domestic Receipt Book* appeared in 1846) that were intended to emancipate American women from domestic drudgery and dependence on ignorant servants. She emphasized the importance of intelligent design, good taste, and careful physical organization in household architecture. The *Treatise* is recognized as one of the earliest attempts to achieve the "rational household" by organization of the work process to increase efficiency. Like the textile magnates of Boston in their Lowell mills, Beecher sought to apply industrial techniques to a female environment.

Catharine Beecher's major concern was not efficiency, however, but significance. Her American sisters, she believed, felt unimportant and unappreciated because their chief duties, centered in the domestic establishment, were undervalued. In her *Treatise* Beecher hoped to raise women's morale, convincing them that their work was important. She wrote reassuringly:

> Surely it is a pernicious and mistaken idea, that the duties which tax a woman's mind are petty, trivial, or unworthy of the highest grade of intellect and moral worth. She, who is the mother and housekeeper in a large family, is the sovereign of an empire, demanding as varied cares, and involving more duties than are really exacted of her . . . who wears the crown . . . of the greatest nation on earth. . . . [1]

In order to have their important duties appreciated and understood, Beecher urged that women obtain professional training. Her *Treatise* was intended as a textbook for such instruction and she later founded a school which, according to her plan, would make systematic study of domestic economy a reality.

Another purpose of Beecher's *Treatise* was to respond to the growing agitation over woman's rights, to provide an alternative model for woman which would appeal to a wide audience. Discussion of the equality of the sexes she considered "both frivolous and useless." Leading off with a chapter called "The Peculiar Responsibilities of American Women," she gave religious validity to woman's vocation, identifying democracy with Christianity. The United States, she assured her readers, was appointed by the "Eternal Lawgiver" to show the way for "the destiny of the whole earth." This destiny, she supposed, was largely in the hands of woman:

> The mother writes the character of the future man; the sister bends the fibres that hereafter are the forest tree; the wife sways the heart, whose energies may turn for good or for evil the destinies of a nation. Let the women of a country be made virtuous and intelligent, and the men will surely be the same. [2]

Although indirect, exercised through man, woman's power would be profound.

In thus approaching the spectre of woman's rights, Beecher attempted to mediate between an ideal of subordination and confinement and the newer aspirations for full equality announced by the abolitionists and other reformers. By interpreting domestic reform in the context of progressive change, she hoped to rationalize woman's inequality and deflect the growing appeal of feminism. Surely when woman had indirect authority over the nation's destiny, they had no need for political rights or specious claims to equality.

One of Catharine Beecher's major co-workers in holding back the feminist tide was Sarah Josepha Hale, editor of the most popular woman's magazine of the 1840s, *Godey's Lady's Book*. One of the leading conservative theorists of woman's "sphere," Hale commanded an empire of taste, popular literature, and values which penetrated thousands of middle-class households. Faced with widowhood and the need to support five young children, Hale began writing and editing, and in 1828 moved to Boston to edit the *Ladies' Magazine*, becoming one of the nation's first professional woman editors. Louis Godey, proprietor of the *Lady's Book* in Philadelphia, recognized her talents and in 1836 invited her to take over the editorship of *Godey's*, a position offering far greater monetary rewards and a wider realm of influence than her position in Boston. The offer was too good to refuse.

Through her power as editor, Hale became an overseer of women's writing during the decade, encouraging a host of sentimental authors, headed by the genial, beloved "Sweet Singer of Hartford," Lydia H. Sigourney. Most of her contributors are deservedly forgotten, although several male writers, grateful for the generous fees paid by Louis Godey, achieved lasting importance through the *Lady's Book*. Hale gave consistent support to improvements in woman's education, publishing kind notices of new schools and approaches to instruction, so long as they respected the true and separate sphere of action belonging to woman. Forced by popular demand to picture the latest fashions of Paris, she advocated dress reform in the interests of health, economy, and good morals. She looked with favor upon women's property legislation as protection of wives against dissolute husbands. Two of her favorite crusades illustrate Hale's cultural outlook and concept of woman's influence. In 1840, she sponsored a successful woman's campaign to raise money for completion of the Bunker Hill Monument. During later years of the decade she urged in the pages of the *Lady's Book* that the celebration of Thanksgiving, a New England holiday, be extended to the nation. Her efforts culminated in 1863 with Abraham Lincoln's proclamation of a national Thanksgiving.

Although she opposed the perverse women who would not accept their divinely appointed sphere, Sarah Hale enjoyed celebrating the accomplishments of her sex. In 1848, *Godey's Lady's Book* published a series of sketches by Elizabeth Ellet, "Heroic Women of the Revolution." Revised, expanded, and entitled *The Women of the American Revolution,* this work made a pioneering contribution to women's history. In the last year of the decade Hale initiated another project designed to exhibit more fully the historical influence of woman. Published in 1853, *Woman's Record,* was a volume of biographical sketches of eminent women, showing their achievements through the ages. In *Woman's Record* Hale responded directly to the issue of woman's rights. "I have no sympathy," she wrote, "with those who are wrangling for 'woman's rights'; nor with those who are foolishly urging women to strive for equality and competition with men."

Refuting the proponents of equality, she used the familiar weapons employed to prove woman's inequality to man in the late 1830s — orthodox religious and scriptural interpretations:

> What I seek to establish is the Bible doctrine, as I understand it, that woman was intended as the teacher and inspirer for man, morally speaking of "whatsoever things are lovely, and pure, and of good report." The Bible does not uphold the equality of the sexes. When created, man and woman were unlike in three important respects.
> 1st. The mode of their creation was different.
> 2d. The materials from which each was formed were unlike.
> 3d. The functions for which each was designed were dissimilar. [3]

But "WOMAN . . . God's appointed agent of morality," had immense power: "Woman cannot create, or make, like man; but, better than he, she worships God in spirit and in truth. . . . She has a better, a holier vocation. She works in the elements of human nature . . . these she must build up in the character of her children... often, too, she is called to repair... the mind and heart of the husband she reverences and obeys." Woman would gain influence through the renunciation of self, to "raise humanity towards the angelic." [4]

Here was the argument for separate spheres, elaborated in exhaustive, repetitive detail. By serving her grand religious purpose, and submitting to masculine power, woman would be preserved from becoming unsexed, as the advocates of woman's rights would have her.

Hale's influence, although conservative, was widespread because of her position as a popular writer and editor. Like Catharine Beecher, she hoped to reassure her readers by pointing to the religious and moral importance of woman's subordinate status.

The popular literature written during the 1840s for a female audience had little to say directly concerning the debate over woman's rights. Implicitly, however, in its overriding concern with domesticity, it reinforced conservative views. Poetry — bad, sentimental doggerel — appealed in nearly every popular periodical or anthology to the emotions of domestic middle-class women. Caroline May, in *The American Female Poets: With Biographical and Critical Notices* (Philadelphia, 1848), boasted of the great number of women poets in the United States and commented on the concentration of this poetry on commonplace domestic experience:

> Hence, the themes which have suggested the greater part of the . . . poems have been derived from the incidents and associations of everyday life. And home, with its quiet joys, its deep pure sympathies, and its secret sorrows, with which a stranger must not intermeddle, is a sphere by no means limited for woman, whose inspiration lies more in her heart than her head. [5]

Two other species of popular literature fed a growing feminine audience — the literary annual or gift book, and the domestic novel. Between 1825 and 1865, more than 1000 separate gift books were published — anthologies of poetry, sketches, essays, and stories, embellished with handsome, often fanciful engravings, generally enclosed within elaborately embossed bindings. Gift-book authors included many of the same men and women who wrote for popular magazines. To their readers, predominantly women, gift books were reassuring, "highly moral and polite," "refined," "pure." Their sentimental, exotic content responded to romantic impulses and stereotypes so popular in the 1840s. The heyday of the domestic novel came in the next decade, but before then its influence was clear. Set within the household, focusing on family relationships, transforming ordinary experience into exciting fantasy, the domestic novel was written especially for women. Its most popular creators, too, were women, This popular literature offered entertainment and escape for thousands of readers who were bored or tied down to their households, all the while encouraging them to believe in the importance of their roles.

Of the women who represented the spirit of rebellion during the 1840s, none had more lasting impact than Margaret Fuller. Testing the limits of her gender, Fuller became the symbol of the potential but untried talents of womanhood. Her feminist writings summed up the grievances of a generation of women, although she never lived to join the organized woman's rights movement. Reared in precocious circumstances, reading Latin and Greek before she was an adolescent, she wanted to write "like a man of the world of intellect and action." [6] Yet when the future seemed bright, her father's death forced her to support her widowed mother and younger siblings by teaching school. Experimental as a teacher, and speculative as a thinker, she joined New England's loftiest intellectual circle, that of the Transcendentalists. She soon became the foremost woman intellectual of her generation, as well as one of its major rebels.

In November, 1839, Margaret Fuller undertook her first efforts to rectify the injustices done to woman, beginning her famous Conversations with some of New England's most socially prominent and gifted women. Her powers during the Conversations were dedicated to the advancement of woman's intellect:

> She held that women were at a disadvantage as compared with men, because the former were not called on to test, apply or reproduce what they learned; while the pursuits of life supplied that want to men. Systematic conversation, controlled by a leading mind, would train women to make definite statement, and continuous thought; they would make blunders and gain by their mortification; they would seriously compare notes with each other, and discover where vague impression ended and clear knowledge began. [7]

Fuller was the "leading mind," the brilliant guide for Boston's eminent women as they attempted "to answer the great questions. What are we born to do? How shall we do it?" [8] Her Conversations were related to the earlier, humbler attempts of women's literary societies and discussion groups to improve woman's intellect, and also to similar experiments tried by Elizabeth Peabody and Delia Bacon—other women intellectuals.

The Conversations took place during five winters until Margaret Fuller left Boston in 1844. Since each participant paid a fee of twenty dollars for the series of ten meetings, Fuller was able to earn a living by talking. In 1841, the group attempted an innovation, holding Conversations which included men, but the mixed group of great minds failed to coalesce around the topic of Greek Mythology and the experiment was not tried again. Possessed with a mystique which acted as a magnet to her admiring audiences, Fuller functioned best with women. Conversation subjects ranged widely but they were intended to exercise the minds of all participants and provoke self-discovery by each member of the group. Her presence raised the consciousness of her listeners, as she indicated in describing the final meeting:

> It was the last day with my class. How noble has been my experience of such relation . . . and with so many and so various minds! Life is worth living, — is it not? We had a most animated meeting. On bidding me good-bye, they all and always show so much good-will and love that I feel I must really have become a friend to them. [9]

Between 1840 and 1842, in addition to conducting the Conversations, Margaret Fuller served as editor of a periodical, the *Dial*, whose short existence gave voice to the Transcendentalist intellect. In this task, too, she operated as the peer of Ralph Waldo Emerson and other great minds of New England. In the *Dial* in 1843 she published her first essay on women, "The Great Lawsuit: Man versus Men, Woman versus Women," an outgrowth of the consciousness of woman's possibilities achieved in the Conversations. Two years later an expanded version of this important essay was published as a book, *Woman in the Nineteenth Century*, giving Fuller widespread notoriety and prestige as one of America's first feminist theoreticians.

The author's receptive intellect translated her own frustrations, absorbed the most liberal influences of the 1840s, and produced a tract of timely significance. Like Mary Wollstonecraft's *Vindication of the Rights of Woman*, Fuller's work clarified basic issues, but, unlike the earlier essay, it appeared when an enthusiastic audience existed ready to confront the issues and overcome obstacles. Fuller noted the desire for change expressed widely in her time: "Many women are considering within themselves what they need and what they have not, and what they can have if they find they need it." [10] Signs of the times were everywhere — in the press, in the utterances of public speakers, in the legislatures of some states.

The environment of the 1840s also exhibited the handicaps which limited women, publicized by conservative advocates of woman's "sphere":

> The numerous party, whose opinions are already labeled and adjusted too much to their mind to admit of any new light, strive, by lectures on some model-woman of bride-like beauty and gentleness, by writing and lending

little treatises, intended to mark out with precision the limits of Woman's sphere and Woman's mission, to prevent . . . the flock from using any chance to go astray. [11]

Although she mentioned no names, Fuller's description could have applied to the advice of Catharine Beecher, Sarah Hale, or their imitators. Their repressive theme appeared thus:

Woman is, and *shall remain*, inferior to Man and subject to his will. . . . The lot of Woman is sad. She is constituted to expect and need a happiness that cannot exist on earth. She must stifle such aspirations within her secret heart, and fit herself, as well as she can, for a life of resignations and consolations. [12]

Fuller wrote extensively and bitterly of marriage. In America the institution was deeply flawed, and compared unfavorably with the open practice of polygamy in the East and among American Indians. The double standard debased American women who "should know nothing about such things" as man's immoral and profligate sexual behavior. Virtuous women had a great responsibility for their fallen sisters: "Seek out these degraded women, give them tender sympathy, counsel, employment. Take the place of mothers, such as might have saved them originally." Pure women should protect innocence by direct action, deciding which men "were fit for admission to their houses and the society of their daughters." Reject men as "fathers, lovers, husbands, sons of yours," who are impure, Fuller preached. [13]

Margaret Fuller urged basic changes in assumptions underlying marriage: woman should "lay aside all thought, such as she habitually cherishes, of being taught and led by men." Equality in marital relationships could lead to the highest development of both individuals, free intellectual and spiritual communion, the achievement of freedom in union, and the greatest enjoyment of sexual relations. Motherhood, too, needed reconsideration: "Earth knows no fairer, holier relation than that of a mother," Fuller wrote. But woman needed to think of possibilities beyond maternity; she was "a being of infinite scope. . . . Give the soul free course, let the organization, both of body and mind be fully developed, and the being will be fit for any and every relation to which it may be called." [14]

"Be ye perfect" was the text to which Margaret Fuller most fully subscribed. The world was developing toward a higher level of consciousness, and woman as the best representative of this higher spirit, would help to inaugurate the new era:

> Now the time has come when a clearer vision and a better action are possible—when Man and Woman may regard one another as brother and sister, the pillars of one porch, the priests of one worship.
>
> I believe that, at present, women are the best helpers of one another. Let them think; let them act; till they know what they need.
>
> We only ask of men to remove arbitrary barriers. Some would like to do more. But I believe it needs that Woman show herself in her native dignity, to teach them how to aid her; their minds so encumbered by tradition.
>
> But if you ask me what offices they may fill, I reply—any. I do not care what case you put; let them be sea-captains, if you will. I do not doubt there are women well fitted for such an office....
>
> I think that women need, especially at this juncture, a much greater range of occupation than they have, to rouse their latent powers. [15]

Individual talents, not gender prescriptions, would be the basis of a new social order. Each life demanded "the perfection of each being in its kind ... Woman as Woman. . . . Had I but one more moment to live I must wish the same." [16] Contradicting timid critics, both men and women, Fuller insisted that women would be themselves if given the opportunity:

> Ye cannot believe it, men; but the only reason why women assume what is more appropriate to you, is because you prevent them from finding out what is fit for themselves. Were they free, were they wise fully to develop the strength and beauty of Woman, they would never wish to be men, or manlike. [17]

Woman in the Nineteenth Century articulated the patterns of feminine discontent prevalent during the late 1830s and 1840s, absorbing ideas from moral reform, abolitionism, and popular literature, and adding a particular quality of moral idealism which was Margaret Fuller's own strength and her gift to the woman's movement. Undoubtedly her work influenced virtually all advocates of woman's rights in this country. It provided ammunition and inspiration for the writers and rebels who sparked the organized crusade for woman's emancipation after 1850. Paulina Wright Davis, chief organizer of the national woman's rights convention at Worcester in 1850, hoped that Fuller might be persuaded to lead the new movement.

Not only her work but her life challenged contemporaries. From provincial New England she traveled through the pressured atmosphere of New York City, and from there to Europe to experience deeper cultural influences. Finally, in Italy during the revolution of 1848, she found love and fulfillment. In 1850, returning to the United States and on the verge of what might have been a new career as an advocate of woman, Margaret Fuller died in a shipwreck off the shore of Fire Island. "Her life," wrote an admirer, "thus did more for the intellectual enfranchisement of American women than was done by even her book on the subject. . . ." [18] No other woman of her time so embodied the quest for personal autonomy.

Other protagonists and other issues entered into the complex question of woman's rights during the 1840s. A handful of women assaulted the privileges of the medical profession, seeking the right to study and practice medicine. Harriot K. Hunt, Mary Gove Nichols, and Elizabeth Blackwell pioneered as women physicians and health reformers in this decade. They shared several assumptions about health and medical care that later gained wide influence in the woman's movement. The diseases peculiar to women, they believed, should be treated by women physicians. It was "indelicate" for men to be dealing with the most intimate difficulties of women suffering from disease. Extending their logic, they justified and demanded professional training for women doctors and were among the earliest members of their sex to work as physicians. Finally, the three were active in the health reform or hygiene movement, teaching good health habits and preventive medicine to other women, so as to improve their general physical conditions, reduce suffering, and make women less dependent on men doctors.

Both Harriot Hunt and Mary S. Gove studied medical books and began practicing during the 1830s. Both became involved in the profession when conventional doctors failed to ease women's sufferings, in the case of Hunt, those of her sister, in Mary Gove's case, her own. Both women arrived at the conclusion that male doctors lacked understanding of women's illnesses. Hunt insisted that medical care be drastically overhauled in favor of more reliance on natural processes of healing and recovery. Discerning a close relationship between mental attitudes and physical health, she worked to restore patients' confidence as she treated their bodily afflictions. She was especially concerned that women learn the "laws of life" in order to prevent illness: "Setting aside medication, we endeavored to trace diseases to violated laws, and learn the science of prevention. That word—prevention—seemed a great word to me; curative was small beside it." [19]

Describing her reasons for becoming a physician, Harriot Hunt gave a high place to the sympathy she felt toward other women and the failure of male doctors to understand women patients:

> There must be always oneness between the doctor and the patient. The prevailing idea as before remarked is, that the *doctor* is to cure the disease. It is not so. The doctor and the patient *together*, are to cure or mitigate the disease. They must be coworkers. In order to be so, there must be the fullest—the most cordial sympathy and frankness between them. It is rarely that this can be so between a male physician and a female patient. Therefore, the female physician is, *the* physician for the female patient. [20]

Her interest in preventing disease and spreading knowledge about health led Hunt in 1843 to assist in forming the Ladies' Physiological Society of Charlestown, Massachusetts, to which she offered lectures on physiology and health improvement. She lectured to this and other groups in succeeding years.

In 1847, urged by her patients, Harriot Hunt applied to attend medical lectures at the Harvard University Medical School. She was peremptorily refused on the grounds that it would be "inexpedient" to admit a woman. To Hunt, this decision reflected the low state of society in nineteenth-century Boston:

> The facts are on record—when civilization is further advanced, and the great doctrine of human rights is acknowledged, this act will be recalled, and wondering eyes will stare, and wondering ears will be opened, at the semi-barbarism of the middle of the nineteenth century.

But it had set the people stirring: "the subject of woman as physician was before the public—the conversation on this and kindred topics increased tenfold, and teatables and evening parties were made merry with criticisms and raillery...." [21] In the course of her life and medical career, Harriot Hunt became an active feminist and advocate of women physicians. At the 1850 women's rights convention in Worcester she spoke in favor of this purpose.

Mary Gove Nichols felt obliged to treat herself after the failure of male doctors. As a result of her experience, in 1838 at Lynn, Massachusetts, she began lecturing to women on anatomy, physiology, and hygiene. Her lectures became popular, enabling her to make a living by public speaking in northeastern cities and towns. As the first recorded American woman to lecture on anatomy and physiology to others of her sex, Mary Gove played a significant role in educating her contemporaries. Like many health reformers, she attributed most ill health to corrupt customs and bad habits — "violation of the laws of health . . . excessive eating, by improper food, and poisonous drinks; by neglect of healthful employment and exercise. . . ." [22] Her bold public lectures naturally aroused opposition from prudish guardians of virtue who considered any discussion of the human body by women to be "indelicate." Yet woman's general ignorance on these subjects "of vast importance" justified the lectures to their defenders.

Mary Gove published the substance of her discussions as *Lectures to Ladies on Anatomy and Physiology* (Boston, 1842), containing innocuous advice against heavy dosing with medicines and drugs, fashionable occupations, and in favor of dress reform. Four of Gove's Lectures concern improved nutrition and condemn meats, condiments, tobacco, alcohol, coffee, and tea, following recommendations of Sylvester Graham, the dietary reformer. Gove also took a stand against all forms of sexual abuse. During the 1840s she began practicing water-cure medicine as a highly beneficial approach to the most widespread women's diseases. In 1846, hoping both to set an example as a water-cure physician, and to train women in the system, she opened a clinic specializing in women's diseases in New York City. A water-cure medical school was later attached to this establishment. By this time her interests had expanded in more radical directions and her clinic had become "a general depot of Ultraisms in thought." She combined health reform and feminism, believing that freedom of women from disease and poor medical care would be the basis of other freedoms. Several other women, including two vigorous feminists, Paulina Wright Davis and Jane Elizabeth Jones, followed her example as a lecturer on medical subjects.

Elizabeth Blackwell entered the medical profession because of sympathy for a friend who had received inadequate care from a male physician. Terminally ill, the friend wished she had been able to obtain treatment from a woman doctor. This circumstance sent Elizabeth Blackwell, somewhat against her better judgment, to seek medical instruction. After a long struggle to obtain training, she enrolled in 1847 in the medical department of Geneva University in New York State. Her obviously serious purpose and gentle demeanor evidently subdued opposition to her presence, although townspeople would not accept her until after she graduated in 1849. She quickly became a symbol and a heroic figure to the advocates of woman's rights. After additional difficulties in obtaining clinical experience and becoming established,

Blackwell went on to found the New York Infirmary for Women and Children, devoting much of her life to training women physicians and serving women patients.

The movement to reform medical care for women at first seemed not to conflict with the notions of modesty and "delicacy" characterizing conservative attitudes toward woman's "sphere." Even Catharine Beecher and Sarah Hale supported improvements in woman's health and better medical care for their sex. However modest they supposed their efforts to be, women health reformers created lively opposition. Some of the enmity to their cause arose from ignorance and fear, but certainly when they began to practice and tried to enter medical schools, another reason for hostility became evident. As doctors, women threatened an established male profession, and the power and prestige of its members. Harriot Hunt's rejection by the faculty and students of Harvard's medical school was a measure of the hostility of male professionals. So too, women who embraced the water-cure as patients and physicians exhibited their lack of trust in traditional medicine and threatened to erect a rival system.

Opposition only goaded the more militant reformers to try harder at circulating medical information and opening the profession to women, an effort which after 1850 became part of the larger movement for woman's rights. The health reform effort sought to expand woman's power and assert her autonomy. It charged women with becoming guardians of their own bodies and promised to release them from the bondage of disease and the tyranny of male physicians.

One of the decade's most dramatic crusades relating to health was carried out almost single-handedly by a lonely, somewhat eccentric New England woman, Dorothea Dix. In 1841, teaching a prisoners' Sunday school class, she discovered with horror that mentally ill persons suffered extremely by being confined in jails. For the next eighteen months she surveyed all the jails, prisons, and almshouses in Massachusetts; verifying her first impressions of the unhappy fate of "lunatics" there. A detailed memorial to the legislature in 1843 resulted from her work, stirring that body to appropriate funds to support better care for mentally ill citizens. Responding to the same kind of sisterly ties which united other reformers, Dix sympathized particularly with suffering girls and women in the prisons. Her crusade continued through the 1840s and beyond, with investigations in Rhode Island, New York, New Jersey, and other states, resulting in greatly improved care for the mentally ill wherever she worked. Here was a clear display of woman's power to achieve humanitarian aims by creating a sympathetic public opinion and enlisting strong support from men and women.

Numerous women in the 1840s, conservatives and reformers alike, moved toward autonomy — conducting their own lives. Sarah Hale, Catharine Beecher, Margaret Fuller, Harriot Hunt, Mary Gove Nichols, Elizabeth Blackwell, and Dorothea Dix all worked vigorously as independent professional women. Each one contributed to the expansion of feminine influence, as did scores of other writers, lecturers, performers, and agitators. They shared a moralistic frame of reference and a preoccupation with the needs and influence of women, as each interpreted these. Increasingly aware of the importance of what they were doing, many of these women grew frustrated with limitations that seemed artificial. The experience of autonomy and its potential consequences encouraged proponents of women to organize their strength and take the offensive against limiting attitudes and conditions. In so doing they established the woman's rights movement.

10

THE WOMAN'S RIGHTS MOVEMENT

AFTER more than fifty years during which Americans discussed issues relating to women, beginning with arguments over their education in the post-Revolutionary period, the woman's rights movement took form as a distinct crusade between 1847 and 1850. By the mid-nineteenth century a substantial group of adherents had rallied around the new cause and were prepared to go forward in an organized fashion to seek a range of goals which some described not simply as woman's rights but as human rights.

In the late 1830s and early 1840s, the *rights* with which leading advocates of women were concerned included the acceptance of their roles as speakers, writers, and agitators in the antislavery movement, and recognition of their equality with men in reform organizations. Later in the decade the emphasis shifted toward eliminating woman's legal disabilities, as reformers sought legislation enabling women to hold their own property after marriage, to act as guardians of their children, to vote and participate in government.

The key state for woman's rights legislation in the 1840s was New York, where an early proposal to give married women the right to hold independent property was made in 1836. Ernestine Rose, a Polish immigrant, submitted the first women's petition in favor of this bill. Thereafter, other women, including Paulina Wright Davis and Elizabeth Cady Stanton, joined in petitioning for the legislation. In 1840, Ernestine Rose addressed committees of the New York assembly in favor of a woman's property law, and pressure built up, not only from reformers but from conservatives who hoped to preserve family estates against improvident husbands. In the mid-1840s, other bills were introduced in New York. Supported by a number of woman's rights activists, legislation was passed on April 7, 1848.

143

Other states also considered and passed legislation favorable to women during the decade. In 1848, Pennsylvania acted on a woman's property law after much petitioning in its favor. In Vermont, a woman newspaper editor, Clarina Howard Nichols, wrote a series of editorials in behalf of woman's property legislation in 1847, contributing to the success of bills granting married women the right to inherit, own, and bequeath property. Nichols worked also for other legislation passed in Vermont to improve the financial position of married women and widows. Mary Upton Ferrin of Salem, Massachusetts, circulated petitions appealing for liberalized women's property legislation beginning in 1848. These state and local efforts, without any central direction or organization, suggested growing support at the grass-roots for advancing woman's status under the law.

An important addition to the woman's movement appeared in January, 1848, with the first issue of the Pittsburgh *Saturday Visiter*, edited by Jane Grey Swisshelm. Although she was not the first woman to edit a reformist paper—Maria Weston Chapman and Lydia Maria Child had earlier served as editors of antislavery papers—Swisshelm was more particularly concerned in defending women than any previous editor. Possessing a sharp mind and scathing wit, Swisshelm enjoyed jousting with rival editors. She also roasted backward clergymen, like the Reverend James H. Fairchild of Oberlin whose views in a lecture on "Woman's Rights and Duties" she considered antiquated.

Swisshelm documented several aspects of the emerging woman's rights movement. Answering the question "Why do Women Never Excel?" in 1849, she explained:

> Society has ordained that woman's first duty is to follow some certain set of rules; and these are always so minute and complicated that it requires an ordinary capacity to be fully exercised to remember them. These rules are begun to be taught in infancy; and respectability, honor, love depend upon their observance. After her mind has been completely chained down . . . society wonders she has not been off exploring the regions of space for new ideas. [1]

Godey's Lady's Book for May, 1849, she described as "wishy-washy-milk-and-water, pointless and unmeaning, like the great mass of the literature of the day." In a piece comparing housewives to slaves, she explained why Pittsburgh's mothers did not excel at childrearing: "A *slave* is not the person to bring up a family aright! Your domestic drudge is no more fit to train up a family than she is fit for a heaven where there is no scrubbing brushes!'' [2]

Taxation without representation challenged her scorn: "I recognize the obligations of the moral law, because its giver had a right to dictate laws to me, but Congress and the State Legislature have no such right. I am not represented there, although I do pay taxes to support both." [3] Swisshelm summarized approvingly the work of E. P. Hurlburt, "Essays on Human Rights and Their Political Guaranties," which supported woman's suffrage. She gave recognition and praise to achievements by women such as Lucy Stone, Elizabeth Oakes Smith, and Elizabeth Blackwell, but she could not resist poking occasional fun at the achievers.

Although not exclusively a feminist paper, the *Saturday Visiter* was a forerunner of woman's rights periodicals that circulated in the following decades.

To its organizers, the great event of the early woman's rights movement was the first convention at Seneca Falls, New York, in 1848. Consequently, official historians of the suffrage movement give the Seneca Falls meeting an exaggerated role in establishing the woman's movement. In order to understand the significance of this early convention, it is important to comprehend its personal and social origins. The two prime movers, Elizabeth Cady Stanton and Lucretia Mott, had discussed woman's grievances at the London World's Anti-Slavery Convention in 1840, but both women were occupied in the years following it—Stanton with childbearing and housekeeping, Mott with religious controversies and missionary tours.

Stanton's experience played a key part in the background of Seneca Falls. A newcomer to reformist activities in 1840, she soon became acquainted with the Garrisonian abolitionists and their views of woman. In her first lecture on the temperance issue in 1842, she "infused into her speech a homeopathic dose of womans rights, & does the same in many private conversations." About this time she began to circulate Sarah Grimké's pamphlet, *The Equality of the Sexes*, and was deeply "oppressed with the reality" of woman's degradation. [4] Between 1843 and 1847, Elizabeth Stanton lived principally in the Boston area, a young matron enjoying frequent contact with radical abolitionists and other progressive thinkers. Undoubtedly meeting often with people like Maria Weston Chapman and Abby Kelley, she heard much discussion of woman's rights. Here also she was exposed to Margaret Fuller and read Fuller's *Woman in the Nineteenth Century*.

Another factor sometimes overlooked in interpreting the origins of the first woman's rights convention is that of the particular environment where it took place. The mill village of Seneca Falls was located in the heart of that region called the "Burned-Over District"—an area of central New York State peculiarly susceptible to religious revivals, reform movements, and moralistic "isms" of various sorts. Situated near the route of the Erie Canal, long a main thoroughfare for immigrants and traffic in perfectionist ideals—it has been called a "psychic highway" connecting New England with her "colonies" in the West—Seneca Falls had been exposed for years before 1848 to the heady influence of new ideas. [5] Temperance was a particular concern of Seneca Falls women, and Abby Kelley Foster and other Garrisonians had been through the region stirring up opposition to slavery among its women. Many women in Seneca Falls were thus alert to their duties as reformers, ready to discuss new ways of serving moral progress.

Elizabeth Cady Stanton left Boston in 1847 to set up housekeeping in Seneca Falls, where her husband hoped to renew his health and establish a successful law practice. She was quickly overwhelmed by the tedium of small-town life. Seneca Falls offered nothing to compare with the intellectual and social stimulation of Boston, and Stanton soon became bored with her domestic routine. In the spring of 1848 she was delighted to see that a measure she had long advocated, the married women's property law, was enacted. Not long after learning of the new law, she heard of the impending visit of Lucretia Mott to Martha Wright, her sister, in Auburn, near Seneca Falls.

It was a fortuitous decision to organize the first woman's rights convention. On July 13, 1848, Elizabeth Stanton traveled to nearby Waterloo, New York, where Lucretia Mott and Martha Wright were visiting with other Quakers—Jane Hunt and Mary Anne McClintock. The five friends poured out their hearts, expressing grievances freely, then decided to hold a convention dealing with these long-nourished complaints and submitted a "call" for a public meeting to the *Seneca County Courier*. Gathering again the next day, the women searched for models to give form to the meeting. Stanton hit on the Declaration of Independence as a basis for writing woman's Declaration of Sentiments, asserting the self-evident truth "that all men and women are created equal," and describing the "history of repeated injuries and usurpations on the part of man toward woman."

The Seneca Falls convention has been described many times. [6]

On the clear, warm morning of July 19, a crowd assembled at the Wesleyan Chapel. Finding the door locked, perhaps by a fearful clergyman or church elder, the women secured male assistance — "an embryo Professor of Yale College was lifted through an open window to unbar the door" — and the crowd of more than a hundred settled on church benches. The first session had been planned for women only, but due to the timidity felt by some participants, a man, James Mott, was asked to preside, and the meeting admitted both sexes without discrimination. Like most reform meetings of the period, this one included much talk and speech-making — two days and evenings of it. The most interesting moments came with the reading by Stanton of her Declaration of Sentiments. Her paraphrase of Jefferson summarized grievances that had been building up for nearly half a century, announcing a war cry for embattled woman that echoed again and again in the long suffrage struggle.

After cataloging woman's wrongs, the Seneca Falls convention presented a sharp call to action. A series of resolutions denounced all human laws contrary to the law of nature — the law of equality. Woman should claim the right to speak in public, she should demand a single moral standard, she should "move in the enlarged sphere which her great Creator has assigned her," she should secure the franchise and demand "an equal participation with men in the various trades, professions and commerce." It was woman's special duty "to promote every righteous cause by every righteous means; and especially in regard to the great subjects of morals and religion . . . to participate with her brother in teaching . . . by writing and by speaking, and by any instrumentalities proper to be used, and in any assemblies proper to be held. . . ." Stanton's most audacious demand, for suffrage, was so controversial that it became the only resolution not unanimously approved, despite eloquent support from the great abolitionist, Frederick Douglass.

Leaders of the Seneca Falls meeting were so pleased with their accomplishment, finding "there were still so many new points for discussion, and that the gift of tongues had been vouchsafed to them," that they issued the call for another meeting. Douglass's paper, the *North Star*, announced that a woman's rights convention would be held at Rochester on August 2, with a planning meeting scheduled for the first, and that the discussions would be presided over by women. Again Elizabeth Stanton read her Declaration of Sentiments, stimulating animated debates. Several men complained that woman would be removed from her sphere and feared that harmonious family relationships would be disrupted by the new doctrines. Against male opposition, Frederick Douglass again gave vigorous support to the demand for woman suffrage. The proceedings included a lengthy and searching discussion of the economic hardships endured by working women — seamstresses and domestic servants in particular. Lucretia Mott was more outspoken than she had been at Seneca Falls, insisting that oppressed women, like free blacks, must work to take their freedom, must *"themselves feel* and *act."* She attacked the flattery typically used to deceive women, such as "the sickly sentimentality of the 'Ladies Department' " in popular periodicals. Mott found the resolutions of this meeting too tame for her own advanced attitudes. The two first conventions, organized by the same basic group of leaders, depending on the tried experience of Lucretia Mott and the emerging talent of Elizabeth Cady Stanton, gave the woman's rights movement a firm identity.

Reactions around the country were largely critical or sarcastic. Stanton preserved a scrapbook of clippings to show how the press treated the new movement. Typical was the response of a New York State paper, the *Oneida Whig*:

> Seriously we respect woman as woman. She fills a place higher, more useful and far more appropriate when she acts in the sphere she has already enobled, than she could in any other capacity. A highly cultivated intellect has never shown to such advantage in women as when connected with domestic habits and a dignified appreciation of woman's calling. [7]

The New York *Herald* mocked these upstarts, suggesting that one of their "rights" should be to wield the sword: ". . . we confess it would go to our hearts to see them putting on the panoply of war, and mixing in scenes, it is said, the fair sex in Paris lately took a prominent part." Not all comment was unfavorable. The progressive *National Reformer*, of Rochester, urged: "To the ladies we say — act — agitate — bid high, you will not get, in this age, more than you demand." Frederick Douglass, in the *North Star*, expressed strong support for the new cause:

> We . . . express our conviction that all political rights which it is expedient for man to exercise, it is equally so for woman. All that distinguishes man as an intelligent and accountable being, is equally true for woman. . . . Our doctrine is that "Right is of no sex." We therefore bid the women engaged in this movement our humble God-speed. [8]

At least the "amazons" and "insurrectionaries" could gain satisfaction from the attention paid them.

Stanton hoped that the woman's rights movement would follow the course of other reforms, with additional conventions, agents, speakers, petitions to state and national legislatures and widespread publicity. Such a pattern eventually developed, but it came much more slowly than the leaders wished. From her home in Philadelphia, Lucretia Mott wrote to Elizabeth Stanton later in the year 1848:

> I am now trying to awaken sufficient interest, to hold a Woman's Rights Meeting in this city. It is far more difficult than we found it out West — Still there are numbers here, who feel a deep interest in the cause. Few however are accustomed to public speaking.
>
> We have been looking around for a suitable place to hold a meeting or convention in — There will be difficulty in obtaining one for that object. . . . Why cant thou & the McClintocks come on here to attend such a meeting? You are so wedded to this cause, that you must expect to act as pioneers in the work. [9]

The pioneers discovered only limited public sympathy for the new cause. Nevertheless, Stanton and Mott continued to lecture and write in woman's behalf, as their free time permitted.

The Seneca Falls convention stirred up a few women. Emily Collins, an obscure resident of Ontario County, New York, remembered the impact of the first convention on her life. Having long felt the wrongs of woman's condition, Collins appreciated the inspiration of Seneca Falls:

> But, it was the proceedings of the Convention, in 1848 . . . that first gave a direction to the efforts of the many women, who began to feel the degradation of their subject condition, and its baneful effects upon the human race. They then saw the necessity for associated action, in order to obtain the elective franchise, the only key that would unlock the doors of their prison. [10]

Collins and a few associates organized a local Woman's Equal Rights Union which survived for about a year, sending petitions to the state assembly, sponsoring debates and discussions of woman's rights. In 1849, Mrs. Elizabeth Wilson of Cadiz, Ohio, published ''A Scriptural View of Woman's Rights and Duties.'' The next year Frances Dana Gage of Morgan County, Ohio, organized and spoke at several woman's rights meetings in Ohio. Evidence is scattered, yet it suggests that an undercurrent of local woman's organizing took place in the late 1840s.

Publicity was essential to the new movement, not only by means of favorable notices in reform periodicals, but through its own publications.

While pamphlets could carry reports of meetings and speeches, woman's rights advocates wanted a more reliable vehicle to spread their message. This want was supplied by the *Lily*. Begun at Seneca Falls in 1849 as a temperance paper, and edited by Amelia Bloomer, the *Lily* quickly responded to the influence of Elizabeth Cady Stanton. Beginning in 1850, using the pseudonym Sun Flower, Stanton wrote increasingly for the new paper on subjects relating to woman's rights. From its exclusive concern with temperance, the *Lily* shifted its allegiance and soon carried the motto: Devoted to the Interests of Woman. The *Lily* gained national fame in 1851 for its advocacy of dress reform, the new costume being called "Bloomers" after the name of the editor.

1850 was a banner year for the cause of woman's rights. Two woman's conventions met in this year at Salem, Ohio, and Worcester, Massachusetts, signaling the establishment of woman's rights as an independent movement. On March 30, 1850, the *Anti-Slavery Bugle* carried the "call" for a women's convention to meet at Salem on April 19, "to concert measures to secure to all persons the recognition of Equal Rights, and the extention of the privileges of Government without distinction of sex or color." [11] This meeting came about because leading feminists were eager to influence the Ohio constitutional convention, scheduled to meet at Columbus in May to revise the state's charter. "The meeting of a Convention of men to amend the Constitution of *our* (?) State presents a most favorable opportunity for the agitation of this subject. Women of Ohio! We call upon you to come up to this work in womanly strength, and with womanly energy." The *Bugle*'s editor observed that woman's cause "has at length acquired a momentum that can no longer be resisted." [12]

Salem, Ohio, like Seneca Falls, was located in a geographical area highly susceptible to reform. Much of the surrounding territory had been settled by Pennsylvania Quakers of fairly radical persuasion. Interacting with these sympathetic spirits was a small but volatile group of radicals of New England descent. This population operated the Garrisonian Western Anti-Slavery Society and supported its journal, the *Anti-Slavery Bugle*. Here in April, 1850, the Ohio women's convention met, with many of the state's female abolitionists in attendance — Jane Elizabeth Jones, Mary Anne W. Johnson, Emily Robinson, Jane Trescott, Josephine Griffing, and Betsey M. Cowles. They heard letters from several leading feminists, including Lucretia Mott, Lucy Stone, Elizabeth Cady Stanton, Sarah Pugh, and others. Mott's *Discourse on Woman*, read by Jane Elizabeth Jones, was "listened to with marked interest by the whole Convention."

The inevitable "preamble and resolutions" drew their inspiration from the Declaration of Independence, asserting human equality, God-given rights, government by the consent of the governed, and other basic principles. The convention "Resolved, That all laws contrary to these fundamental principles, or in conflict with this great precept of nature, are of no binding obligation, not being founded on equity or justice." Ohio's women remembered arguments that had been discussed for nearly two decades — the comparison of women with slaves as an oppressed group, and the double moral standard as a particularly degrading injustice. They heard two original addresses, one by Jane Elizabeth Jones, entitled "The Wrongs of Woman." For the most part the women's discussions and resolutions covered ground that was widely known.

In two respects was the Ohio women's convention unusual. In accordance with their purpose, the women submitted a Memorial to the Ohio Constitutional Convention urging that they be afforded full legal equality with men, including suffrage. Their plea had no impact on the state constitution, although the issue of giving votes to women and blacks produced a spirited debate among the male constitution-makers in Columbus. Few other feminist meetings had such immediate negative results. The Salem meeting was also characterized by its exclusion of men from participation. The other sex could watch and listen to the proceedings, but they could not discuss or vote.

This convention, like its predecessor at Seneca Falls, received a mixed but generally unfavorable response from the press. Horace Greeley's New York *Tribune* admitted that woman deserved the right to vote as a natural right, and because her interests were not automatically cared for by man, but he speculated that delicate and domestic women would probably be apathetic or indifferent to politics. Woman voters, he feared, would be dominated and exploited by men. If women insisted on voting, they would be taking a "pledge" that their vote would be "faithfully and conscientiously used." He seemed to be applying a double standard to suffrage. In Wisconsin, a liberal editor attacked the ridicule being heaped on the Salem convention by other papers: "There is a kind of contemptible smartness and vulgar witticism, in which some editors indulge, when speaking of the position, rights, and duties of women which is not indicative of a high degree of refinement or virtue." [13] The Salem convention was significant in giving focus and identity to the interest in women's grievances that had grown in Ohio during the 1840s. From 1850 onward, annual meetings were held in the state to agitate for women. In 1852, the convention established the Ohio Woman's Rights Association, giving that state a major role in the woman's movement.

The first convention organized to represent a national interest in woman's rights took place at Worcester, Massachusetts, in October, 1850. Encouraged by the Salem convention and sensing a growing momentum for the new cause, a group of New England abolitionists began to plan for a meeting which would bring together woman's rights advocates from all the states. Paulina Wright Davis, Abby Kelley Foster, Lucy Stone, and four other women constituted a committee of arrangements for the assembly, but Davis, because she had free time and social connections, became the convention's chief organizer. She wrote to Elizabeth Stanton in July, explaining her hopes:

> You are already I presume fully aware of our movements in relation to a womans rights convention to be held in Worcester. . . . The convention is not designed to be a New England Con[vention] but a general one just so far as we can enlist attention to it, hence we ask your name and your husbands to the call and any others in that part of the state which you may think desirable to send me. We anticipate your presence with us with confidence. [14]

Scores of similar letters went to other feminists scattered through the northern states.

The *Liberator* of September 6 announced the convention for October 23 and 24. Ninety-one men and women from six states signed the announcement, whose list of supporters included many of the greatest reformers of the age. Besides such figures as Lucy Stone, Garrison, Wendell and Ann Phillips, and Elizabeth Stanton, it included William H. Channing, A. Bronson Alcott, Adin Ballou, Thomas Wentworth Higginson, Ralph Waldo Emerson, Gerrit Smith, and Maria Giddings, daughter of the noted abolitionist congressman, Joshua Giddings of Ohio.

The proceedings at Worcester typified reform meetings. Several notable speeches were made, including an address by Paulina Wright Davis, who had been chosen president of the convention, dealing with woman's wrongs and disabilities. The roster of speakers was more distinguished than that of any earlier woman's convention, since it included Garrison, Phillips, Douglass, Lucretia Mott, Ernestine Rose, and Sojourner Truth — the ex-slave woman and abolitionist. Dr. Harriot K. Hunt of Boston spoke on woman as physician, and Antoinette Brown, who had completed the theological course at Oberlin College but not been permitted to take a degree, discussed the scriptural basis of woman's equality with man. Several committees were appointed, including a

Central Committee which was authorized to schedule additional meetings in the future and serve as a continuing executive body. Specialized committees on education, industrial vocations, civil and political affairs, and social relations were also formed.

The Worcester convention climaxed the organizing process of the woman's rights movement. Following this occasion, the movement took on the characteristics of an independent, organized reform crusade, much like the antislavery agitation. Although no national society for women formed until after the Civil War, some local and state organizations were established in the 1850s, and the Central Committee, with such familiar leaders as Elizabeth Cady Stanton, Paulina Wright Davis, and Lucy Stone, as members, sponsored a variety of activities. This group saw to it that national woman's rights conventions were held annually, with the exception of 1857, through the decade. By means of conventions, publications, lecture tours, and other efforts, the feminists attracted a corps of able recruits to the movement — Elizabeth Oakes Smith, Caroline Healey Dall, Hannah Tracy Cutler, Susan B. Anthony, and many others. The vigorous activity of this decade is chronicled in the *History of Woman Suffrage* and other accounts and collections.

The successful launching of the independent movement for woman's rights obscured a basic internal problem that would have serious effects in less than two decades. As an outgrowth from the antislavery movement, the woman's rights crusade naturally attracted most of its leaders from the older agitation. For some abolitionists, however, the appeal of woman's rights seemed to conflict with the needs of antislavery. Abby Kelley Foster, a great contributor to the growth of woman's rights sentiment, considered abolition to be the supreme reform of the age and, although she was anxious for woman's emancipation, she devoted her primary energies to the crusade against slavery. Lucy Stone faced a similar dilemma. She hoped, after graduating from Oberlin College, to work for woman's rights. Yet at that time there was no opportunity to earn a livelihood in the new reform.

Jane Elizabeth Jones urged Stone to work as an antislavery lecturer, writing in 1847: "Is it not better to go forward & take our rights — show our independence — establish our equality — make the world feel that we are not intellectually inferior rather than tarry to discuss the question? ..."[15] It was the argument used by Theodore Weld a decade earlier in an unsuccessful attempt to dissuade the Grimké sisters from lecturing on woman's rights. During the 1850s Lucy Stone shifted back and forth between the two reforms. When, after the Civil War, she was pressed to choose between woman and the former slaves, in deciding which had the greater need for suffrage, she would not sacrifice Negro voting by opposing the fifteenth amendment.

Other abolitionists and feminists reacted differently to the priorities of woman's cause versus black rights. Jane Elizabeth Jones eventually saw no inconsistency in advocating both, and spoke well at the first Ohio women's convention. She later served as a lecturer on women's anatomy and physiology, then returned to advocating both woman's rights and abolition. Lucretia Mott moved easily between the two reforms. Another wing of the woman's movement had far less commitment to the antislavery cause and gave its dedicated allegiance to women. Paulina Wright Davis and Elizabeth Cady Stanton were more concerned for women's interests than for the needs of blacks, and when offered a choice in the struggle over the fifteenth amendment, between giving the vote to black males and denying it to women, they turned against the Negro.

The half-century leading up to its organization gave the woman's rights movement many goals and characteristics that would dominate its conduct into the twentieth century. Its basic aim, to achieve human rights, was inherited directly from the antislavery movement. All humans are equal in the sight of God and nature, was the assumption, equal not necessarily in talents or endowments, but in basic rights and responsibilities. Aileen Kraditor has identified this approach as the argument for *justice*, eternal and undifferentiated, not dependent on gender. [16]

This fundamental demand subsumed a long list of specific wants which evolved out of woman's experiences between 1800 and 1850, and were reflected in the feminist writings and addresses of Frances Wright, Angelina and Sarah Grimké, Margaret Fuller, Lucretia Mott, and Elizabeth Cady Stanton. Woman's most obvious claims for justice involved legal rights. Some victories had already been won with the enactment of statutes enabling married women to control their own property, and feminists were optimistic about legislating reform of the rights of contracts, guardianship of children, divorce, financial and other legal rights. The right to vote was not yet the single issue dominating all others, but it had been asserted as a basic symbol of and means of access to real power in a government deriving its authority from the people.

Feminists also applied the argument for justice to woman's economic situation. They observed an apparent deterioration in woman's economic worth as new industries employed female operatives and as a cash-oriented economy replaced older patterns of exchange. In the textile mills women received much less pay than men for doing the same or similar work. In other occupations employing both sexes, such as the needle trades or schoolteaching, women earned half or a third of the wages paid to men. Educational reformers, in promoting the employment of women teachers, boasted of the lower pay and cost reductions made possible by hiring women. In some occupations self-supporting women could not earn subsistence income. Hence, equal pay for equal work became a significant feminist drive for justice.

The argument for justice led to demands for equal education. Most feminists had been well educated for their time, yet the educational system frustrated many women's ambitions to study the classics, the sciences, or other demanding intellectual disciplines. It is little wonder, then, that throughout the nineteenth century advocates of women sought educational opportunities equal to those of men, including access to all studies at every level of instruction, and an institutional environment that would encourage women to strive for learning. Another related campaign for justice was the effort to open wider professional opportunities for women in fields such as medicine, the ministry, law, or college teaching. Both educational barriers and prejudice kept able women out of these fields.

Moral equality was still another application of the justice argument. Feminists fought against the double moral standard in several ways. The female moral reform movement included a drive to eliminate prostitution and the sexual exploitation of women by men, including immorality within marriage. Moral reformers insisted that both sexes be governed by a single moral standard, that men be condemned like women for sexual misconduct. They would bring man *up* to the moral standards of woman. Moral equality, not superiority or subordination, was the feminist principle. The double standard served in other ways to discriminate against woman. On the grounds of "impropriety," she had been refused the right to speak or participate in "promiscuous" assemblies of reformers, or even to pray aloud in religious meetings. In the name of justice, woman's advocates argued against these disabilities and for freedom of speech and action as basic human rights.

Underlying the woman's rights movement was another basic attitude at variance with the ideology of women's "appropriate sphere" and its complex limitations. Feminists wanted women to achieve *autonomy*. Men, they felt, were free to decide for themselves how they would conduct their lives, by having access to social, economic, and political power. By means of this power they also determined for women the circumstances of their lives. Aileen Kraditor has described the craving for autonomy: "The feminists' desire has, consequently, been for women to be recognized, in the economic, political, and/or social realms, as individuals in their own right." And further, "The essential change demanded has always been that women's 'sphere' must be defined by women." [17]

Autonomy, of course, was closely tied to justice. In order to define their own lives women needed equality with men in each area where choice existed. The drive for autonomy aimed particularly at modifying the concept of woman's subordinate "sphere," removing useless and binding restrictions. Before 1850 the advocates of woman's rights protested against the limitations placed on women by orthodox religious interpretations of their "sphere" and enforced by clergymen. The feminists argued that woman had the same rights of conscience as man, and the same responsibilities to practice her religious and moral convictions. If these practices interfered with men's privileges and power, men had no business in denying her autonomy. So, too, the feminists argued that woman had the right to govern her own body, to reject her husband's sexual advances and limit her fertility.

Health reform also supported autonomy and woman's control of her body. Health reformers and feminists agreed that the right to good health was basic to other demands of women. They sought to spread information about the causes of disease, the means of prevention, and they attempted to organize new systems of treatment, using women as physicians. The right to health also required reform of various fashionable but injurious practices. Thus dress reform was necessary to eliminate the constricting garments which endangered health and impeded mobility and exercise for women. Assumptions about woman's "delicacy" and inability to endure physical or mental exertion also came under attack. Feminists differed markedly with the majority of their contemporaries in believing that corrupt custom, not natural limitations or inferiority, undermined and deformed the lives of American women. Autonomy would be the antidote to woman's degradation.

A few generalizations can be made about characteristics of the woman's rights movement. Like most other contemporary efforts to bring about change, the crusade originated and gained its adherents from the middle class. Middle-class women were not the most downtrodden Americans of their gender, but they felt more need to articulate their grievances than women of greater or lesser social standing. Some students of the woman's movement have recently explained the appeal of woman's rights in terms of status deprivation. Americans of the nineteenth century experienced rising levels of aspiration. For enterprising middle-class males, opportunities seemed wide open. In an expanding economy they could enter the professions; as restrictions on suffrage were relaxed, they could vote more freely; or they might go west and build new communities.

For women, on the other hand, life was quite different. With their expectations severely constrained by attitudes toward their "appropriate sphere," they had to be onlookers in the race for success, dependent on men for their status. Unlike lower-class women, who had no energy to spare from the struggle to survive, middle-class women were generally supported in decent style with leisure to become involved in religious and reformist activities if they felt so inclined. The status of middle-class women tended also to be more insecure than that of other groups because they belonged to families whose situations in life might easily change, reducing them to genteel poverty or raising them to *nouveau riche*. Yet they themselves could in no way, except by marrying well, contribute to their own advancement or achieve goals which came readily to men. Relative to men they had lost ground during the first half of the nineteenth century. Thus they had cause to feel status anxiety and status deprivation keenly.

The advocates of woman's rights had other experiences in common. They usually came to the cause from kindred movements—most often antislavery and temperance. Many had gone through religious crises in which they grew alienated from the orthodox faith of their upbringing and became more evangelical, or liberal, or both. Often the religious change was associated with new attitudes about women. Lucretia Mott joined the liberal evangelical Hicksite sect of the Society of Friends when the Society divided during the 1820s. Elizabeth Cady Stanton, who had been reared in a rigidly Presbyterian home, moved after 1840 toward Unitarianism and free thinking. Rejecting the aristocratic and patriarchal Episcopal church, Sarah and Angelina Grimké joined the Society of Friends, then drifted into a humanitarian faith of their own devising. In Pennsylvania and New England, many feminists were liberal Quakers, in Massachusetts and New York, Unitarianism was the denomination of many, and elsewhere Universalism and other liberal doctrines attracted many women's advocates.

Their experience with religious and reformist enterprises provided most supporters of woman's rights with a sense of sisterhood essential to the new undertaking. Leaders of the movement were also much more highly educated than typical middle-class women. None was satisfied, however, with the educational opportunities available to them. Advanced training only widened the gap between their aspirations and their achievements within woman's limited sphere.

Geographically, the sources of this reform were similiar to those of its sister movements. The most fertile center of woman's rights agitation was the belt of Yankee settlements extending westward from Boston, through central Massachusetts, through central New York State, through northern Ohio (the Western Reserve or "New Connecticut"), into northern Indiana, southern Michigan, central and northern Illinois, Wisconsin, Iowa, and Kansas. A secondary distribution of feminist sentiment had grown up in the area connecting Philadelphia and its Quaker offshoots into western Pennsylvania, Ohio, Indiana, and Michigan. Evidence suggests that the woman's rights agitation took hold more readily in smaller and medium-sized cities—Worcester, Rochester, Syracuse, Akron, Seneca Falls, Salem, Ohio—than in great metropolitan centers. But there was constant movement between the large cities and smaller places, and a continual interchange and flow of reform energies. The South, with its plantation economy and its "peculiar institution" of slavery, was closed to the agitation of woman's rights until a much later period.

The struggle for woman's rights was a product of change—the spirit of perfectionism demanding improvement in established institutions and in human individuals, industrialization and modernization, changing the patterns of women's work and elevating their aspirations, and the consciousness among many middle-class women that they as a group had common goals requiring collective action to achieve. In its turn, the woman's rights movement became an engine of change, challenging conventional attitudes, demanding the end of restrictions, expanding opportunities for women, and helping to organize them nationally. The movement's purposes, momentous yet simple, were described by an advocate in 1850:

> I shall claim nothing for ourselves because of our sex. . . . We should demand *our* recognition as equal members of the human family; as persons to whom pertain all the rights which grow out of our relations to God, and to each other, as human beings; and when this point is once established, the term "Woman's Rights" will become obsolete, for none will entertain the idea that the rights of women differ from the rights of men. It is then *human* rights for which we contend. [18]

The early feminists began a struggle for equality and autonomy which continued through the nineteenth and into the late twentieth century. What they aimed to achieve was nothing less than a revolution in human attitudes. We have not yet seen the culmination of this revolution, but the ideals and accomplishments of its pioneers remain alive and significant today.

NOTES

CHAPTER 1

1. Maria J. McIntosh, *Woman in America: Her Work and Her Reward* (New York: 1850), pp. 22-3.

2. *Ohio Observer* (Hudson, Ohio), April 13, 1837, p. 14.

3. Margaret Coxe, *Claims of the Country on American Females* (Columbus, Ohio: 1842), 1: 29.

4. Edith Abbot, *Women in Industry* (New York: 1910), p. 47.

5. Harriet H. Robinson, *Loom and Spindle, or Life Among the Early Mill Girls...*(New York: 1898), pp. 69, 77; Harriet Martineau, *Society in America*, 2nd ed. (New York: 1837), 2: 41-3, 54, 138-9.

6. Abbott, *Women in Industry,* pp. 66-83, 352-382; different statistics are offered in W. Elliot Brownlee and Mary M. Brownlee, *Women in the American Economy: A Documentary History, 1675-1929* (New Haven, Conn.: 1976), pp. 1-31, 153-83.

7. Joseph Story, *Commentaries on Equity Jurisprudence, As Administered in England and America* (Boston: 1836), 1: 32-3; Mary R. Beard, *Woman as Force in History* (New York: 1946), chs. 4-8.

8. Story, *Commentaries,* 2: 655.

9. On the New York women's property law, see Thomas Hertell, *Remarks Comprising in Substance Judge Hertell's Argument in the House of Assembly...1837, in Support of the Bill to Restore to Married Women "The Right of Property"...*(New York: 1839); Elizabeth Cady Stanton, Susan B. Anthony, and Matilda Joslyn Gage, *History of Woman Suffrage* (New York: 1881), 1: 63-7, 99-100; Yuri Suhl, *Ernestine L. Rose and the Battle for Human Rights* (New York: 1959), chs. 6-7; Charles Z. Lincoln, *Constitutional History of New York* (Rochester, N.Y.: 1906),2: 112-4. For Pennsylvania, see Ward W. Pierson, "Property Rights of Married Women in Pennsylvania," *University Lectures Delivered by Members of the Faculty in the Free Public Lecture Course, 1915-1916* (Philadelphia: 1916), 3: 348-353.

10. Beard, *Woman as Force, p. 109.*

11. Sir William Blackstone, *Commentaries on the Laws of England* (London: 1813), 1: 444.

12. Thorstein Veblen, *The Theory of the Leisure Class* (New York: 1953), pp. 46, 68-70, 232.

13. *American Freeman* (Prairieville, Wisc.), April 2, 1845. For an analysis of woman's "sphere," see Barbara Welter, "The Cult of True Womanhood: 1820-1860," *American Quarterly* 18 (Summer 1966): 151-74.

14. Daniel Chapin, *A Discourse Delivered Before the Charitable Female Society in Groton, Oct. 19, 1814* (Andover, Mass.: 1814), p.8.

15. Elizabeth Erskine, "Female Education, Its Importance, and in What it Should Consist," *Common School Assistant* (June 1839): 44.

16. W. R. DeWitt, *Woman: Her Excellence and Usefulness* (Harrisburg, Penn.: 1841), p. 41.

17. *Signal of Liberty* (Ann Arbor, Mich.), July 4, 1846, p. 42; Constitution of the Marietta, Ohio, Bethel Association, Ms., Ohio Historical Society.

18. Coxe, *Claims...on American Females,* 1: 32.

19. Lydia Maria Child, *The Mother's Book,* 6th ed. (New York: 1844): on motherhood in general, see Anne L. Kuhn, *The Mother's Role in Childhood Education: New England Concepts, 1830-1860* (New Haven, Conn.: 1947).

20. Catharine E. Beecher, "Suggestions Respecting Improvements in Education" (1829), quoted in Clifton J. Furness, ed., *The Genteel Female: An Anthology* (New York: 1931), pp. 210-11.

21. Hannah Mather Crocker, *Observations on the Real Rights of Women, with their Appropriate Duties Agreeable to Scripture, Reason and Common Sense* (Boston: 1818), pp. 17, 20.

22. Lydia Sigourney, *Letters to Young Ladies* (New York: 1837), p. 15.

23. There is a large and growing literature on the history of childhood. Pertinent to this discussion are Philippe Ariés, *Centuries of Childhood: A Social History of Family Life,* tr. Robert Baldick (New York: 1962); Ross W. Beales, Jr., "In Search of the Historical Child: Miniature Adulthood and Youth in Colonial New England," *American Quarterly* 27 (October 1975): 379-98; Lloyd deMause, ed., *The History of Childhood* (New York: 1974); John Demos, *A Little Commonwealth; Family Life in Plymouth Colony* (New York: 1970); Bernard Wishy, *The Child and the Republic: the Dawn of Modern American Child Nurture* (Philadelphia: 1968).

24.   Jessie Bernard, *The Future of Motherhood* (New York: 1975), p. 12; see also Anne F. Scott, "Woman's Perspective on the Patriarchy in the 1850s," *Journal of American History,* (June 1974): 52-64.

25.   Lydia Sigourney, *Letters to Mothers* (Hartford, Conn.: 1838), preface; see also John S. C. Abbott, *The Mother at Home; or the Principles of Maternal Duty Familiarly Illustrated* (New York: 1833), pp. 117-33.

CHAPTER 2

1.   L. H. Butterfield et al., eds., *The Book of Abigail and John: Selected Letters of the Adams Family, 1762-1784* (Cambridge, Mass.: 1975), p. 218.

2.   Lawrence A. Cremin, *American Education: The Colonial Experience 1607-1783* (New York: 1970), p. 561; see also pp. 375-412, 479-543.

3.   Catharine E. Beecher, "Female Education," *American Journal of Education 2,* no. 4 (April 1827): 221.

4.   Emma Willard, *An Address to the Public; Particularly to the Legislature of New York, Proposing a Plan for Improving Female Education* (Middlebury, Vt.: 1819), pp. 28-40.

5.   *Ibid.,* pp. 19-20.

6.   *Ibid.,* pp. 3-4.

7.   Beecher's most popular work, a manual of housekeeping and domestic economy, went through many reprintings and revisions: *Treatise on Domestic Economy for the Use of Young Ladies at Home and at School* (Boston: 1841). The present interpretation of Beecher's career is indebted to Kathryn Kish Sklar, *Catharine Beecher, A Study in American Domesticity* (New Haven: 1973).

8.   L. T. Guilford, comp., *The Use of a Life: Memorials of Mrs. Z. P. Grant Banister* (New York: 1886). A great many letters, documents, and other manuscripts in the Mount Holyoke College Archives deal with Zilpah Grant's and Mary Lyon's work at Ipswich Seminary.

9.   Mary Lyon, "Schools for Adult Females," Ms., Mount Holyoke College Archives, p. 11.

10.   [Mrs. Russel Sage] *Emma Willard and her Pupils or Fifty Years of Troy Female Seminary 1822-1872* (New York: 1898) pp. 14-5.

11.   Betsey M. Cowles to her sister Cornelia, October 13, 1838, Ms., courtesy of Mrs. Robert Ticknor, Austinburg, Ohio.

12.   *American Annals of Education and Instruction 3* (August 1833): 361-7, and (September 1833): 404-17; *Common School Assistant*

3 (September 1838): 69.

13. *Connecticut Common School Journal 1* (September 1, 1838): 10; also ibid., 1 (May 1838): 4.

14. Quoted in the *Common School Journal 1* (July 15, 1839): 224, and *Connecticut Common School Journal 2* (April 1, 1840): 168.

15. *Common School Journal 1* (June 1, 1839): 161. Mann frequently discussed the employment of female teachers in glowing terms, as in his Fourth Annual Report as Secretary of the Massachusetts Board of Education, *Common School Journal 3* (October 1, 1841): 303-4.

16. *Ibid.*

17. Statistics are abstracted from the *Common School Journal, Common School Assistant,* and *Connecticut Common School Journal,* 1838-1841.

18. *Connecticut Common School Journal 2* (March 1, 1840): 155; ibid., 1 (March 15, 1839): 118-9.

19. Michael Katz, *The Irony of Early School Reform: Educational Innovation in Mid-Nineteenth Century Massachusetts* (Cambridge, Mass.: 1968). pp. 58, 224; Thomas E. Woody, *A History of Women's Education in the United States* (New York and Lancaster, Penn.: 1929), 1: 496-500; Barnard's *American Journal of Education 1* (March 1856): 371-80.

20. *Connecticut Common School Journal 3* (May 1, 1841): 141-2.

21. Numerous letters in the Betsey Mix Cowles Papers, in the possession of Mrs. Robert Ticknor of Austinburg, Ohio, and many examples of correspondence of teachers in the Mount Holyoke College Archives indicate the enthusiasm and sense of purpose of these early nineteenth-century schoolmarms.

22. Gerda Lerner, "The Lady and the Mill Girl: Changes in the Status of Women in the Age of Jackson," *Midcontinent American Studies Journal 10* (Spring 1969): 11-15.

CHAPTER 3

1. Quoted in Mason Wade, *Margaret Fuller: Whetstone of Genius* (New York: 1940), pp. 90-1.

2. William R. Taylor and Christopher Lasch, "Two Kindred Spirits: Sorority and Family in New England," *New England Quarterly 36* (March 1963): p. 31, 23-41.

3. Carroll Smith-Rosenberg, "The Female World of Love and Ritual: Relations Between Women in Nineteenth-Century America,"

Signs: Journal of Women in Culture and Society 1 (Autumn 1975): 15.

4. On the Grimké sisters, see Gerda Lerner, *The Grimké Sisters from South Carolina, Rebels Against Slavery* (Boston: 1967); on the Blackwell family, see Alice S. Rossi, ed., *The Feminist Papers From Adams to de Beauvoir* (New York: 1973), pp. 323-46.

5. Catharine Beecher to Mary Dutton, February 8, 1830, Ms., Yale University Library.

6. Rossi, *The Feminist Papers*, p. 378.

7. Zilpah P. Grant, "The character of Ipswich Fem. Sem...." Ms. ca. 1835, Mount Holyoke College Archives; see also Zilpah P. Grant to Rev. Rufus Anderson, February 23, 1837, Mount Holyoke College Archives.

8. "Candidates for Mount Holyoke Female Seminary" (circular, n.p., n.d.); Mary Lyon to Rev. Theron Baldwin, July 12, 1838, Ms., Mount Holyoke College Archives.

9. M. A. Gillett to Sarah Rowland, July 21, 1832, Ms., Mount Holyoke College Archives.

10. Sabrina Jennings to Mary Lyon, October 3, 1844, Ms., Mount Holyoke Archives.

11. D. P. Labaree to Mary Lyon, December 12, 1831, Ms., Mount Holyoke College Archives.

12. Journal of Lydia Ann Stow, August 16, 1842, January, 18, 1840, Ms., Framingham State College Archives, Framingham, Mass.

13. Constitution and Record Book of the "Ladies Reasoning Assembly" of Cazenovia, New York, October 19, 1818—July 10, 1819, Ms., Ohio Historical Society Library, Columbus, Ohio, Preamble to the Constitution.

14. *Ibid.,* entry of November 3, 1818, July 10, 1819.

15. Minutes of the Young Ladies Society for Intellectual Improvement (later the Literary Society for Young People of Austinburg), Ms., Betsey Cowles Papers. Constitution of the Society.

16. Almira Eaton to Weltha Brown, August 23, 1816, Ms., Weltha Brown correspondence, Schlesinger Library; other letters by the same young woman exhibit religious concerns. Southern women also shared religious anxieties: see Ann Firor Scott, *The Southern Lady: From Pedestal to Politics* (Chicago: 1970), pp. 10-14.

17. Susan Burnham to Zilpah P. Grant, December 8, 1837, Ms., Mount Holyoke College Archives.

18. Mary Lyon to Zilpah P. Grant, July 25, 1826, Ms., Mount Holyoke College Archives.

19. Maria Cowles to Rev. Henry Cowles, July 14, 1831, typed

copy, Mount Holyoke College Archives.

20. *Christian Repository* (Utica, N.Y.), 2 (May 1823): 156; *A Narrative of the Revival of Religion in the County of Oneida Particularly in the Bounds of the Presbytery of Oneida, in the Year 1826* (Utica, N.Y. 1826), pp. 17-8; Whitney R. Cross, *The Burned-Over District: The Social and Intellectual History of Enthusiastic Religion in Western New York, 1800-1850* (Ithaca, N.Y.: 1950), pp. 84-9.

21. "Narrative of the State of Religion within the bounds of the General Assembly of the Presbyterian Church...," *Religious Intelligencer* (New Haven, Conn.), June 15, 1816, p. 45.

22. *A Narrative of the Revival...in ...Oneida...*, p. 30.

23. Stephen Peet to Rev. Milton Badger, February 24, 1825, Ms. letter (copy) in the Presbyterian Historical Society Library, Philadelphia.

24. Sarah Trimmer, *The Oeconomy of Charity, or, An Address to the Ladies Concerning Sunday Schools, etc.* (London: 1787), p. 48.

25. Ethan Smith, *A Sermon Preached to the Ladies of the Cent Institution, in Hopkinton, New Hampshire, August 14, 1814* (Concord, N.H.: 1814), p. 8; also *Report on the Concerns of the New Hampshire Cent Institution, for September, 1816 by the Committee of the Missionary Society* (Concord, N.H.: 1816): Edwin J. Aiken, *The First Hundred Years of the New Hampshire Bible Society, 1812-1912* (Concord, N.H.: 1912), pp. 66-7.

26. *The Fourth Annual Report of the...American Bible Society....* (New York: 1820),pp. 97-8.

27. Thomas Barnard, *A Sermon Preached Before the Salem Female Charitable Society...*(Salem, Mass.: 1803), p. 17.

28. *National Anti-Slavery Standard* (New York), July 15, 1841, p.22

29. Lucy Larcom, *A New England Girlhood* (New York: 1889), pp. 178-9. See also Hannah Josephson, *The Golden Threads: New England's Mill Girls and Magnates* (New York: 1949), chs. 4-5, 9.

30. *Lynn Record,* June 4, June 18, 1834.

31 *Lynn Record,* February 19, 1834.

32. Quoted in Keith E. Melder, "Woman's High Calling: The Teaching Profession in America, 1830-1860." *American Studies 13* (Fall 1972); 30.

CHAPTER 4

1. John L. Thomas, "Romantic Reform in America, 1815-1865," *American Quarterly 17* (Winter 1965): 662, 656-81; Perry

Miller, *The Life of the Mind in America from the Revolution to the Civil War* (New York: 1965), pp. 3-35.

2. *Annual Report of the Directors to the Penitent Females' Society,* in Justin Edwards, *Joy in Heaven over the Penitent. A Sermon...Before the Penitent Females' Refuge Society* (Boston: 1826), p.24.

3. *Second Annual Report of the Boston Female Moral Reform Society* (Boston: 1837), pp. 10-11.

4. *Third Annual Report of the Boston Female Moral Reform Society* (Boston: 1838), p.7.

5. New England Golden Rule Association, *Prospectus for Publishing a New Periodical, to be Called the Golden Rule* (Boston: 1839). See also Carroll Smith Rosenberg, "Beauty, the Beast and the Militant Woman: A Case Study in Sex Roles and Social Stress in Jacksonian America," *American Quarterly 23* (Fall 1971), pp. 562-84.

6. *Temperance Almanac...1834* (Albany, N.Y.: 1833), p. 48, also pp. 15-24. See also the *Journal of Humanity; and Herald of the American Temperance Society,* September 23, 1830, p. 70. John A. Krout, *The Origins of Prohibition* (New York: 1925) is a good general study of this period of temperance agitation.

7. Alice Felt Tyler, *Freedom's Ferment* (Minneapolis, Minn.: 1944), pp.324-7; American Temperance Society, *Permanent Temperance Documents* (New York: 1852), 1: 156-61, 342, 344; Krout, *Origins of Prohibition,* pp. 143-4, 148-150, 215-6.

8. *Massachusetts Cataract and Worcester County Waterfall,* vol.3, April 23, 1845.

9. *Journal of Humanity,* August 16, 1832, p. 49.

10. William Lloyd Garrison to Helen Garrison, September 21, 1838, in Wendell P. and Francis J. Garrison, *William Lloyd Garrison 1805-1879, The Story of his Life Told by his Children* (New York: 1885), 2: 227-8. See also Merle E. Curti, "Non-Resistance in New England," *New England Quarterly 2* (January 1929), pp. 34-57.

11. Boston *Liberator,* January 7, 1832, p. 2; November 2, 1833, p. 173.

12. *Ibid.,* July 13, 1833, p. 111.

13. Theodore Dwight Weld, comp., *American Slavery As It Is: Testimony of a Thousand Witnesses* (New York: 1839), p. 15.

14. *Liberator,* March 3, 1832. p. 34; August 27, 1836, p. 138; January 2, 1837, p. 2: Address of the Boston Female Anti-Slavery Society, Ms., Boston Public Library, Department of Rare Books and Manuscripts.

15. Ms. speech, undated, probably given during the late 1840s by Betsey M. Cowles, Cowles Papers. Another narrative describing the "Influence of Slavery on the Character of the Mistress," and a fervent poem, "The Slave Mother & Child," are in the Cowles Papers, suggesting the great appeal of this theme.

16. *Liberator,* January 14, 1832, p. 6.

17. *Ibid.,* January 2, 1837, p.2; May 21, 1836, p. 81.

18. Maria Weston Chapman, ed., *Harriet Martineau's Autobiography and Memorials of Harriet Martineau* (Boston: 1877), 2: 252. See also 1: 335-80, 2: 252-65, 273-7; Rossi, *Feminist Papers,* pp. 118-24.

19. A. A. Guthrie to Betsey M. Cowles, October 29, 1835, Ms., Betsey Cowles Papers.

20. Augustus Wattles to Betsey Cowles, April 9, 1836, Ms., Betsey Cowles Papers.

CHAPTER 5

1. Lydia Maria Child, *An Appeal in Favor of That Class of Americans Called Africans* (Boston: 1833), p. 232.

2. Samuel J. May, *Some Recollections of Our Antislavery Conflict* (Boston: 1869), p. 98.

3. Sarah Josepha Hale, *Woman's Record; or Sketches of All Distinguished Women...*(New York: 1853), p. 620.

4. *Liberator,* September 7, 1833, pp. 141-2.

5. *Ibid.,* August 29, 1835, p. 136.

6. *Sixth Annual Report of the Philadelphia Female Anti-Slavery Society* (Philadelphia: 1840), p. 10.

7. James Forten, Jr., *An Address Delivered Before the Ladies Anti-Slavery Society of Philadelphia, on the Evening of the 14th of April, 1836* (Philadelphia: 1836), p. 13.

8. Minutes of the Philadelphia Female Anti-Slavery Society, December 8, 1836, Mss., Historical Society of Pennsylvania.

9. Theodore D. Weld to Lewis Tappan, March 18, 1834, in *Letters of Theodore Dwight Weld, Angelina Grimké Weld and Sarah Grimké; 1822-1844* (hereafter referred to as *Weld-Grimké Letters),* ed. Gilbert H. Barnes and Dwight L. Dummond (New York: 1934), 1: 132-5; see also Gilbert H. Barnes, *The Anti-Slavery Impulse 1830-1844* (New York: 1964), pp. 68-9.

10. Emeline Bishop to Theodore Weld, March, 1835, *Weld-Grimké Letters,* 1: 214; see also *Weld-Grimké Letters,* 2: 995-9.

11.   Samuel Wells to Weld, December 15, 1834, January 8, 1835, *ibid.*, pp. 179, 191-2.

12.   Susan B. Wattles to Betsey M. Cowles, June 30, 1838, Ms., Betsey M. Cowles Papers, in the possession of Mrs. Robert Ticknor, Austinburg, Ohio. See also Jennett Raymond to Betsey Cowles, September 5, 1839, Betsey Cowles to Martha I. Root, September 28, 1842, Mss., Cowles Papers.

13.   Massachusetts Anti-Slavery Fair of 1840, Ms., Report, Boston Public Library.

14.   Abby Kelley to Henry G. Chapman, 2nd mo. 22, 1837 and Abby Kelley to Anne W. Weston, 6th mo. 17, 1837, Mss.; Anne W. Weston To Deborah Weston, February 13, 1837, Ms.; Lucy M. Ball, Treasurer of the Boston Female Anti-Slavery Society, to William Lloyd Garrison, January 30, 1836, Ms., Boston Public Library.

15.   "Address of the Boston Female Anti-Slavery Society to the Women of New England," *Right and Wrong in Boston, Number Three: Annual Report of the Boston Female Anti-Slavery , Society... 1837* (Boston: 1837), p. 97.

16.   Juliana Tappan to Anne W. Weston, July 21, 1837, Ms. Boston Public Library.

17.   *Memorial of Sarah Pugh, A Tribute of Respect From her Cousins* (Philadelphia: 1888), p. 22.

18.   Mary Grew, in "Anti-Slavery Album," Ms., Library of Congress, p. 153.

19.   Gilbert H. Barnes, *The Anti-Slavery Impulse*, p. 141.

20.   Samuel Flagg Bemis, *John Quincy Adams and the Union* (New York: 1956), p. 368.

21.   *Ibid.*, p. 369; see also the *Emancipator*, July 19, 1838, p. 47.

22.   Mary Grew, "Anti-Slavery Album," p. 153.

23.   *Proceedings of the Anti-Slavery Convention of American Women, New York, 1837* (New York: 1837), pp. 8-9; Minutes of the Philadelphia Female Anti-Slavery Society, September 14, 1837, Ms.

24.   American Anti-Slavery Society Records, Minutes of the Committee on Agencies for July 13, 1836, Ms., Boston Public Library.

CHAPTER 6

1.   Angelina to Sarah Grimké, August 1, 1836, Ms., Weld-Grimké Papers. Clements Library, University of Michigan. The pamphlet was published by the American Anti-Slavery Society.

2.   American Anti-Slavery Society Records, Minutes of the

NOTES 169

Committee on Agencies, July 13, August 2, 1836, Mss., Boston Public Library. See also Angelina Grimké to Jane Smith, September 18, 1836, Ms., Weld-Grimké Papers.

3. Angelina Grimké to Jane Smith, February 4, 1837, Ms., Weld-Grimké Papers.

4. Angelina Grimké to Jane Smith, November 19, and not dated, 1836, Mss., Weld-Grimké Papers. See also Benjamin P. Thomas, *Theodore Weld: Crusader for Freedom* (New Brunswick, N.J.: 1950), pp. 118-21.

5. Theodore Weld to Sarah and Angelina Grimké May 22, 1837, *Weld-Grimké Letters*, 1: 389.

6. *Proceedings of the Anti-Slavery Convention of American Women...May...1837* (New York: 1837), pp. 8-9, 18, see also Angelina Grimké, *An Appeal to the Women of the Nominally Free States, Issued by an Anti-Slavery Convention of American Women* (New York: 1837), pp. 5-6, 10, 19.

7. Angelina Grimké to Jane Smith, May 29, 1837, Ms., Weld-Grimké Papers.

8. Letter dated Boston, May 6, 1837, published in the *Proceedings of the Anti-Slavery Convention of American Women...1837*.

9. *Right and Wrong in Boston, Number Three: Annual Report of the Boston Female Anti-Slavery Society for 1837* (Boston: 1837), pp. 42-3.

10. Angelina Grimké to Jane Smith, May 29, 1837, Ms., Weld-Grimké Papers; see also Henry C. Wright, Journal, vol. 35, July 31, 1837, Ms., Boston Public Library.

11. Henry C. Wright, Journal, vol. 35, June 29, 1837, Ms., Boston Public Library.

12. Angelina Grimké to Jane Smith, September 15, 1837, Ms., Weld-Grimké Papers.

13. Angelina Grimké to Jane Smith, October 6, 1837, Ms., Weld-Grimké papers.

14. Boston *Recorder*, July 14, 1837, pp. 109-10.

15 Parsons Cooke, *Female Preaching Unlawful and Inexpedient...*(Lynn, Mass.: 1837), pp. 9-10.

16. Angelina Grimké to Theodore Weld, n.d. 1837, Ms., Weld-Grimké Papers.

17. Angelina Grimké to Theodore Weld, August 12, 1837, *Weld-Grimké Letters*. 1: 418. Other correspondence on this subject in the published *Weld-Grimké Letters* are John G. Whittier to the Grimké sisters, August 14, 1837, 1:411; Theodore Weld to the sisters, July 22 and

August 15, 1837, 1: 423-7; Angelina Grimké to Weld and Whittier, August 20, 1837, 1: 428-9; Sarah Grimké to Henry C. Wright, August 12, 1837, 1: 420.

18. Angelina Grimké to George C. Chase of Claremont, N.H., August 20, 1837, Ms., Weld-Grimké Papers; see also Henry C. Wright, Journal, vol. 35, July 9, 12, 24, 26, 27, 1837, Ms., Boston Public Library.

19. Sarah Grimké to Amos A. Phelps, August 3, 1837, Ms., Boston Public Library.

20, Angelina Grimké to Jane Smith, October 26, 1837, Ms., Weld-Grimké Papers; see also Angelina Grimké to Jane Smith, October 6, 1837, Ms., Weld-Grimké Papers.

21. Catharine E. Beecher, *An Essay on Slavery and Abolition-ism...* (Philadelphia: 1837), pp. 101-102, 98.

22. Angelina E. Grimké, *Letters to Catharine E. Beecher, in Reply to An Essay on Slavery and Abolitionism, Addressed to A. E. Grimké* (Boston: 1838), pp. 104, 112-3.

23. *Ibid.*, p. 119.

24. Sarah Grimké's letters appeared in the *New England Spectator* and the *Liberator,* and were collected and published as a pamphlet: *Letters on the Equality of the Sexes and the Condition of Women, Addressed to Mary S. Parker, President of the Boston Female Anti-Slavery Society* (Boston: 1838), from which the present quotations are extracted. The quoted passages appear on pp. 4, 5, 7-8, 11, and 21; see also pp. 18-20.

25. *Ibid.*, pp. 111, 119, 24-5, 46-7.

26. *Ibid.*, pp. 122, 125-6.

27. *Ibid.*, p. 42.

28. Gerda Lerner, *The Grimké Sisters from South Carolina: Rebels Against Slavery* (Boston: 1967), p. 194. Eleanor Flexner, *Century of Struggle: the Women's Rights Movement in the United States* (Cambridge, Mass.: 1959), p. 344, calls this work "the first serious discussion of woman's rights by an American woman." See also Anne Firor Scott, *The Southern Lady, From Pedestal to Politics 1830-1930* (Chicago: 1970), p. 61, for a similar evaluation.

29. Lucy Stone to Francis Stone, August 31, 1838, Ms., Lucy Stone Papers, Library of Congress.

30. Elizabeth Robinson to Lucy M. Wright, January 1, 1838, Ms., Elizur Wright, Jr., Papers, Library of Congress.

31. Anne W. Weston to "The Female Anti-Slavery Society." August 21, 1837, Ms., Boston Public Library.

32. Anne W. Weston to Caroline Weston, August 7, 1837; Sarah

C. Rugg to Anne W. Weston, February 16, 1838, Mss., Boston Public Library.

33. *Liberator*, November 3, 1837, p. 178.

34. Juliana Tappan to Anne Warren Weston, July 21, 1837, Ms., Boston Public Library.

35. *Liberator*, December 15, 1837, p. 203.

36. *Ibid.*, January 12, 1838, p. 7.

37. Angelina Grimké to Theodore Weld, February 11, 21, 22, 1837, *Weld-Grimké Letters*, pp. 538, 564-8.

38. *Liberator*, March 2, 1838, p. 35.

39. Lydia Maria Child to Theodore Weld, July 10, 1880, *Letters of Lydia Maria Child* (Boston: 1883), p. 259.

40. Excerpts from the diary of Samuel Philbrick, 1837-38, Ms., Weld-Grimké Papers.

41. Sarah Grimké to Jane Smith, March 24, 1838, Ms., Weld-Grimké Papers.

CHAPTER 7

1. *Liberator*, January 12, 1838, p. 7.

2. Sarah Baker, of the Dorchester Female Anti-Slavery Society, to Abby Kelley, May 31, 1838, Ms., Abby Kelley Foster Papers, American Antiquarian Society.

3. Elizabeth Cady Stanton et al, *History of Woman Suffrage* (Rochester, N.Y.: 1881), 1: 333-42; see also *History of Pennsylvania Hall, Which Was Destroyed by a Mob...* (Philadelphia: 1838); *Report of a Delegate to the Anti-Slavery Convention of American Women, May, 1838* (Boston: 1838); and Anna D. Hallowell, *James and Lucretia Mott: Life and Letters* (Boston: 1884), pp. 128-34.

4. *Liberator*, June 8, 1838, p. 90.

5. *Ibid.*, June 22, p. 97; see also James Mott to Anne Warren Weston, June 7, 1838, Sophia Davenport to Anne Warren Weston, November 20, 1838, Mss., Boston Public Library.

6. *Liberator*, June 8, 1838, pp. 90-1.

7. *Ibid.*, July 27, 1838, p. 119; July 6, p. 106. See also Wendell P. and Francis J. Garrison, *William Lloyd Garrison* (New York: 1885), 2: 221.

8. *Liberator*, September 7, 1838, p. 142.

9. *Ibid.*, June 29, 1838, p. 102; July 6, p. 107.

10. Aileen S. Kraditor, *Means and Ends in American Abolitionism: Garrison and His Critics on Strategy and Tactics, 1834-1850* (New

York: 1969), pp. 106, 56, ch. 3. See also Gerda Lerner, *The Grimké Sisters from South Carolina, Rebels Against Slavery* (Boston: 1967), pp. 184-203.

11.   Maria Weston Chapman, *Right and Wrong in Massachusetts* (Boston: 1839), pp. 96-114; *Liberator,* February 1, 1839, pp. 18-9.

12.   Charles Torrey to Francis Jackson, January 12, 1839, Ms., Boston Public Library.

13.   *Liberator,* January 25, 1839, p. 15; also January 18, p. 11.

14.   William Smyth to Amos A. Phelps, April 25, 1839, and Rufus A. Putnam to Phelps, April 27, 1839, Mss., Boston Public Library.

15.   Orange Scott to the American Anti-Slavery Society, April 12, 1839; Alanson St. Clair to Amos A. Phelps, February 21 and March 30, 1839, Mss., Boston Public Library.

16.   *Liberator,* April 19, 1839, p. 63; May 17, 1839, p. 79.

17.   *Ibid.,* May 31, p. 87; June 7, 1839, p. 98.

18.   Amos. A. Phelps, Recording Secretary of the Massachusetts Abolition Society, Circular Letter, dated Boston, June, 1839, Boston Public Library.

19.   Gerrit Smith to Amos A. Phelps, July 11, 1839, Ms., Boston Public Library.

20.   Chapman, *Right and Wrong in Massachusetts,* pp. 53, 156; also pp. 12-3.

21.   *Liberator,* November 22, 1839, p. 186; Lucretia Richardson to Maria Weston Chapman, September 30, 1839, Ms., Boston Public Library.

22.   *Liberator,* February 15, 1839, p. 27; February 22, p. 30; March 1, p. 33; March 15, pp. 41-3; March 22, p. 47; March 29, p. 51.

23.   *Ibid.,* April 19, 1839, p. 62; April 26, p. 67.

24.   Lydia Maria Child to Lucretia Mott, March 5, 1839, in Hallowell, *James and Lucretia Mott,* p. 136.

25.   "Report of Delegates to the Anti-Slavery Convention of American Women," Lucretia Mott, Chairman, Minutes of the Philadelphia Female Anti-Slavery Society, May 9, 1839, Ms., Historical Society of Pennsylvania.

26.   Abby Kelley Foster, Reminiscences, January 26, 1885, Ms., Abby Kelley Foster Papers, Worcester Historical Society.

27.   *Liberator,* April 10, 1840, p. 57.

28.   *Ibid.,* March 6, 1840, pp. 38-9.

29.   Henry C. Wright to John A. Collins, April 23, 1840, Ms., Boston Public Library.

30. W.P. and F.J. Garrison, *Garrison*, 2; 346-7, 355.

31. Lewis Tappan to James G. Birney, May 13, 1840, Ms., letterbooks, Tappan Papers, Library of Congress.

32. *Liberator*, July 3, 1840, p. 106.

33. *Ibid.*, June 19, 1840, p. 97.

34. *Ibid.*, May 22, 1840, p. 83.

35. Cincinnati *Philanthropist*, June 30, 1840.

36. Augustus and Susan Wattles to Garrison, February 26, 1840, *Liberator*, February 28, 1840, p. 34.

CHAPTER 8

1. Abbie Graham, *Ladies in Revolt* (New York: 1934), p. 83.

2. Wendell P. and Francis J. Garrison, *William Lloyd Garrison* (New York: 1885), 2: 351–2; Gilbert H. Barnes, *The Anti-Slavery Impulse 1830-1844* (New York: 1964), p. 171.

3. Sarah Grimké to Elizabeth Pease, May 1840, Ms., Boston Public Library.

4. Frederick B. Tolles, ed., *Slavery and "The Woman Question": Lucretia Mott's diary of Her visit to Great Britain to attend the World's Anti-Slavery Convention of 1840* (London and Haverford, Penna.; 1952), pp. 22–3, 27–9.

5. W.P. and F.J. Garrison, *Garrison* 2; 370.

6. *Ibid.*, 374-6; W.H. Ashurst to Wendell Phillips, June 17, 1840, W.H. Ashurst to William Lloyd Garrison, July 26, 1840, Mss., Boston Public Library; John Bowring to Garrison, November 9, 1840, in W.P. and F.J. Garrison, *Garrison*, 2; 378.

7. Lucretia Mott to Maria Weston Chapman, July 29, 1840, Ms., Boston Public Library; Tolles, *"The Woman Question,"* pp. 35–8.

8. Tolles, *"The Woman Question,"* pp. 50–2, 58–60, 73–7.

9. James Mott, *Three Months in Great Britain*, (Philadelphia: 1841), pp. 19–22, 25–7, 43–8.

10. Anne Knight to Maria Weston Chapman, August 4, 1840, Ms., Boston Public Library.

11. Minutes of the Philadelphia Female Anti-Slavery Society, October 8, 1840, Mss., Historical Society of Pennsylvania.

12. *Memorial of Sarah Pugh, A Tribute of Respect from her Cousins* (Philadelphia; 1888), pp. 26–7.

13. Stanton et al., *History of Woman Suffrage*, 1: 62.

14. Elizabeth Cady Stanton to Angelina Grimké Weld and Sarah Grimké, June 25, 1840, *Weld-Grimke' Letters*, 2; 347; Stanton et al.,

History of Woman Suffrage, 1: 420.

15. Tolles, *"The Woman Question,"* p. 75.

16. Edmund Quincy to Caroline Weston, July 9, 1840, Ms., Boston Public Library.

17. New York *National Anti-Slavery Standard*, April 29, 1841, p. 185.

18. Lynn *Record*, December 30, 1840; *Liberator*, January 1, 1841, p. 3.

19. Alice Welch Cowles to Rev. Henry Cowles, July 19, 1840, typed copy, Fletcher Papers, Oberlin College Archives.

20. J.C. Jackson to Oliver Johnson, August 2, 1840, Ms., Boston Public Library. See also Jerusha S. Bird to Maria Weston Chapman, November 1, 1840, Ms., Boston Public Library; T.P. Beach, June 1841?, Ms., Abby Kelley Foster Papers, American Antiquarian Society; Andrew Hanna to John A. Collins, January 24, 1843, Ms., Boston Public Library; John A. Collins to Abby Kelley, July 16, 1842, Ms., Abby Kelley Foster Papers, Worcester Historical Society.

21. Edward M. Davis to Maria Weston Chapman, December 16, 1844, Mss., Boston Public Library; Eliza Hambleton to Abby Kelley, n.d., 1844–45, Ms., Abby Kelley Foster Papers, Worcester Historical Society.

22. Jane Elizabeth Hitchcock to Maria Weston Chapman, October 16, 1845, Ms., Boston Public Library.

23. Arvine Wales to Arvine C. Wales, September 29, 1845, Ms., courtesy of Mrs. Horatio Wales, Massillon, Ohio; see also *Anti-Slavery Bugle*, June 20, July 25, and October 24, 1845.

24. Abby Kelley to Sydney H. Gay, March 1, 1846, Ms., Sydney H. Gay Papers, Columbia University; Lucy Stone to Abby Kelley Foster, March 25, July 3, 1846, Ms., American Antiquarian Society; Oberlin *Evangelist*, September 30, 1846, p. 158.

25. Hartford *Connecticut Observer and New-York Congregationalist*, March 7, 1840, p. 38, March 28, p. 50; Abby Kelley Foster to Lucy Stone, April 20, 1846, Ms., Lucy Stone Papers, Library of Congress.

26. Abby Kelley Foster to Betsey M. Cowles, January 28, 1846, typed copy, Fletcher Papers, Oberlin College Archives.

27. Parker Pillsbury to Abby and Stephen S. Foster, January 1, 1846, Ms., American Antiquarian Society; Sarah Pugh to Elizabeth Pease, April 27, 1846, Ms., Boston Public Library.

28. Jane Elizabeth Hitchcock to Maria Weston Chapman, October

16, 1845, Ms., Boston Public Library.

30. Lucy Stone to Abby Kelley Foster, July 3, 1846, Ms., American Antiquarian Society; Lucy Stone to her family, July 4–15, 1845, Ms., Lucy Stone Papers, Library of Congress; Lucy Stone to her sister Sarah, March 13, 1846, Ms., Library of Congress.

31. Abby Kelley Foster to Lucy Stone, April 20, 1846; Francis Stone (father) to Lucy Stone, January 10, 1847; Lucy Stone to W. B. Stone, June 9, 1848, Mss., Library of Congress.

32. Lucretia Mott to Elizabeth Pease, February 18, 1841, Ms., Friends' Historical Society, Swarthmore College.

33. *Liberator*, October 15, 1841, p. 168.

34. Edward M. Davis to Maria Weston Chapman, October 29, 1845, Ms., Boston Public Library.

35. Lucretia Mott, *Discourse on Woman, Delivered at the Assembly Building, December 17, 1849* (Philadelphia: 1850), pp. 12, 21.

36. *Wisconsin Free Democrat*, March 13, 1850, p. 257; see also *American Freeman*, January 22, 1845.

CHAPTER 9

1. Catharine E. Beecher, *A Treatise on Domestic Economy, for the Use of Young Ladies at Home and at School* (Boston: 1841), p. 144.

2. *Ibid.*, p. 19.

3. Sarah Josepha Hale, *Woman's Record: or, Sketches of all Distinguished Woman . . .* (New York: 1853), p. xxxvii.

4. *Ibid.*, pp. xxxv, xlvi, 753.

5. Caroline May, *The American Female Poets: With Biographical and Critical Notices* (Philadelphia: 1848), p. vi.

6. Extract from the reading journals of Margaret Fuller, undated Ms., Houghton Library, Harvard University.

7. Thomas Wentworth Higginson, "Margaret Fuller Ossoli," *Eminent Women of the Age* (Hartford, Conn.: 1869), p. 180.

8. Barbara M. Cross, ed., *The Educated Woman in America* (New York: 1965), p. 113.

9. Higginson, *Eminent Women*, p. 182.

10. Margaret Fuller Ossoli, *Woman in the Nineteenth Century, and Kindred Papers Relating to the Sphere, Condition and Duties, of Woman*, ed. Arthur B. Fuller (Boston: 1855), p. 30.

11. *Ibid.*, p. 31.

12. *Ibid.*, pp. 158–9.

13. *Ibid.*, pp. 133–6, 147, 152, 167.

14. *Ibid.*, pp. 123, 71–82, 96.

15. *Ibid.*, pp. 172–4.

16. *Ibid.*, p. 177.

17. *Ibid.*, p. 63.

18. Higginson, *Eminent Women*, p. 195.

19. Harriot K. Hunt, *Glances and Glimpses; or Fifty Years Social, including Twenty Years Professional Life* (Boston; 1856), pp. 122, 139, 170–180.

20. *Ibid.*, pp. 156–7, 150–9.

21. *Ibid.*, pp. 218–9.

22. Mary S. Gove, *Lectures to Women on Anatomy and Physiology. With an Appendix on Water Cure* (New York: 1846), p. 245. See also John B. Blake, "Mary Gove Nichols: Prophetess of Health," *Proceedings of the American Philosophical Society* 106 (June 29, 1962), pp. 219–34.

CHAPTER 10

1. *Pittsburgh Saturday Visiter*, September 15, 1849, p. 137.

2. *Ibid.*, April 28, 1849, p. 58; May 5, 1849, p. 62.

3. *Ibid.*, May 19, 1849, p. 70.

4. Lucretia Mott to Richard and Hannah Webb, February 25, 1842; Elizabeth J. Neall to Richard Webb, May 28, 1841; Elizabeth Cady Stanton to Elizabeth Pease, February 12, 1842, Mss., Boston Public Library.

5. Whitney R. Cross, *The Burned-Over District: The Social and Intellectual History of Enthusiastic Religion in Western New York, 1800–1850* (Ithaca, N.Y., 1950), pp. 3–6, 237; Alice S. Rossi, ed., *The Feminist Papers from Adams to deBeauvoir* (New York: 1973), pp. 265–70.

6. For descriptions of the Seneca Falls convention, see Stanton et al., *History of Woman Suffrage*, 1:69-74; Eleanor Flexner, *Century of Struggle: The Woman's Rights Movement in the United States* (Cambridge, Mass.: 1959), pp. 76-7; Alma Lutz, *Created Equal: A Biography of Elizabeth Cady Stanton* (New York: 1940), pp. 47-50; Elizabeth Cady Stanton, *Eighty Years and More,* (New York: 1898) ch. 9; Robert S. Riegel, ed., " 'Woman's Rights and Other Reforms in Seneca Falls': A Contemp-

orary View," *New York History* 46 (January 1965),: 42-6; *Report of the Woman's Rights Convention Held at Seneca Falls, N.Y., July 19th & 20th, 1848* (Rochester, N.Y.: 1848); *Address of Mrs. Elizabeth Cady Stanton, Delivered at Seneca Falls & Rochester . . .* (Rochester, N.Y.: 1848).

7. "Scrapbook Made by Elizabeth Cady Stanton in 1848 of clippings of press comments, etc. on the Woman's Rights Conv., 1848," Elizabeth Cady Stanton Papers, Library of Congress; Susan B. Anthony scrapbook, vol. 1, Rare Book Division, Library of Congress.

8. *Ibid.*

9. Lucretia Mott to Elizabeth Cady Stanton, October 3, 1848, Ms., Elizabeth Cady Stanton Papers, Library of Congress.

10. Stanton et al., *History of Woman Suffrage*, 1: 88–94, 103, 117–8.

11. *Anti-Slavery Bugle*, March 30, 1850, p. 115.

12. *Ibid.*, March 30, 1850, pp. 114–5; B.B. Hunter to L.M. Cowles, May 13, 1850, Ms., Betsey Cowles Papers, in the possession of Mrs. Robert Ticknor, Austinburg, Ohio.

13. *Wisconsin Free Democrat*, May 22, 1850, pp. 295–6; May 29, p. 301.

14. Paulina Wright Davis to Elizabeth Cady Stanton, July 7, 1850, Ms., Elizabeth Cady Stanton Papers, Library of Congress.

15. Jane Elizabeth Jones to Lucy Stone, July 1, 1847, Ms., Lucy Stone Papers, Library of Congress.

16. Aileen S. Kraditor, *The Ideas of the Woman Suffrage Movement 1890–1920* (New York: 1965), pp. 38–43.

17. Aileen S. Kraditor, ed., *Up From the Pedestal: Landmark Writings in the American Woman's Struggle for Equality* (Chicago: 1968), p. 8. The opposition, consisting of doctors and others united against woman's autonomy, is forcibly described in G.J. Barker-Benfield, *The Horrors of the Half-Known Life: Male Attitudes Toward Women and Sexuality in Nineteenth-Century America* (New York: 1976).

18. Jane Elizabeth Jones, *The Wrongs of Woman. An Address...in Proceedings of the Ohio Women's Convention* (Salem, Ohio: 1850), p. 30.

SELECTED BIBLIOGRAPHY

Manuscript Collections and Unpublished Materials
American Antiquarian Society, Worcester, Mass.
   Abigail Kelley Foster Papers
Boston Public Library, Boston, Mass.
   American Anti-Slavery Society Records
   Margaret Fuller Papers
   William Lloyd Garrison Papers
   Amos A. Phelps Papers
   Weston Family Papers
   Henry C. Wright Papers
William L. Clements Library, University of Michigan
   Weld-Grimké Papers
Collection of American Literature,
 The Beinecke Rare Book and Manuscript Library, Yale University
   Catharine E. Beecher-Mary Dutton Correspondence
Columbia University Library, New York
   Sidney Howard Gay Papers
Framingham State College, Framingham, Mass.
   Framingham State College–Lexington Normal School Archives
Friends' Historical Society, Swarthmore College Library, Swarthmore, Penn.
   Lucretia Mott Papers
Historical Society of Pennsylvania, Philadelphia
   Minutes of the Philadelphia Female Anti-Slavery Society
Houghton Library, Harvard University
   Margaret Fuller Papers
   Henry C. Wright Papers
Library of Congress, Washington, D.C.
   Susan B. Anthony Scrapbooks, Rare Book Division
   Anti-Slavery Album, Manuscript Division
   Elizabeth Cady Stanton Papers
   Elizabeth Cady Stanton Scrapbook
   Lucy Stone Papers
   Lewis Tappan Papers
   Western Anti-Slavery Society Minute Book
   Elizur Wright, Jr., Papers
Oberlin College, Oberlin, Ohio
   Charles G. Finney Papers

Robert S. Fletcher Papers
Oberlin College Archives
Ohio Historical Society, Columbus
    Constitution of the Marrietta, Ohio, Bethel Association
    Constitution and Record Book of the "Ladies Reasoning Assembly" of Cazenovia,
        N.Y., 1818–1819
Arthur and Elizabeth Schlesinger Library, Radcliffe College, Cambridge, Mass.
    Poor Family Papers
    Weltha Brown Papers, Hooker Collection
Syracuse University Library
    Gerrit Smith Papers
Western Reserve Historical Society, Cleveland, Ohio
    Antislavery Collections
Williston Memorial Library, Mount Holyoke College, So. Hadley, Mass.
    Zilpah P. Grant Banister Papers
    Mary Lyon Papers
    Mount Holyoke College Archives
Worcester Historical Society, Worcester, Mass.
    Kelley-Foster Collection, 1837–1893
By courtesy of Mrs. Robert Ticknor, Austinburg, Ohio
    Betsey Mix Cowles Papers

Newspapers and Periodicals

American Annals of Education and Instruction (Boston), 1830–1833
American Freeman (Prairieville, Wisc.), 1845–1846
American Journal of Education (New York), 1856
Anti-Slavery Bugle (Salem, Ohio), 1845–1852
Christian Repository (Utica, N.Y.), 1822–1823
Common School Assistant (Albany, N.Y.), 1836–1840
Common School Journal (Boston), 1838–1842
Connecticut Common School Journal (Hartford), 1838–1842
Connecticut Observer and New-York Congregationalist (Hartford), 1840
Journal of Humanity; and Herald of the American Temperance Society (Andover, Mass.),
    1829–1833
Liberator (Boston), 1831–1850
Lynn Record (Lynn, Mass.), 1834–1840
Massachusetts Abolitionist (Boston), 1839–1840
Massachusetts Cataract and Worcester County Waterfall (Worcester, Mass.), 1843–1845

Massachusetts Spy (Worcester, Mass.), 1835–1841
National Anti-Slavery Standard (New York), 1840–1850
New Hampshire Patriot and State Gazette (Concord, N.H.), 1838
Oberlin Evangelist (Oberlin, Ohio), 1838–1846
Ohio Observer (Hudson, Ohio), 1836–1837
Philanthropist (New Richmond and Cincinnati, Ohio), 1836–1840
Pittsburgh Saturday Visiter (Pittsburgh, Pa.), 1848–1850
Religious Intelligencer (New Haven, Conn.), 1816
Signal of Liberty (Ann Arbor, Mich.), 1845–1847
Temperance Almanac (Albany, N.Y.) 1834
Vermont Gazette (Bennington, Vt.), 1839
Wisconsin Free Democrat, 1850

Reports and Proceedings of Organizations

Anti-Slavery Convention of American Women, *Proceedings . . . May . . . 1837*. New York:
    W. S. Dorr, 1837
Anti-Slavery Convention of American Women. *Report of a Delegate . . . May, 1838*.
    Boston: Isaac Knapp. 1838.
Boston Female Anti-Slavery Society. *Right and Wrong in Boston: Report of the . . . Society
    . . . 1835*. 2nd ed., Boston: 1836
———, *Right and Wrong in Boston, Number Three: Annual Report . . .1837*. Boston: 1837.
Ladies New York Anti-Slavery Society. *Annual Report . . 1836*. New York: W. S.
    Dorr, 1836.
———, *Annual Report . . . 1837*. New York: W. S. Dorr, 1837.
Philadelphia Female Anti-Slavery Society, *Sixth Annual Report*. Philadelphia; 1840.
———, *Thirty-sixth Annual Report*, Philadelphia: 1870.
Woman's Rights Convention, Seneca Falls. *Report of the Woman's Rights Convention
    Held at Seneca Falls, N.Y., July 19th & 20th, 1848*. Rochester: J. Dick, 1848.
Women's Convention, Ohio. *Proceedings of the Ohio Women's Convention, at Salem,
    April 19th and 20th, 1850*. Salem, Ohio: 1850.

Published Primary Sources

Barnard, Thomas. *A Sermon Preached Before the Salem Female Charitable Society. . . .*
    Salem, Mass.: W. Carlton, 1803.
Barnes, Gilbert H., and Dwight L. Dummond, eds. *The Letters of Theodore Dwight Weld,
    Angelina Grimké Weld, and Sarah Grimké, 1822-1844*, 2 vols., New York:
    D. Appleton-Century Co., 1934.
Beecher, Catharine E. *An Essay on Slavery and Abolitionism with Reference to the Duty of
    American Females*. Philadelphia: Henry Perkins, 1837.
———, *Suggestions Respecting Improvements in Education, Presented to the Trustees of
    the Hartford Female Seminary, and Published at Their Request*. Hartford, Conn.:
    Packard & Butler, 1829.

————. *A Treatise on Domestic Economy, for the Use of Young Ladies at Home and at School*. Boston: Marsh, Capen, Lyon & Webb, 1841.

Chapin, Daniel. *A Discourse Delivered Before the Charitable Female Society in Groton, Oct. 19, 1814*. Andover, Mass.: 1814.

Chapman, Maria Weston. *Right and Wrong in Massachusetts*. Boston: Dow & Jackson's Anti-Slavery Press, 1839.

Child, Lydia Maria. *An Appeal in Favor of That Class of Americans Called Africans*. Boston: Allen and Ticknor, 1833.

————. *Letters of Lydia Maria Child*. Boston: Houghton Mifflin Co., 1883.

Cooke, Parsons. *Female Preaching Unlawful and Inexpedient. . . .* Lynn, Mass.: James R. Newhall, 1837.

Coxe, Margaret. *Claims of the Country on American Females*. 2 vols. Columbus, Ohio: Isaac N. Whiting, 1842.

Crocker, Hannah Mather. *Observations on the Real Rights of Women, With Their Appropriate Duties Agreeable to Scripture, Reason and Common Sense*. Boston: the author, 1818.

DeWitt, W.R. *Woman: Her Excellence and Usefulness*. Harrisburg, Penna.: 1841.

Dumond, Dwight L., ed. *The Letters of James Gillespie Birney, 1831-1857*. 2 vols. New York: D Appleton-Century Co., 1938.

Edwards, Justin. *Joy in Heaven over the Penitent, A Sermon . . . Before the Penitent Females' Refuge Society. . . .* Boston: T.R. Marvin, 1826.

Forten, James, Jr. *An Address Delivered Before the Ladies Anti-Slavery Society of Philadelphia, on the Evening of the 14th of April, 1836*. Philadelphia: Merrihew and Gunn, 1836.

Gove, Mary S. *Lectures to Ladies on Anatomy and Physiology*. Boston: Saxton & Peirce, 1842.

————. *Lectures to Women on Anatomy and Physiology. With an Appendix on Water Cure*. New York: Harper & Bros., 1846.

Grimké, Angelina E. *An Appeal to the Christian Women of the South*. New York: American Anti-Slavery Society, 1836

————. *An Appeal to the Women of the Nominally Free States: Issued by an Anti-Slavery Convention of American Women. . . .* New York: W.S. Dorr, 1837.

————. *Letters to Catherine E. Beecher, in Reply to an Essay on Slavery and Abolitionism Addressed to A.E. Grimké*. Boston: Isaac Knapp, 1838.

Grimké, Sarah. *Letters on the Equality of the Sexes and the Condition of Women; Addressed to Mary S. Parker, President of the Boston Female Anti-Slavery Society*. Boston: Isaac Knapp, 1838.

Martineau, Harriet. *The Martyr Age of the United States*. Boston: Weeks, Jordan & Co., 1839.

————. *Society in America*. 2 vols. 2nd. ed. New York: Saunders & Otley, 1837.

May, Caroline. *The American Female Poets: With Biographical and Critical Notices*. Philadelphia: Lindsay and Blakiston, 1848.

May, Samuel J. *The Rights and Condition of Women; Considered in "The Church of the Messiah,"* Syracuse, N.Y.: Stoddard & Babcock, 1846.

————, *Some Recollections of Our Antislavery Conflict*. Boston: Fields, Osgood and Co.,
     1869.

McIntosh, Maria J. *Woman in America: Her Work and Her Reward*. New York: D.
     Appleton & Co., 1850.

Mott, James. *Three Months in Great Britain*. Philadephia: J. M. McKin, 1841.

Mott, Lucretia. *Discourse on Woman, Delivered at the Assembly Building, December 17,
     1849*. Philadelphia: T. B. Peterson, 1850.

————, *Slavery and "The Woman Question": Lucretia Mott's Diary of Her Visit to Great
     Britain to attend the World's Anti-Slavery Convention of 1840*. Edited by Frederick B.
     Tolles. Haverford, Penn.: Friends' Historical Society, 1952.

Ossoli, Margaret Fuller. *Woman in the Nineteenth Century, and Kindred Papers Relating
     to the Sphere, Condition and Duties, of Woman*. Edited by Arthur B. Fuller. Boston:
     J. P. Jewett & Co., 1855.

[Pennsylvania Hall]. *History of Pennsylvania Hall, Which Was Destroyed by a Mob*.
     Philadelphia: Merrihew & Gunn, 1838.

Sigourney, Lydia. *Letters to Mothers*. Hartford: Hudson & Skinner, 1838.

————, *Letters to Young Ladies*. New York: Harper & Bros., 1837.

Smith, Ethan. *Daughters of Zion Excelling. A Sermon Preached to the Ladies of the Cent
     Institution, in Hopkinton, New Hampshire, August 14, 1814*. Concord, N.H.: George
     Hough, 1814.

Stanton, Elizabeth Cady, *Address of Mrs. Elizabeth Cady Stanton, Delivered at Seneca
     Falls & Rochester, N.Y., July 19th & August 2d, 1848*.New York: R.J. Johnston, 1870.

————, Susan B. Anthony, and Matilda Joslyn Gage. *History of Woman Suffrage*, Vol. 1.
     New York: Fowler & Wells, 1881.

Weld, Theodore Dwight, comp. *American Slavery As It Is: Testimony of a Thousand
     Witnesses*. New York: American Anti-Slavery Society, 1839.

Willard, Emma. *An Address to the Public: Particularly to the Legislature of New York,
     Proposing a Plan for Improving Female Education*. 2nd ed. Middlebury, Vt.: J.W.
     Copeland, 1819.

Biographical Works

Birney, Catherine H. *The Grimké Sisters*. Boston: Lee & Shepard, 1885.

Blackwell, Alice Stone. *Lucy Stone, Pioneer of Woman's Rights*. Boston: Little, Brown,
     1930.

Blackwell, Elizabeth. *Pioneer Work in Opening the Medical Profession to Women*. New
     York: Longmans, Green & Co., 1895.

Bloomer, Dexter C. *Life and Writings of Amelia Bloomer*. Reprint. New York: Schocken Books, 1975.

Chapman, Maria Weston, ed. *Harriet Martineau's Autobiography and Memorials of
     Harriet Martineau*. 2 vols. Boston: James R. Osgood & Co., 1877.

Cromwell, Otelia. *Lucretia Mott*. Cambridge, Mass.: Harvard University Press, 1958.

Emerson, Ralph. *Life of Rev. Joseph Emerson*. Boston: Crocker & Brewster, 1834.

Entrikin, Isabelle W. *Sarah Josepha Hale and Godey's Lady's Book*. Philadelphia; n.p.,
     1946.

Finney, Charles G. *Memoirs of Rev. Charles G. Finney, Written by Himself*. New York: A.S. Barnes & Co, 1876.

Flexner, Eleanor. *Mary Wollstonecraft: A Biography*. New York: Coward, McCann & Geoghegan, 1972.

Garrison, Wendell P., and Francis J. Garrison. *William Lloyd Garrison 1805–1879; The Story of His Life Told By his Children*. Vols. 1–2, New York: The Century Co., 1885.

Goodsell, Willystine, ed. *Pioneers of Women's Education in the United States*. New York: McGraw-Hill, 1931.

Guilford, Lucinda T., comp. *The Use of a Life: Memorials of Mrs. Z.P. Grant Banister*. New York: American Tract Society, 1885.

Hale, Sarah Josepha. *Women's Record; or, Sketches of all Distinguished Women.* . . . New York: Harper & Bros., 1853.

Hallowell, Anna D. *James and Lucretia Mott; Life and Letters*. Boston: Houghton Mifflin, 1884.

Hays, Elinor Rice. *Those Extraordinary Blackwells*. New York: Harcourt, Brace & World, 1967.

Higginson, Thomas Wentworth. "Margaret Fuller Ossoli," *Eminent Women of the Age*. Hartford, Conn.: S. M. Betts & Co., 1869.

Hunt, Harriot K. *Glances and Glimpses; or Fifty Years Social, including Twenty Years Professional Life*. Boston: J.P. Jewett & Co., 1856.

James, Edward T., Janet W. James, and Paul S. Boyer, eds. *Notable American Women 1607–1950; A Biographical Dictionary*. 3 vols. Cambridge, Mass.: Harvard University Press, 1971.

Larcom, Lucy. *A New England Girlhood*. Boston: Houghton Mifflin, 1890.

Lerner, Gerda. *The Grimké Sisters From South Carolina; Rebels Against Slavery*. Boston: Houghton Mifflin, 1967.

Lundy, Benjamin. *The Poetical Works of Elizabeth Margaret Chandler; With a Memoir of her Life and Character*. Philadelphia: L. Howell, 1836.

Lutz, Alma. *Created Equal: A Biography of Elizabeth Cady Stanton*. New York: John Day Co., 1940.

————, *Emma Willard, Daughter of Democracy*. Boston: Houghton Mifflin, 1929.

Marshall, Helen E. *Dorothea Dix: Forgotten Samaritan*. Chapel Hill, N.C.: University of North Carolina Press, 1937.

Merrill, Walter M. *Against Wind and Tide: A Biography of William Lloyd Garrison*. Cambridge, Mass.: Harvard University Press, 1963.

Perkins, Alice J. G., and Theresa Wolfson. *Frances Wright, Free Enquirer: The Study of a Temperament*. New York: Harper & Bros., 1939.

[Pugh, Sarah]. *Memorial of Sarah Pugh. A Tribute of Respect from her Cousins*. Philadelphia: J.B. Lippincott, 1888.

Riegel, Robert E. *American Feminists*. Lawrence, Kans.: University of Kansas Press, 1963.

Sklar, Kathryn Kish. *Catharine Beecher, A Study in American Domesticity*. New Haven, Conn.: Yale University Press, 1973.

Stanton, Elizabeth Cady *Eighty Years and More*. New York: European Publ. Co., 1898.

Swisshelm, Jane Grey. *Half a Century*. 2nd ed. Chicago: Janson, McClurg & Co., 1880.

Tappan, Lewis. *The Life of Arthur Tappan*. New York: Hurd & Houghton, 1870.

Thomas, John L. *The Liberator, William Lloyd Garrison: A Biography*. Boston: Little, Brown, 1963.

Thorp, Margaret Farrand. *Female Persuasion: Six Strong-Minded Women*. New Haven, Conn.: Yale University Press, 1949.

Wade, Mason. *Margaret Fuller: Whetstone of Genius*. New York: Viking Press, 1940.

Wardle, Ralph M. *Mary Wollstonecraft: A Critical Biography*. Lawrence, Kan.: University of Kansas Press, 1951.

Wyatt-Brown, Bertram. *Lewis Tappan and the Evangelical War Against Slavery*. Cleveland: Press of Case Western Reserve University, 1969.

Secondary Works

Abbott, Edith. *Women in Industry: A Study in American Economic History*. New York: D. Appleton & Co., 1910.

Ariès, Philippe. *Centuries of Childhood: A Social History of Family Life*. Translated by Robert Baldick. New York: Alfred A. Knopf, 1962.

Bailyn, Bernard. *Education in the Forming of American Society: Needs and Opportunities for Study*. Chapel Hill, N.C.: University of North Carolina Press, 1960.

Barker-Benfield, G.L. *The Horrors of the Half-Known Life: Male Attitudes Toward Women and Sexuality in Nineteenth-Century America*. New York: Harper & Row, 1976.

Barnes, Gilbert H. *The Anti-Slavery Impulse 1830–1844*. Introduction by William G. McLoughlin. New York: Harcourt, Brace & World, 1964.

Beard, Mary R. *Woman as Force in History: A Study in Traditions and Realities*. New York: Macmillan, 1946.

Benson, Mary S. *Women in Eighteenth-Century America: A Study of Opinion and Social Usage*. New York: Columbia University Press, 1935.

Bernard, Jessie. *The Future of Motherhood*. New York: Dial Press, 1974.

Brownlee, W. Elliot, and Mary M. Brownlee. *Women in the American Economy: A Documentary History, 1675–1929*. New Haven, Conn.: Yale University Press, 1976.

Cole, Arthur C. *A Hundred Years of Mount Holyoke College: The Evolution of an Educational Ideal*. New Haven, Conn.: Yale University Press, 1940.

Cremin, Lawrence. *American Education: The Colonial Experience 1607–1783*. New York: Harper & Row, 1970.

Cross, Barbara M., ed. *The Educated Woman in America*. New York: Teacher's College Press, 1965.

Cross, Whitney R. *The Burned-Over District: The Social and Intellectual History of Enthusiastic Religion in Western New York, 1800–1850*. Ithaca, N.Y.: Cornell University Press, 1950.

Dexter, Elizabeth A. *Career Women of America, 1776–1840*. Francestown, N.H.: N.H.M. Jones Co., 1950.

———, *Colonial Women of Affairs*. Boston: Houghton Mifflin, 1924.

Filler, Louis. *The Crusade Against Slavery 1830–1860*. New York: Harper & Bros., 1960.

Fletcher, Robert S. *A History of Oberlin College from its Foundation Through the Civil War*. 2 vols. Oberlin, Ohio: Oberlin College, 1943.

Flexner, Eleanor. *Century of Struggle: The Woman's Rights Movement in the United States*. Cambridge, Mass., Harvard University Press, 1959.

Josephson, Hannah. *The Golden Threads: New England's Mill Girls and Magnates*. New York: Russell and Russell, 1949.

Katz, Michael, *The Irony of Early School Reform: Educational Innovation in Mid-Nineteenth Century Massachusetts* Cambridge, Mass.: Harvard University Press. 1968.

Kraditor, Aileen. *The Ideas of the Woman Suffrage Movement 1890-1920*. New York: Columbia University Press, 1965.

———*Means and Ends in American Abolitionism: Garrison and His Critics on Strategy and Tactics, 1834-1850*. New York: Pantheon Books, 1969.

———, *Up From the Pedestal: Landmark Writings in the American Woman's Struggle for Equality*. Chicago: Quadrangle Books, 1968.

Krout, John A. *The Origins of Prohibition*. New York: Knopf, 1925.

Kuhn, Anne L. *The Mother's Role in Childhood Education: New England Concepts, 1830-1860*. New Haven, Conn: Yale University Press, 1947.

Lockridge, Kenneth A. *Literacy in Colonial New England: An Enquiry into the Social Context of Literacy in the Early Modern West*. New York: Norton, 1974.

Lutz, Alma. *Crusade for Freedom: Women of the Antislavery Movement*. Boston: Beacon Press, 1968.

Morris, Richard B. *Studies in the History of American Law, With Special Reference to the Seventeenth and Eighteenth Centuries*. New York: Columbia University Press, 1930.

O'Neill, William L. *Everyone Was Brave: The Rise and Fall of Feminism in America*. Chicago: Quadrangle Books, 1969.

O'Sullivan, Judith, and Rosemary Gallick, *Workers and Allies: Female Participation in the American Trade Union Movement, 1824-1976*. Washington D.C.:Smithsonian Institution Press, 1975.

Papashvily, Helen W. *All the Happy Endings: A Study of the Domestic Novel in America* New York: Harper & Bros., 1956.

Robinson, Harriet H. *Loom and Spindle, or Life Among the Early Mill Girls*. Boston: T.Y. Crowell & Co., 1898.

Rossi, Alice, ed. *The Feminist Papers From Adams to deBeauvoir*. New York: Columbia University Press, 1973.

Schlesinger, Arthur M., Sr. *The American As Reformer*. Cambridge, Mass: Harvard University Press, 1950.

———, *New Viewpoints in American History*. New York: Macmillan, 1922

Scott, Anne Firor. *The Southern Lady: From Pedestal to Politics 1830-1930*. Chicago: University of Chicago Press, 1970.

Sinclair, Andrew. *The Emancipation of the American Woman*. New York: Harper & Row, 1965.

Sizer, Theodore, ed. *The Age of the Academies*. New York: Teacher's College Press, 1965.

Smith, Page. *Daughters of the Promised Land:Women in American History.*Boston:Little,
    Brown, 1970.
Spruill, Julia Cherry. *Women's Life and Work in the Southern Colonies.* Chapel Hill,N.C.:
    University of North Carolina Press, 1938.
Tyler,Alice Felt.*Freedom's Ferment: Phases of American Social History from the Coloni-
    al Period to the Outbreak of the Civil War.* Minneapolis,Minn.:University of Minnesota
    Press, 1944.
Walters, Ronald G. *Primer for Prudery: Sexual Advice to Victorian America,* Englewood
    Cliffs, N.J.:Prentice-Hall, 1974.
Woody, Thomas E. *A History of Women's Education in the United States.* 2 vols. New
    York and Lancaster, Penn.: The Science Press, 1929.

Articles and Essays

Blake,John B., "Mary Gove Nichols,Prophetess of Health, "*Proceedings of the American
    Philosophical Society* 106 (June 29, 1962): 219-34.
Cott,Nancy F."Young Women in the Second Great Awakening in New England. *"Femin-
    ist Studies 3* (1975).
Curti, Merle E. "Non-Resistance in New England."*New England Quarterly 2* (January
    1929):34-57.
Hogeland, Ronald W. "Coeducation of the Sexes at Oberlin College: A Study of Social
    Ideas in Mid-Nineteenth Century America." *Journal of Social History* 6 (Winter 1972-
    73): 160-76
            "The Female Appendage: Feminine Life Styles in America, 1820-
    1860." *Civil War History* 17 (June 1971): 101-15
Kerber,Linda K. "Daughters of Columbia: Educating Women for the Republic, 1787-
    1805." *The Hofstadter Aegis: A Memorial,* Edited by Stanley Elkins   and Eric
    McKitrick: New York, Knopf, 1974, pp. 36-59.
Lerner, Gerda."The Lady and the Mill Girl:Changes in the Status of Women in the Age of
    Jackson."*Midcontinent American Studies Journal* 10 (Spring 1969):5-15.
———."New Approaches to the Study of Women in American History." *Journal of
    Social History 3 (*Fall 1969) 53-62.
Mathews, Donald G. "The Second Great Awakening as an Organizing Process 1780-
    1830." *American Quarterly* 21 (Spring 1969): 23-43.
Melder, Keith E. "Forerunners of Freedom: The Grimké Sisters in Massachusetts, 1837-
    38."*Essex Institute Historical Collections* 103 (July 1967):223-49.
———."Ladies Bountiful: Organized Women's Benevolence in Early 19th Century
    America."*New York History* 48 (July 1967): 231-54.
———,"Mask of Oppression: The Female Seminary Movement in the United States, *"New
    York History* 55 (July 1974):261-79.
———. "Woman's High Calling: The Teaching Profession in America, 1830-1860."
    American Studies 13 (Fall 1972): 19-32.
Potter, David M."American Women and the American Character." In *History and Amer-
    ican Society: Essays of David M. Potter,* edited by Don E. Fehrenbacher: New York:
    Oxford University Press, 1973,pp.278-303.

Riegel, Robert S., ed. "Woman's Rights and Other Reforms at Seneca Falls": A Contemporary View." *New York History* 46 (January 1965): 41-59.

Rosenberg, Charles E. "Sexuality, Class and Role in 19th-Century America." *American Quarterly* 25 (May 1973): 131-53.

Ruchames, Louis. "Race, Marriage, and Abolition in Massachusetts." *Journal of Negro History* 40 (July 1955): 250-73.

Small, Edwin W., and Miriam Small, "Prudence Crandall,Champion of Negro Education." *New England Quarterly* 17 (December 1944):506-29.

Sicherman, Barbara. "Review Essay:American History," *Signs* 1 (Winter 1975):461-85.

Smith-Rosenberg, Caroll, "Beauty, the Beast and the Militant Woman: A Case Study in Sex Roles and Social Stress in Jacksonian America." *American Quarterly* 23 (October 1971): 562-84.

————,"The Female World of Love and Ritual:Relations Between Women in Nineteenth-Century America,"*Signs* 1 (Autumn 1975): 1-29.

Taylor, William R.,and Christopher Lasch. "Two Kindred Spirits:Sorority and Family in New England." *New England Quarterly* 36 (March 1963): 23-41.

Thomas, John L. "Romantic Reform in America, 1815-1865." *American Quarterly* 17 (Winter 1965):656-81.

Welter, Barbara. "The Cult of True Womanhood: 1820-1860." *American Quarterly* 17 (Winter 1965):656-81.

————,"The Feminization of American Religion: 1800-1860."In *Clio's Consciousness Raised: New Perspectives on the History of American Women*, edited by Mary Hartman and Lois W. Banner. New York: Harper & Row, 1974,pp137-57.

Unpublished Doctoral Dissertation

James, Janet Wilson. "Changing Ideas About Women in the United States, 1776-1825." Phd.D. dissertation,Radcliffe College, 1954.

INDEX